"[Ben] Macintyre so seamlessly fuses so many different accounts that their compilation creates something more profound than a simple escape yarn: a biography of the prison itself and the world detainees built there."
    —*The Washington Post*

"My book of the year . . . [a] masterful history of Colditz . . . It's absurdly readable (and at times just absurd) as well as being informative, hilarious and deeply moving."
    —Geoff Dyer, *Literary Hub*

"Like watching a black-and-white photograph being colourised . . . rich in humour and quirky detail . . . another compelling narrative."
    —*The Spectator*

"Nuanced . . . gripping . . . told with sensitivity and insight, with an eye for telling detail."
    —*The Times*

"Fascinating."
    —*The Sun*

"Un-putdownable. . . . Macintyre has a genius for taking war stories that seem familiar and breathing new life into them. . . . The escapers' stories are told with great style, verve and brio."
    —*Daily Mail*

"Whipped along in classic Macintyre style . . . the book is an engaging retelling."
    —*The Times Literary Supplement*

"Macintyre is a superb writer, with an eye for the telling detail as fine as any novelist's."
    —*The Dallas Morning News*

"Macintyre is a master storyteller."
    —*San Francisco Chronicle*

"Macintyre writes with the diligence and insight of a journalist, and the panache of a born storyteller."
    —John Banville, *The Guardian*

"Macintyre at once exalts and subverts the myths of spycraft, and has a keen eye for absurdity."
    —*The New Yorker*

"With Macintyre in charge, you're virtually guaranteed a history book that reads like a spy novel."
    —*Richmond Times-Dispatch*

"A scrupulous and insightful writer—a master historian."
    —Alan Furst, author of *A Mission to Paris*

"Macintyre is a master at leading the reader down some very tortuous paths while ensuring they never lose their bearings."
    —*Evening Standard*

"Macintyre . . . has that enviable gift, the inability to write a dull sentence."
    —*The Spectator*

BY BEN MACINTYRE

Prisoners of the Castle
Agent Sonya
The Spy and the Traitor
Rogue Heroes
A Spy Among Friends
Double Cross
Operation Mincemeat
The Last Word
For Your Eyes Only
Agent Zigzag
Josiah the Great
The Englishman's Daughter
The Napoleon of Crime
Forgotten Fatherland

PRISONERS
OF THE CASTLE

PRISONERS OF THE CASTLE

AN EPIC STORY OF SURVIVAL AND ESCAPE FROM COLDITZ, THE NAZIS' FORTRESS PRISON

BEN MACINTYRE

CROWN
NEW YORK

2023 Crown Trade Paperback Edition

Published in the United States by Crown, an imprint of Crown Publishing
Group, a division of Penguin Random House LLC, New York.

CROWN and the Crown colophon are registered trademarks of
Penguin Random House LLC.

Originally published in hardcover in the United States by Crown,
an imprint of Random House, a division of
Penguin Random House LLC, in 2022.

Photography credits can be found on page xiii.

Library of Congress Cataloging-in-Publication Data
Names: Macintyre, Ben, 1963– author.
Title: Prisoners of the castle / Ben Macintyre.
Description: New York: Crown, 2022 | Includes bibliographical
references and index.
Identifiers: LCCN 2022026350 (print) | LCCN 2022026351 (ebook) |
ISBN 9780593136355 (tradepaper) | ISBN 9780593136348 (ebook)
Subjects: LCSH: Oflag IVC (Concentration camp) | World War,
1939–1945—Prisoners and prisons, German. | Schloss Colditz (Colditz,
Germany)—History. | Prisoner-of-war escapes—Germany—Colditz—
History. | Prisoners of war—Germany—Colditz.
Classification: LCC D805.5.O37 M22 2022 (print) | LCC D805.5.O37
(ebook) | DDC 940.54/7243—dc23/eng/20220603
LC record available at https://lccn.loc.gov/2022026350

crownpublishing.com

2 4 6 8 9 7 5 3 1

In the fell clutch of circumstance
I have not winced nor cried aloud.
Under the bludgeonings of chance
My head is bloody, but unbowed.
  —"Invictus," William Ernest Henley
    (1849–1903)

Preface

The myth of Colditz has stood unchanged and unchallenged for more than seventy years: prisoners of war, with mustaches firmly set on stiff upper lips, defying the Nazis by tunneling out of a grim Gothic castle on a German hilltop, fighting the war by other means. Yet, like all legends, that tale contains only a part of the truth.

The soldier-prisoners of Colditz were courageous, resilient, and astonishingly imaginative in the ways they tried to get out of the high-security camp holding the most troublesome captives of the Third Reich. There were more attempted escapes from Colditz than any other camp. But life in Colditz was about more than escaping, just as its inmates were more complicated, and far more interesting, than the cardboard saints depicted in popular culture.

Colditz was a miniature replica of pre-war society, only stranger. It was a close-knit community intensely divided over issues of class, politics, sexuality, and race. In addition to the resolute warriors, the participants in the Colditz drama included communists, scientists, homosexuals, women, aesthetes and philistines, aristocrats, spies, workers, poets, and traitors. Many of these have hitherto been excluded from history because they did not fit the traditional mold of the white male Allied officer, dedicated to escaping. Moreover, roughly half the population of Colditz was German: the guards and their officers have also tended to be painted in one uniform color, yet this group also contained a rich cast of characters, including some men of culture and humanity far removed from the brutal Nazi stereotype.

The inside story of Colditz is a tale of the indomitable human spirit, and much else besides: bullying, espionage, boredom, insanity, tragedy, and farce. Colditz Castle was a frightening prison, but it was also frequently absurd, a place of suffering but also of high comedy, an idiosyncratic and eccentric crucible that evolved its own culture, cookery, sports, theater, and even a distinct internal language. But this heavily guarded cage, surrounded by barbed wire and cut off from the world, changed everyone who entered it, as life inside the castle evolved, and the war ground on. Some prisoners were heroic, but they were also human: tough and vulnerable, brave but terrified, by turns cheerful, determined, and despairing.

This is the core of the real Colditz story: how ordinary people, on both sides, responded to dramatic and demanding circumstances not of their making. It asks a simple question: What would you have done?

Contents

1944

1945

List of Illustrations

All photographs credited to Johannes Lange, the official photographer at Colditz, are reproduced from an unpublished scrapbook in a private collection.

INSERT ONE

Europe, 1937–42

Copenhagen

DENMARK

North Sea

Hamburg

□ Marlag und Milag Nord

Elbe

Weser

Amsterdam

Berlin

NETHERLANDS

GERMANY

Mulde —

Rhine

Kassel

Halle

Leipzig

Leisnig

Colditz

Dresden

Brussels

Berrendorf

Penig

Eschweiler

Zwickau

Chemnitz

Königs

Sa

BELGIUM

BOHEM

Prag

Nürnberg

□Weinsberg

Regensburg

□Eichstätt

Strasbourg

Ulm

FRANCE

Munich

Danub

Basel

Singen

(Ramsen salient)

□Tittmoning

Laufen□ Salzburg

Dôle

Berchtesgaden

Innsbruck

Markt Pongau

Bern

AUSTRIA

SWITZERLAND

Geneva

ITALY

0   50   100   150 miles

0   100   200 km

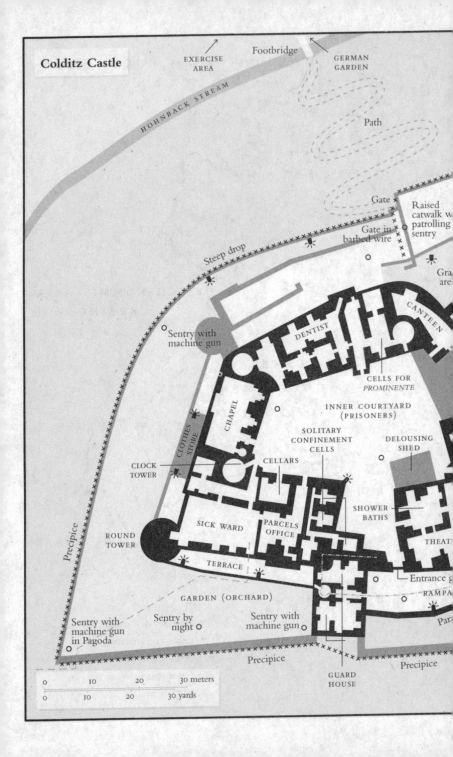

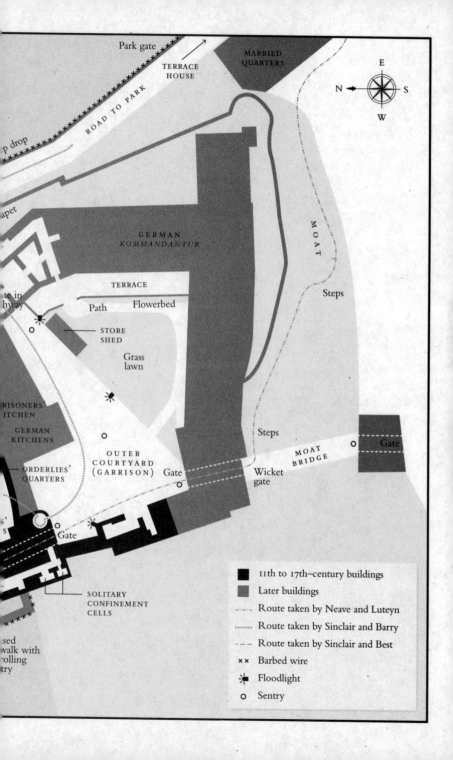

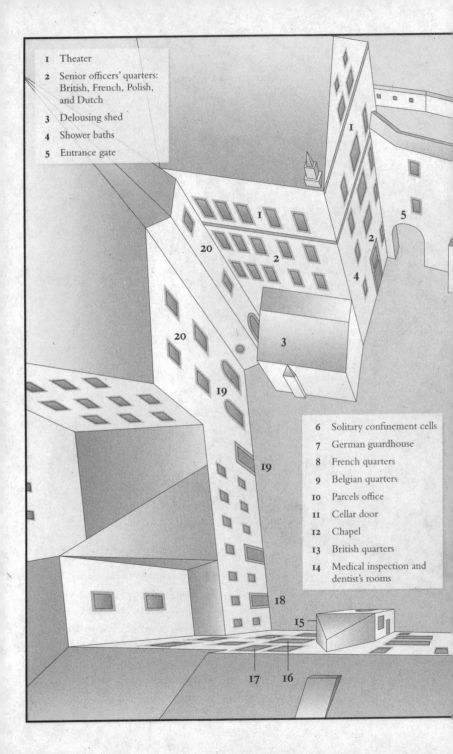

1 Theater
2 Senior officers' quarters:
   British, French, Polish,
   and Dutch
3 Delousing shed
4 Shower baths
5 Entrance gate

6 Solitary confinement cells
7 German guardhouse
8 French quarters
9 Belgian quarters
10 Parcels office
11 Cellar door
12 Chapel
13 British quarters
14 Medical inspection and
   dentist's rooms

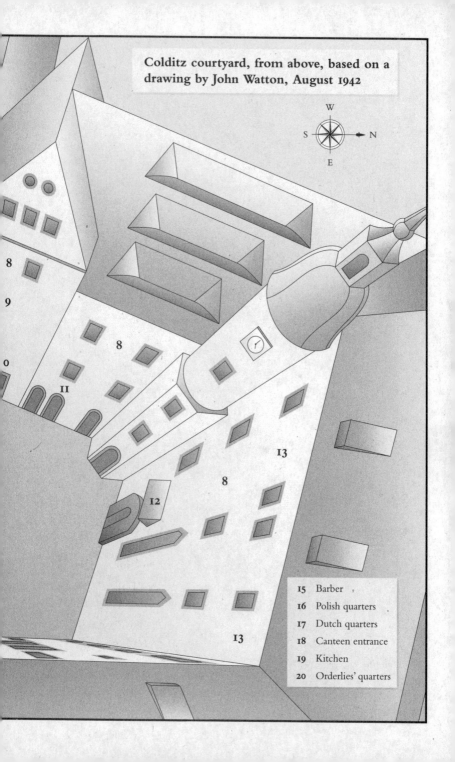

Colditz courtyard, from above, based on a drawing by John Watton, August 1942

8

9

0

11

8

8

12

13

8

13

15 Barber
16 Polish quarters
17 Dutch quarters
18 Canteen entrance
19 Kitchen
20 Orderlies' quarters

PRISONERS
OF THE CASTLE

Franz Josef

Every evening, Sergeant Major Gustav Rothenberger carried out an inspection of the castle perimeter, checking that the sentries were alert at their posts and hoping to catch one napping. Rothenberger was a stickler for routine, and the last stop on his rounds was always the east side of the building, where a narrow walkway, with a sheer drop on one side and the mighty castle wall rising on the other, led to a barbed wire gate. Beyond that lay the park and the woods. Guards with machine guns were posted at intervals of thirty feet along the length of the terrace. Two more sentries guarded the gate itself, one patrolling a raised metal catwalk with a clear line of fire down the terrace.

Shortly before midnight on a warm September night in 1943, the Sergeant Major (or Stabsfeldwebel in German) appeared on the terrace as usual, accompanied by two soldiers with slung rifles. The prisoners had been locked into their quarters two hours earlier. Colditz was quiet. Powerful floodlights threw the guards' distorted silhouettes against the granite face of the castle.

Rothenberger cut an unmistakable figure. A native of Saxony, he had won the Iron Cross during the First World War and was said to wear his campaign medals in bed. He was feared and admired by the men under his command in Number 3 platoon of the guard company. The prisoners took every opportunity to mock their captors, but treated this bristling martinet with cautious respect, as a soldier from an earlier age: battle-scarred, disciplined, and extravagantly hairy. The most distinctive thing about Rothenberger was his facial plumage, a spectacular mustache and mutton-chop combination. The old soldier was immensely proud of his huge gingery whiskers, brushing, clipping, and waxing them to points, as if grooming an exotic pet. The British POWs called him "Franz Josef" [*sic*], after the Austro-Hungarian emperor with the handlebar mustache, but never, ever to his face.

Rothenberger marched up smartly to the first guard on the terrace and barked: "There is an attempted escape on the west side. Report to the guardhouse immediately." The startled sentry saluted, clicked his heels, and took off; the officer dismissed the second guard, and then the third. The two sentries manning the gate were surprised to see Rothenberger rounding the corner of the terrace with two replacement guards in tow. They were not due to go off duty for another two hours. "You're relieved early," snapped the mustachioed sergeant major. "Give me the key." Rothenberger appeared to be particularly irritable tonight; but appearances can be deceptive.

A close inspection of Rothenberger's facial hair would have revealed that it was made from dismantled shaving brushes, colored ginger-gray with watercolor paints from the prison shop and attached with glue; his uniform, like those of his escorts, was stitched with precision out of prison blankets, and dyed the correct shade of German field gray; the Iron Cross on his breast was made from zinc stripped off the castle roof and molded into shape with a hot kitchen knife; his headgear had been fashioned out of a peaked RAF cap using felt and string; his pistol holster was cardboard, shined up with brown boot polish, from which poked a piece of wood painted to look like the butt of a 9mm Walther P38 pistol; the two soldiers in greatcoats carried dummy rifles with wooden barrels polished with pencil lead, bolts fashioned from bits of steel bedstead, and tin triggers formed from metal cutlery.

The sergeant major was a replica Rothenberger, a fake Franz Josef. His name was Michael Sinclair, a twenty-five-year-old British lieutenant who had already escaped twice from Colditz before being caught and brought back. Sinclair was fluent in German, a talented amateur actor, and an obsessive. He thought only of escaping, and talked about nothing else. "I'm getting out of here," he insisted, repeatedly. This was not an expression of hope, but a statement of belief. Some of the other prisoners found his single-mindedness off-putting: There was something desperate in Sinclair's determination. For four months, he had studied Rothenberger's gait, posture, and accent, his routine, his mannerisms, and the way he swore when angry, which was often.

High above the terrace, thirty-five more British officers waited in the darkness. The bars on the windows of the sixth floor had already been sawn through. The men wore handmade civilian clothes. Each carried a counterfeit travel pass, forged using a typewriter of wood and wire, a photograph taken with a camera made from a cigar box and spectacles, and authorized with the official German eagle stamp carved out of a shoe heel using a razor blade. "It's going to work," someone whispered, as the first guard hurried off. "It's really going to work."

The plan was simple: with the sentries out of the way, a first group of twenty would climb down the outside of the building on ropes made from knotted bedsheets, Sinclair would unlock the gate to the park, and they would all scramble down the slope into the nearby woods. If they got away, the rest would follow a few minutes later. Once in the trees, they would split into pairs and spread out into the countryside, before making for Germany's borders by a variety of prearranged routes. The "Franz Josef plan" depended on ingrained German habits of military obedience, preparation, timing, luck, and the credibility of Sinclair's false whiskers. The escapers calculated it would take four and a half minutes before the dismissed guards reached the guardhouse and found the real Rothenberger. At which point all hell would break loose. Many of the prisoners crouching in the dark had been captives for almost three years. During that time numerous escapes had been attempted with only a small handful of successes. In the escalating internal war between the guarded and the guards, a major victory beckoned. If it worked, this would be the first mass breakout in Colditz history.

The *Kommandant* of Colditz had recently issued orders that everyone, without exception, entering or leaving the castle must produce a pass, with a different color for each day. The sentry at the gate was sticking to the rules. Later, he would claim that the mustache before him "did not quite curl properly"; in truth he was merely obeying orders, even though Rothenberger had issued those orders and was now apparently telling him to disobey them. The sentry's voice floated up to the windows above: "Nein, Herr Stabsfeldwebel. *Nein!*" Sinclair cursed him for his insolence. "Are you daft? Don't you know your own sergeant?" But finally, he reached into his pocket and handed over an exit pass, or *Ausweis,* dated, signed, and stamped.

This was a copy of a real pass obtained from a bribed German guard. It was a perfect duplicate in every respect. Except it was the wrong color. The fake pass was gray. It was supposed to be yellow.

The sentry stared at it for a moment, and back at "Franz Josef" Rothenberger. Then he slowly raised his rifle.

1940

1

The Originals

On the afternoon of November 10, 1940, Captain Pat Reid gazed up at the castle on the cliff and experienced the combination of admiration and anxiety its builders had intended. "We saw looming above us our future prison," he later wrote. "Beautiful, serene, majestic and yet forbidding enough to make our hearts sink . . . a sight to make the bravest quail."

Quailing was not in Pat Reid's nature. Indeed, he saw faint-heartedness of any sort as a moral failing, and refused to countenance it, in himself or anyone else. An officer in the Royal Army Service Corps, he had been captured in May, one of thousands of soldiers unable to get away after the fall of France. Initially held in Laufen Castle in Bavaria, he had immediately supervised the digging of a tunnel from the basement to a small shed outside the prison walls, and then made a break for the Yugoslavian border with five other officers. They were on the run for five days before they were caught and sent to Colditz, a new camp for incorrigible prisoners, and therefore a place for which Reid was amply qualified.

Born in India to an Irish father, Reid was at twenty-nine years old a natural contrarian and a born exhibitionist, a most dependable ally, and as an opponent, obstinate and insufferable. He had once climbed the rugby posts during an England-Ireland international at Twickenham to plant a bunch of shamrocks at the top. Described as "a thick-set, wavy-haired fellow with a mischievous look in his eyes" by one fellow inmate, Reid spoke and wrote exclusively in the argot of the *Boy's Own Paper*. He displayed, at all times, a relentless, chirpy optimism. With a strong sense of his own place in the drama, Reid would become the first and most extensive chronicler of Colditz. He hated the place on sight and spent most of the rest of his life thinking and writing about it.

The British officers, later known as the "Laufen Six," were marched across the moat, and then under a second stone archway, "whose oaken doors closed ominously behind us with the clanging of heavy iron bars in true medieval fashion." In peacetime, Reid had been a civil engineer and he cast a professional eye over the battlements. The ground fell away in a sheer precipice on three sides, below terraces festooned in barbed wire. As the day faded, the castle walls were lit by a blaze of searchlights. The nearest city was Leipzig, twenty-three miles to the northwest. The closest border to a country outside Nazi control was 400 miles away. "Escape," Reid reflected, "would be a formidable proposition." The little group was marched under another gated arch, and into the inner courtyard. Only the sound of their boots ringing on the cobbles broke the silence. It was, wrote Reid, "an unspeakably grisly place."

Colditz Castle stands on a hilltop 150 feet above the Mulde River, a tributary of the Elbe in the east of what is now Germany. Before it became a German province in the tenth century, the Serbian Slavs who inhabited the area had called it *Koldyese,* meaning "dark forest." The first stone of what would become a mighty fortress was laid in about 1043, and over the next millennium it was repeatedly expanded and modified, destroyed and rebuilt by the great dynasties that tussled for power and prominence in the area. Fire, war, and pestilence changed the castle's shape over the centuries, but its purposes remained constant: to impress and oppress the ruler's subjects, demonstrate his might, frighten his enemies, and incarcerate his captives.

The hereditary rulers of the region, the Electors of Saxony, converted it into a hunting lodge, with a chapel and banqueting hall, and in 1523 the surrounding parkland became a game reserve encircled by high stone walls; white stags were held in a special enclosure in the park or *Tiergarten,* before being released and hunted down. The electors kept their dowagers, turbulent relatives, and unmarried daughters within the castle walls. In the early eighteenth century under Augustus II, Elector of Saxony, King of Poland, and Grand Duke of Lithuania, the *Schloss* was enlarged with additional fortifications and pleasure gardens, and a theater. "Augustus the Strong" was a man of immense physical stamina, skilled in the sport of fox-tossing (which was exactly as nasty as it sounds), and a prodigious womanizer said to have fathered somewhere between 365 and 382 children. The castle was expanded to 700 rooms in order to house them.

By the nineteenth century the Saxon princes had turned their attention elsewhere, and the castle on the hill became a poorhouse, a remand home, and then a hospital for the "incurably insane." The most expensive lunatic asylum in Germany, Colditz was a dumping ground for the mentally disturbed members of wealthy and notable families, including the composer Robert Schumann's son Ludwig, who arrived, deranged, at the age of twenty, and never left. By the twentieth century it had become a place of death, a vast mausoleum of freezing stone floors, drafty corridors, and hidden misery. During the First World War it housed tuberculosis and psychiatric patients, of whom 912 died from malnutrition. Before the war, the Nazis used it as a concentration camp for communists, social democrats, and other political opponents of Hitler. More than 2,000 such "undesirables" were imprisoned there in a single year. Some were tortured in its dank cells. After a brief period as a camp for Reich Youth Workers, in 1938 it became an asylum again, but this time a lethal one: eighty-four physically and mentally disabled people were deliberately starved to death, a testing ground for Hitler's full-scale euthanasia program.

But in 1939 it became what it will always be remembered as: a camp for prisoners of war. The *Oberkommando der Wehrmacht* (OKW), or German Army High Command, turned Colditz into a special camp (*Sonderlager*) for a particular breed of captured enemy officers: prisoners who had tried to escape from other camps, or otherwise displayed a markedly negative attitude toward Germany. These were designated *deutschfeindlich*, or "German-unfriendly," a word that has no parallel in any other language and is virtually untranslatable: in Nazi Germany, insufficient friendliness was a crime. Being *deutschfeindlich* merited a red tab on a prisoner's record: a mark of demerit in German eyes, but a distinction of note among POWs. The castle was henceforth a camp for captured officers, an *Offizierslager,* designated Oflag IV-C.

The denizens of Colditz Castle, over the centuries, had been many and varied, but almost all had this in common: They were not there out of choice. The dowagers, lunatics, Jews, virgins, tubercular patients, war prisoners, and white stags in the park had all been brought to the castle by others, and could not get out. Even the bastard progeny of Augustus the Strong were trapped in this huge hilltop compound. The great castle had supposedly been built to protect the people, but it was always a projection of power, a vast castellated giant dominating the skyline, erected to awe those living below and keep its occupants securely inside. It was either magnificent or monstrous, depending on which side of its walls you were on.

The building consisted of two adjoining courtyards. The inner, older space, no bigger than a tennis court, was cobbled and surrounded by four walls ninety feet high. On the north side were the chapel and clock tower; on the west the *Saalhaus,* or great hall, with the theater, parcels office, and senior officers' quarters above; on the south was the prisoners' kitchen, adjoining the German quarters; the east wing was the *Fürstenhaus,* or Prince's House, which would accommodate the British prisoners. The sun penetrated the inner courtyard for only a few hours around noon. A single gateway led to the larger outer courtyard, which itself had only two exits: one over the dry moat leading down to the town of Colditz in the valley below, and the other through a tunnel under the barracks, sloping down toward the park and woods that had once been the gardens and hunting grounds of the mighty electors. The prisoners were contained in the inner courtyard, while the German guards, men of the 395th Defense Battalion, occupied the outer one: the garrison headquarters known as the *Kommandantur.*

Colditz Castle looked as solid and unyielding as the rock it stood upon. In reality, it was full of holes. The colossal stone warren had been built in layers, one on another, rooms expanded, windows opened up or filled in, corridors blocked, drains diverted and re-dug, by men who had been dead for centuries. It was riddled with hidden compartments, abandoned attics, doors secured by medieval locks, and long-forgotten fissures. Over the next four years, Reid and the other inhabitants of the inner courtyard sought to exploit these openings, while those in the outer courtyard struggled, just as energetically, to plug them.

A tall, sharp-faced German officer saluted crisply as the British prisoners entered the courtyard. "Good evening, my English friends," he said, in impeccable English. "You must be tired after so long a day."

Leutnant Reinhold Eggers was the antithesis of Pat Reid in every possible way, being formal, self-disciplined, and humorless, as patriotic as Reid was *deutschfeindlich*. The two men detested each other on sight: their meeting marked the start of a long and bitter contest.

The son of a blacksmith from Brunswick, Eggers had fought at Ypres and the Somme, and finished the war after "fifty-one dreadful months" with an Iron Cross and a bullet wound in his leg. Eggers described himself as a "German patriot, devoted to my country." But Eggers was no Nazi, and had briefly fallen foul of the party before the war for failing to show sufficient enthusiasm for National Socialism. Already forty-nine years old when the second war started, he was called up again and, like many older soldiers, deployed in the army prison service as deputy to the senior duty officer at Oflag IV-C. He would go on to become the supreme security chief of Colditz.

A schoolteacher by profession, Eggers retained all the attributes of an old-fashioned Prussian headmaster: an orderly, fastidious disciplinarian, as brittle and stiff as a stick of chalk, but even-handed, unflappable, and insistent on good manners. He believed that a career spent educating disobedient children ideally suited him to maintaining control over the rowdiest POWs in Germany, and he applied his rules for teaching to running a prison camp: "Never show any emotion; keep smiling whatever happens; punish disobedience with energy." A man of principle, he strongly disapproved of using violence against inmates, except in self-defense. His diary and other writings offer a remarkable insight into Colditz from the German perspective.

Eggers was also an ardent anglophile, a risky enthusiasm in Nazi Germany. He made no secret of his admiration for the British countryside, courtesy, language, food, and good sportsmanship. The dissertation for his teacher's diploma was entitled *The Theory and Practice of School Reform in England from Victorian Times to the Present Day*. In 1932, he had organized a school exchange between the Johann-Gottfried-Herder-Gymnasium in Halle and the Cheltenham Grammar School. While Nazism was on the rise in Germany, he had spent several happy months in the Gloucestershire spa town lapping up British culture and English beer. But the experience had left him with a warped perception of England, and he emerged with the impression that all Britons were like those he had encountered in Cheltenham: polite, interested in Germany, and incapable of unfair play. He was about to get a rude surprise.

Even before the first prisoners arrived, Eggers had spotted two major flaws in the Wehrmacht's plan to create a super-prison for difficult prisoners from which it would be impossible to escape. The first was the building itself: it looked daunting, to be sure, but the sheer complexity of its medieval layout made it extremely hard to render secure. "The place was impregnable," Eggers wrote, "but a more unsuitable place to hold prisoners will probably never again be chosen." The second was the nature of the inmates: *deutschfeindlich,* "the bad types," as Eggers put it, "undesirables [with] established reputations as disturbers of the peace." Removing troublemakers might make the other prison camps easier to manage, but Eggers the schoolmaster was acutely aware that if you put all the naughtiest boys in one class they pool their resistance, egg one another on, and soon your classroom is on fire.

Every school and prison needs a rule book, and for Eggers this was the Geneva Convention on POWs, signed by Germany and thirty-six other nations in 1929, laying down regulations governing the feeding, housing, and punishment of POWs. Prisoner welfare was monitored by a neutral "protecting power," initially America and then Switzerland. Under the Convention, captured officers enjoyed certain privileges, including being "treated with the regard due to their rank." Unlike prisoners from "other ranks," who were held in a labor camp known as a *Stammlager*, or Stalag, officers imprisoned during the Second World War could not be forced to work for the Reich. The most senior officer among them was recognized as an official intermediary between the camp authorities and the prisoners. The inmates of Colditz might have lost their freedom but they knew their legal rights, and so did the Germans. The paramilitary SS operated the concentration camps with an inhuman disregard for international law, but in the army-run POW camps most senior German officers saw it as a matter of soldierly pride to uphold the Convention, and took offense at any suggestion they were failing to do so. In the midst of an increasingly brutal war, the German army guards were still sticking to the rules, for now. "They do not resort to petty tyranny," wrote one British inmate, "but treat us, after they have taken every precaution to prevent escapes, as gentlemen who know the meaning of honour and possess a gentleman's dignity."

As he looked around the courtyard for the first time, Pat Reid felt he had entered "some ghostly ruin," and sure enough, as his eyes grew accustomed to the gloom, eerily pale faces began to appear at the upper windows. A contingent of 140 Polish officers had arrived a week earlier, and now welcomed the new prisoners with a slow-rising chant: "*Anglicy, Anglicy . . .*" The English, the English . . .

As POWs, the Poles occupied an anomalous position. Some 420,000 Polish soldiers were captured by the Germans in 1939, and their country had been carved up between Germany and the Soviet Union. In German eyes they were not protected by the Convention. "Poland no longer exists," Polish officers were told upon arrival in Colditz. "It is only due to the magnanimity of the Führer that you are benefiting temporarily from the privileges accorded to prisoners-of-war of the other belligerent powers. You should be grateful." The Poles did not feel grateful. Most felt only visceral loathing for the Germans, which they did little to disguise. The Polish officer contingent was led by General Tadeusz Piskor, who had been sent to Colditz for refusing to shake the proffered hand of a camp Kommandant. "The Poles seethed with hatred of us," wrote Eggers.

Reid and his five companions were marched up a narrow staircase, and locked into an attic room, where they found three more inmates: Canadian RAF officers who had been shot down over Germany the previous April and escaped from another camp, only to be swiftly recaptured, comprehensively beaten up, and taken to Colditz.

The British were settling into their new quarters when they heard a scratching at the door, which swung open to reveal four smiling Polish officers carrying several large bottles of beer. It had taken the Poles less than a week to work out that the ancient locks on the castle's internal doors could be opened with ease using "a couple of instruments that looked like button hooks." A small party now took place, conducted in fractured English, with snatches of French and German, the founding ceremony of an enduring Anglo-Polish alliance in Colditz. As he fell asleep on a straw-stuffed mattress in a narrow wooden bunk, Reid reflected that the Poles must have opened at least five locks to reach the British quarters from their own billet on the other side of the courtyard: "If they could get from one place to another through locked doors, well, so could we."

The first few weeks in Colditz resembled another phony war, similar to the period of tense inaction just after war itself was officially declared, as the different nationalities, the guards and the prisoners, carefully assessed one another and their new shared home. Compared with some of their previous camps, the castle seemed almost comfortable, despite the peeling walls and pervasive smell of mold. One new inmate felt he had joined a "sort of club." The British and Canadian contingent was moved to permanent quarters in the east wing, with flushing lavatories, showers, spasmodic hot water, electric light, a stove, and a long hall used as a mess room for eating and recreation. They could circulate in the courtyard during daylight, but the rest of the huge castle was strictly off-limits. The food produced by the German kitchen down in the courtyard was unappetizing—ersatz acorn coffee, thin soups, and black bread—but it was edible. As officers, the prisoners were theoretically entitled to pay, which came in the form of "camp money" to be spent in the prison shop or canteen on cigarettes, razor blades, blankets, and, at least initially, weak beer. Three times a day, the prisoners were assembled for a roll call, or *Appell,* in the courtyard: having formed up in ranks by nation, they were counted, laboriously recounted, addressed by the Germans if there was anything worth saying, and then dismissed. The first roll call was at 8 a.m., and the last at 9 p.m., shortly before "lights out," when the electricity was cut off, the staircases were locked, and the courtyard was shut off. The 200-strong German guard contingent outnumbered the inmates, but over the first few weeks prisoner numbers steadily increased: more British and Polish officers, a handful of Belgians, and a growing contingent of Frenchmen. Each nation was assigned to separate quarters.

At first the prisoners of different nations were kept forcibly apart, but the Germans soon realized this was going to be impossible, and so the inmates mixed and mingled in the courtyard during the day, and covertly at night. For many, this was their first prolonged exposure to people of different nationalities and cultures. National rivalries persisted, but some were rather surprised to discover how much they had in common. "The Poles and the French are excellent fellows," observed one British inmate. "They are all of the difficult-prisoner type, but difficult prisoners make interesting prison companions."

The *Blitzkrieg* invasions of Poland and Western Europe were so swift and successful they had created an unanticipated problem for the German war machine: a vast army of prisoners to be housed, fed, and, in the case of "other ranks," put to work in the service of Hitler's Reich. More than 1.8 million Frenchmen were made captive during the Battle of France between May and June 1940, around 10 percent of the entire adult male population. The rescue operation at Dunkirk had ferried 300,000 soldiers of the cornered British Expeditionary Force across the Channel to safety, but for every seven men who escaped, one was left behind as a prisoner. Thousands more would be captured in June after the Anglo-French force surrendered at Saint-Valery. By the end of 1940, some 2,000 British officers and at least 39,000 other ranks were "in the bag," including many from the British Dominions: Canada, Australia, New Zealand, and South Africa. As the war progressed, these would be supplemented by prisoners shot down or otherwise captured in battle.

The first Colditz prisoners were the cream of their nations' professional armed forces, new graduates from Sandhurst and Saint-Cyr, as well as veterans of the First World War. Marching off to war in 1939, they had been told to expect a swift victory. None had seriously contemplated the possibility of being captured, let alone herded into Germany and locked up indefinitely in a dismal fortress. Laying down their lives for king and country was one thing; risking, and losing, their liberty was quite another, and most were entirely unprepared for captivity.

Christmas 1940 was a strange, oddly peaceful time. Cut off from the outside world, the prisoners knew nothing of the progress of the wider war. There were no letters from home, no orders from higher command, and no sense of the future. Sealed up behind medieval walls, they found their perception of time began to elongate. The war might end tomorrow, or never. They might live here for years. They might grow old here. Or die here. After the adrenaline of combat, the trauma of capture, and the uncertainty of being transferred here from other camps, Colditz seemed a place apart, almost surreal: "a fairytale castle floating high above the town." The optimists predicted they would soon be released; the restless ones were not prepared to wait for a liberation that might never come; the realists settled in for the long haul. The dank corridors were suffused with the "smell of musty decay." At night, rats could be heard scuttling over attic floorboards. Most of the castle remained empty and locked, occupied only by the ghosts of former inmates. "The walls looked as if they had smallpox." But on a clear night, when the snow-clad countryside rolled away into the distance and the sound of church bells floated up from the village below, the place was serene, and almost beautiful.

The Poles laid on a Christmas dinner of sorts, and staged a puppet show of *Snow White and the Seven Dwarfs* that ended, unlike the traditional version of the fairy tale, with the glorious restoration of the Polish nation and a rousing rendition of the Polish national anthem. The Germans distributed wine and beer to the prisoners. Leutnant Eggers was delighted to discover his

Christmas rations included a pound of real coffee beans, "the last of it I saw for years," he would note.

As he sipped his Christmas coffee, Eggers jotted down his own reports, as if assessing the latest intake of pupils at the start of a new school year: "The Polish officers were top in morale at the end of that year 1940, although they had been in our hands for over fifteen months. The French were still solemn after their defeat. The British were digging themselves in."

They were also exploring how to dig themselves out.

1941

2

Le Ray's Run

Pat Reid believed that escaping from POW camps was "the sworn duty of all officers." He believed this with passionate intensity, and he disdained those who did not share his conviction. But he was wrong.

In fact, no such obligation was incumbent on those who were captured. Most inmates of Colditz were there because they had already tried to escape from somewhere else and so, unsurprisingly, many arrived determined to get out again. For some, escape became an obsession, and the dominant topic of conversation. But not everyone was equally keen on escaping. Some were prepared to sit out the war in captivity and lead, as one disdainful escaper put it, "a vegetable existence." In certain circumstances officers gave their word of honor, or "parole," that they would not attempt to escape; they might borrow tools, for example, to build a stage set, on a solemn promise these would not be used for escaping. Non-combatant officers, including medics and clergymen, were occasionally permitted to take "parole walks," under guard, in the countryside around the castle, on the strict understanding that they would not abuse this privilege by running away. Not once did a prisoner give such a guarantee and then break his word.

Escaping was not only difficult, but dangerous. Under the Geneva Convention, a POW caught on the run was liable to a maximum punishment of one month in solitary confinement. But not all German officers were as punctilious as Eggers in sticking to the rules. Sentries carried arms and were prepared to use them, and the choice of when to deploy force was frequently left to the discretion and inclination of individual officers or guards. Anyone found outside the camp in civilian clothes or, worse, wearing a German uniform, ran the risk of being shot as a spy. If an escapee was handed over to the Wehrmacht military authorities, he was usually sent back to Colditz for a stint in the solitary cells. But if he fell into the clutches of the Gestapo or the SS, his fate was far more uncertain: he might be tortured, sent to a concentration camp, or even shot out of hand. As the Allied bombing of German cities intensified, enraged civilians were increasingly likely to mete out summary punishment to recaptured prisoners.

And just as escaping was not a duty, nor was it a right. One class of prisoner never escaped from Colditz, and was not encouraged to try: the lower class.

Running through the very heart of Colditz ran a wide and almost unbridgeable social divide. This was a camp for captured officers, but it also contained a fluctuating population of orderlies, ordinary soldier-prisoners from the "other ranks" employed by the Germans to perform menial tasks and work as servants for their senior officers: cooking, tidying, cleaning, boot polishing, and other chores. By Christmas 1940, Colditz held seventeen British officers and eight orderlies: a ratio that remained broadly constant throughout the war. Senior officers each had a personal servant, or batman, while more junior officers shared an orderly, usually one to each mess. Some were brought in from other camps and then rotated elsewhere after six months. A few remained in Colditz throughout the war. They received the same rations as the officers, including Red Cross supplies, but occupied different quarters.

The orderlies were not invited to take part in escape attempts, and were not expected to assist them (though some did). Once a week they were taken for a walk in the countryside outside the castle, under guard. None ever tried to escape, and with good reason. A recaptured officer would usually be returned to the castle unharmed, whereas ordinary soldiers were liable to suffer the most draconian punishment: "If an orderly was caught he wouldn't get the same treatment as an officer," said one batman. "He'd probably get shot." As private soldiers, the lowest rung on the military ladder, they were required to obey the orders of the Germans as well as their own officers, without question.

They ate, slept, and lived entirely separately. Less educated than the officers, the orderlies did not write memoirs after the war and their experiences have therefore been almost wholly omitted from the broader Colditz story.

Today it seems bizarre and unjust that one prisoner should have to serve another; that one man should be permitted to seek his liberty and another forbidden to do so on the grounds of rank and class. But under the Geneva Convention every captured officer had a right to be attended by an orderly, as he would if he were free. In the strictly stratified military hierarchy of the time, an officer was more valuable than a private, and therefore more useful to the war effort if he managed to escape and return to Britain. An officer was not permitted to work, but a private soldier was required to; one therefore served the other.

At the start, most orderlies were reasonably content to be in Colditz, where the work was not overly onerous, and the food better than in other camps. Shining an officer's belt buckle was infinitely preferable to forced labor. "After the copper mines, Colditz was a holiday camp," observed one orderly.

Sidney Goldman was batman to the first Senior British Officer (SBO) at Colditz, the confusingly named Guy German. Lieutenant Colonel German had been captured during the Norwegian campaign and sent to Colditz for publicly burning copies of a Nazi propaganda newspaper; his servant went with him. Solly Goldman was a Jewish cockney from London's East End with, as Reid put it, a "lightning wit." Eggers called him "the ace amongst the orderlies," because while Goldman was impudent and entertaining, he was also obedient. "Solly Goldman would be seen regularly in the early morning toting a steaming jug of ersatz coffee across the cobbled courtyard towards the senior officers' quarters." Colonel German was a farmer in civilian life, with a blunt manner and an earthy vocabulary. When the new Senior British Officer was informed that the British prisoners should look smarter during roll calls, German replied with an expletive translated as: "The Germans can jolly well lump it." He was said to be "devoted" to his manservant, Goldman, but there was never any doubt about their respective positions in the prison pecking order.

According to the Colditz myth, all its inmates sought to escape on principle, all the time, in a universal spirit of cooperation, while sadistic and stupid German guards tried to stop them. The reality was more complicated. Many prisoners did try to escape, but a lot did not, either because they were not supposed to, like the orderlies, or because they did not want to. With exceptions, most of the German guards were not brutes, and some, like Eggers, were not even Nazis. There was honor on both sides.

German military thinking tended toward absolutes: total war, total victory, and, in this case, a prison camp that was totally escape-proof. Under the Geneva Convention, the authorities could take special measures to detain particularly difficult prisoners. Pat Reid listed these as: "More roll calls, more searches, more sentries, less exercise space, less privacy, less privileges . . ." From the outset, prisoners at Colditz were not just closely guarded but under round-the-clock surveillance. An escaping prisoner would first have to get out of the inner courtyard, a massive stone box with walls seven feet thick and ninety feet high, and bars on every window; to leave the way he came in, through the main gate, a prisoner would then have to traverse the German garrison courtyard; in the valley to the west was the village of Colditz, its railway station tantalizingly visible; to the east lay the park, with inviting woods beyond. But to get out, the escaper would have to navigate terraces swathed in barbed wire, or clamber down the sheer cliffs on three sides of the fortress. Once beyond the castle perimeter, the escapee faced even greater obstacles: Colditz was a garrison town, and its 6,000 civilian inhabitants were already on alert for fugitive prisoners. As soon as an escape was discovered, the castle Kommandant sent out an emergency alert, with the code word "Mousetrap," to railway stations and police posts for a radius of twenty-five miles; within a few hours, every railway worker, café keeper, forester, and policeman would be on the lookout. Even the Hitler Youth, the Nazi Party youth organization, was mobilized to hunt down the fugitives. Search parties, on foot and mounted on bicycles, scoured the woods and fields, and sentries manned every crossroads. If the escaper managed to reach a frontier, he still had to get through wartime border controls tighter than at any previous time in history. Getting out of Germany was far harder than getting out of Colditz.

It is difficult to escape when starving. An empty stomach fills the mind, sometimes to the point of fixation, with thoughts of where the next meal is coming from. The prisoners of Colditz were not yet famished, but the calorific content of the slop doled out by the prison kitchen was far below what was needed to keep them healthy and active.

The first major boost to prisoner morale came not with a successful escape, but in the form of fifteen rectangular cardboard boxes weighing ten pounds each. A consignment of food parcels arrived in Colditz on Boxing Day 1940, the initial trickle of a great wave of supplies that would supplement the meager prison fare and sustain the prisoners, in body and mind, for most of the rest of the war. After the deprivation of the previous months, the parcels came as manna from heaven or, more precisely, from the International Red Cross charity based in Switzerland: the contents included tea, cocoa, tinned meat, butter, pickled eggs, syrup, and cigarettes. For months, cut off from the outside world, the prisoners had survived on the sparse rations from the German kitchens; here was tangible, edible evidence they had not been forgotten. In prison camps across Germany, the arrival of these first Red Cross parcels was a moment of excitement prisoners savored forever, "as treasure after treasure was revealed, drooled over, fondled, and sampled." Deliveries were at first unpredictable, and stocks had to be teased out over months. But by the spring of 1941 the prisoners were receiving regular deliveries, sometimes as much as one parcel a week. There were English cigarettes, in place of the lung-ravaging German or Polish varieties: "I lit one up and took a big drag," recalled one smoker. "I almost lost my sense in sheer delight." In time, the Red Cross would also supply limited medicines and essential clothing. The prisoners also started to receive letters and personal packages from friends and family back home. These were carefully searched for contraband, before being distributed to each addressee at the parcels office. They were permitted to write back, up to four postcards and two letters a month, with as little as six weeks between dispatch and delivery.

This was a barbaric war, but the provision of food, letters, books, sporting equipment, medicine, and clothing to POWs, on both sides, was a beacon of civilized behavior amid the carnage, insufficiently celebrated and of inestimable value. Many more prisoners in Germany would have died without the Red Cross parcels, and the impact was immediate: "Gone were the hangdog stances of the ragged and starving . . . faces were fuller."

The arrival of limited supplies from outside also presented opportunities for stockpiling, hoarding, and trading, in which one man's consignment of condensed milk might be swapped for another's excess stock of tea. Cigarettes became a currency to be bartered with guards for real money, essential to any escape attempt through Germany. Prison guards faced serious punishment if they were caught trading or accepting bribes, but even the most conscientious sentry might be rendered cooperative by a pound of chocolate and a hundred cigarettes.

Spring saw a steady influx of new arrivals: more British officers and orderlies (including Colonel German and his batman, Solly Goldman), several dozen Poles, two Yugoslav airmen who had volunteered for the RAF before being shot down over France, a handful of Belgians, and more than two hundred Frenchmen. Some had tried to escape from other camps, but twenty of the French officers had no idea why they had been moved to Colditz and therefore called themselves "Les Innocents." Two of the Belgians were labelled *deutschfeindlich* because they had cooked and eaten a cat in their previous camp, a meal they described as "delicious, just like rabbit." The French contingent included some sixty Jewish officers.

"It was a Europe in miniature," said one inmate, and like Europe the prison population was nominally united, but with distinct internal divisions and racial tensions. The French were aggrieved that the Poles got on better with the British; the Poles felt the French had failed to put up sufficient resistance to Nazi invasion; the Belgians resented being thought of as more or less French; the British simultaneously admired and distrusted the French, knowing that many remained loyal to the puppet Vichy regime in unoccupied France. One prisoner saw the Anglo-French tension as "the inevitable clashing impact of French curiosity on British sluggish phlegm." Everyone liked the Yugoslavs. There were strong individual friendships across nationalities— and many paired off for language lessons—but there was inevitably a tendency to fall back on stereotypes. Then, as now, the different European nationalities lived and worked in harmony— except when they didn't.

The new British arrivals included three chaplains, among them a Methodist minister, Joseph Ellison Platt, who had been captured near Dunkirk. Padre "Jock" Platt would keep a daily diary throughout his time in Colditz, a detailed account of everyday life in the prison but also an extended sermon, for Platt was a Christian of iron conventionality who stared sternly at the world through thick horn-rimmed spectacles and found moral instruction wherever he looked. He possessed a "radiant certainty and hope which nothing could destroy," according to the Directory of Primitive Methodist Ministers. This was a polite Christian way of saying he had complete faith in his own rectitude, and never hesitated to correct anyone who disagreed with him. He should not have been in Colditz. In his previous camp, a mysterious metal instrument presumed to be for escape purposes had been found in his locker, and he was packed off to Colditz: it was, in fact, a wire for propping up the lid of his ancient suitcase. The pastor had no intention of escaping: he had a captive flock, and he planned to ensure that whatever trials lay ahead, they did not stray from the path of righteousness. In the boarding school hierarchy emerging at Colditz, Colonel German was Head Boy, Reid the Captain of the First XI, and Platt the school chaplain.

The growing French contingent included some irrepressible personalities, men considered too defiant to be held in a normal camp, of whom the most indomitable, as well as the most enigmatic, was Alain Le Ray, a lieutenant in the Chasseurs Alpins, the elite French mountain infantry force. Le Ray had been wounded and captured during the Battle of France, and then held at a camp on the Oder estuary. An experienced mountaineer with honed survival skills, he had escaped into the teeth of the Baltic winter and headed for France, hiding in a "snow grave" during the day and hopping on freight trains at night. He was just sixty miles short of the French border when he was caught and sent to Colditz.

From the moment of Le Ray's arrival, Pat Reid noticed something distinctive about this "handsome, black-haired, debonair young man," an inner intensity that set him apart from the other Frenchmen. Le Ray teamed up with an English officer to improve his English and willingly recounted his adventures, yet he seldom took part in the talk of escape, despite an undisguised determination to do so. "Some would-be escapers were loners," wrote Reid, who found this secretive and solitary Frenchman both intriguing and unsettling. Reid was the ultimate team player, a backslapping enthusiast who chivvied others to take part in whatever scheme he was hatching. Le Ray was the opposite. As lithe and agile as a cat, he possessed a feline detachment and self-containment. Le Ray had a plan and he had no intention of telling anyone, least of all the garrulous Pat Reid, what it was.

With the exterior of Colditz so heavily guarded, the most logical way to try to get out undetected was underground. Digging a tunnel would take patience, planning, and manpower, all of which were available in abundance. By the spring of 1941, the British, the Poles, and the French were each working on independent tunnels in different parts of the camp, without informing one another: in the ground beneath Colditz, a secret and undeclared contest was underway.

A team of French tunnelers including Le Ray broke into the clock tower in the northwest corner of the courtyard; by early February, they had dug a shaft ten feet into the cellar, from which they began burrowing a horizontal tunnel to the outside, digging quietly at night, in shifts, using pieces of metal bedframe and spreading the spoil in the attics. The Poles, meanwhile, were secretly working on a tunnel at the other side of the courtyard, aiming to connect with the castle sewage system.

A similar thought occurred to Pat Reid. "I was attracted by the drains," he wrote. In the ground floor canteen, where the prisoners lined up to buy the few items it contained, lay a large manhole cover. One afternoon, while the German sergeant on duty was distracted, Reid and a fellow officer levered off the lid, and carried out a swift reconnaissance: in one direction the drain led back to the courtyard, connecting with another manhole, but to the east it curved toward the outer wall for some eighteen feet, where it was blocked by a stone wall. Beyond that lay a triangle of lawn, with a balustrade on one side, and a thirty-foot drop to the roadway leading out to the park. Following the Polish example, the British had already carved a key that opened the old-fashioned lever-lock on the door at the foot of the staircase leading from their quarters into the courtyard. If they could get into the canteen undetected, surmised Reid, they might be able to dig through the stone wall at the end of the drain, construct a horizontal tunnel under the little lawn, and then push a vertical shaft upward through the grass. The escapers could then climb down the parapet with bedsheets, creep past the German quarters, climb over the twelve-foot park wall, and head for the woods. If the opening of the tunnel was concealed by a detachable wooden trapdoor with a turf covering, the exit might be undetected after the first escape, and then used again. If a team of tunnelers could slip in at night and lock the canteen door behind them, they might dig undisturbed until daybreak. The Devil makes work for idle hands, and Padre Platt decided that Reid's tunnel was a wholesome activity deserving of his blessing: "It will occupy about two or three months, working two or three hours a night after lights out."

While the canteen guard was distracted, his key was "borrowed" from the table drawer, pressed into a bar of soap, and then returned. It took just a few days to make a duplicate from part of an iron bedstead. Lookouts, or "stooges," were watching from the upper floors soon after midnight when four men emerged from the British staircase, crossed the ten yards of dark courtyard without being spotted, and entered the canteen. It took a week of nocturnal quarrying to break through the four-foot wall at the end of the drain. Beyond it, the ground consisted of sticky yellow clay.

Then came near-calamity, evidence of how easily one escape attempt could scupper another. In mid-March two Poles broke into the canteen, unaware of the British tunnel being built under their feet, and set about sawing through the bars of the window overlooking the patch of grass. The noise attracted a sentry, and they were caught. A large new floodlight was erected facing directly onto the lawn: henceforth, this dark corner of the castle was lit up every night like a theater stage.

Tunneling by hand is a time-consuming and exhausting business, requiring huge reserves of perseverance, a quality that, like so many others, was unevenly distributed among the prisoners. "Tunnelling did not suit me," admitted Alain Le Ray, the maverick Frenchman. "I was getting too impatient. What I wanted was something quick that I could execute alone."

The courtyard, where prisoners milled around during the day, was far too cramped for any serious exercise. The Geneva Convention, however, stated that prisoners "shall have facilities for engaging in physical exercise and obtaining the benefit of being out of doors," and so the Germans erected two enclosures in the park surrounded by six-foot wire fencing: a large one for running and walking, and a smaller cage for games of soccer or rugby. Two or three times a week saw the "Park Walk," when prisoners who wanted exercise (and not all did) assembled in the courtyard and were carefully counted before being marched past the *Kommandantur,* down a zigzagging path, across the stream, and into the park enclosures. The Park Walk was "a formal affair with a touch of menace," but "march" is an orderly word for an event that was frequently chaotic and became more so as the prison population expanded. The prisoners were counted inside the courtyard, outside it, on arrival in and leaving the park, a laborious rigmarole that the more unruly prisoners did their best to disrupt at every stage. The prisoners never wore the same clothing, failed to form up in neat ranks, and refused to walk in straight lines, "crocodiling around corners, concertinaing on the straight bits, jostling in the gateway, pointing, calling back, calling forward, dropping things." The whole process offended Eggers's sense of order, and gave Alain Le Ray his chance.

At the bottom of the path leading into the park stood a dilapidated building known as the Terrace House, used to store building materials. Shortly before Easter, on the Park Walk, Le Ray noticed that the door had been left ajar. Confiding in only two fellow officers, he assembled his escape kit: a set of civilian clothes, a map of the German railway system, and a few Reichs-marks, obtained by bartering cigarettes with a guard.

On Good Friday, Le Ray put on a greatcoat over a set of homemade civilian clothes and joined the crowd heading down to the park to watch a soccer match. On the way back, as they turned the corner beside the Terrace House, Le Ray's coat was whipped off and put on by the man standing behind him, as he scrambled up the bank and in through the door. He lay panting, listening for sounds of pursuit, but all was silent. "No shouts, no chase, no dogs." Back up at the castle, two accomplices staged a fight; in the confusion the Germans muddled the recount, and Le Ray's absence passed unnoticed. As night fell, he ran down the path and headed for the outer wall. In the open, he felt danger-ously exposed. "The whole park was like a great eye watching me." Le Ray scrambled over the wall and into the trees.

After walking five miles, he reached the town of Rochlitz, where he boarded a train for nearby Penig, and then spent his remaining cash on a train to Zwickau, fifty miles to the south. There he hid in the guard's van of the next train leaving the sta-tion. Twenty-four hours after climbing out of Colditz, he was in Nuremberg, where the Nazi Party had staged huge rallies cele-brating Hitler's rise to power. Le Ray was penniless, freezing, famished, and in the very heart of the Reich. That night he waited in an alleyway: when a lone man approached, Le Ray jumped out of the shadows, knocked him down with two swift punches, stripped off his coat, stole his wallet, and vanished back into the darkness. It was, he conceded, "a brutal act of robbery with vio-lence against a civilian," which he justified as "self-defence under conditions of warfare." The mugging also upped the stakes: he would now face the death penalty if caught.

The stolen money bought him a train ticket to Stuttgart, and then another southward toward the Swiss border. As a moun-taineer, Le Ray had intended to climb into Switzerland across the eastern Alps, but after five days on the run his strength was ebb-ing. Instead, he made for Singen, where the border was long and flat. Setting out from the station toward the frontier through thick woodland, he was spotted by a German border patrol. After a frantic chase, the fugitive evaded capture by shinning up a tree. Aware that the border guards would now be on high alert, he doubled back to the railway station at Gottmadingen, the last stop in Germany before the train crossed into Switzerland. Buying another train ticket was out of the question. Le Ray hid in the undergrowth at the end of the platform. The 11:30 from Singen pulled in, and the train came to a halt just ten feet from where he was concealed. The guard looked up and down the deserted platform, blew his whistle, and turned his back. At that instant, Le Ray clambered over the tracks in front of the locomotive, climbed onto the front, curled up between the headlights, and clung on.

"The driver opened the throttle and the train roared through the fresh air of the spring night," wrote Le Ray, who sat upright on the coupling between the bumpers, his feet dangling inches above the rushing rails. Fear and exhaustion forgotten, the Frenchman felt a wild surge of "hope and pride" as the train picked up speed. "We passed the red lights of the enemy guard post, on under the bridge, and then into Switzerland." Le Ray had spent just forty-six days in Colditz.

Le Ray's "home run" prompted a surge of loud rejoicing among the prisoners, and a corresponding wave of recrimination and investigation by the German authorities. Here was proof that escape, hitherto only a theoretical possibility, was a real and achievable goal. The Germans had built an escape-proof prison, and a Frenchman had climbed out of it within seven weeks of arriving. The Kommandant gave his officers a ferocious dressing down: "We've all been made fools of by one prisoner." Berlin wanted answers and, like all tyrannies, someone to pin the blame on. "Who was responsible? Had he been punished?" Sniffer dogs were brought in, to no effect. Eggers concluded, wrongly, that the French alpinist must have clambered over the roofs and down a ninety-foot lightning conductor. Extra barbed wire was unfurled around the chimneys, a twenty-four-hour guard posted in the inner courtyard, and more powerful searchlights installed. Safe in Switzerland, Le Ray described his escape to the French consul, who told the British, who sent word to London: the Prisoners of War Directorate inside the War Department began to take a closer interest in high-security camp Oflag IV-C.

Le Ray's escape had been a solo effort, of which his senior officers and all but two fellow inmates had been entirely unaware. Not only were individuals planning their own escapes, but the different nationalities were launching plans that overlapped, conflicted, and might prove mutually counterproductive. The different tunnel plans were, almost literally, undermining one another. One night when the British were working on their tunnel, the Germans called a snap nighttime roll call, one of the new security measures brought in by the Kommandant, and discovered four men were missing. By the morning *Appell* the canteen diggers had reappeared, to the baffled fury of the Germans, who launched an intensive search of the castle and uncovered the French tunnel under construction in the base of the clock tower. The Polish attempt to escape through the canteen had already imperiled the British tunnel, which, by the end of March, was approaching a point near the middle of the lawn. Then came a fresh setback. Two more officers, French this time, were caught trying to get out of the canteen window. Eggers was now on the prowl. "We suspected that canteen." The Germans levered off the manhole cover, but found nothing suspicious, as the tunnelers had constructed a false wall at the near end from rubble mortared with mud that looked exactly like the real thing. Eggers had the manhole cemented down with new clasps (which the prisoners loosened before they set), put a new lock on the canteen door, and, worst of all, posted a twenty-four-hour sentry on the lawn outside the window, precisely where the tunnel exit was supposed to emerge. Tunneling was suspended.

Overlapping escape attempts and competing tunnels clearly showed the need for at least a minimal degree of coordination and collaboration. An international escape committee was established, with a set of cardinal principles: individuals would obtain permission from their Senior Officer before attempting to escape, and the senior officers of each nationality would then inform one another. Like many international liaison initiatives, this was a fine idea in principle, but problematic in practice. Secrecy was the central pillar of every escape: plans had to be kept from the Germans, obviously, but also from competitors who could try to steal an idea, and from possible spies or "stool pigeons" who might be lurking among the prison population. "Most escapers were unwilling to share their idea until sometimes at the very last moment," wrote Reid. The French psychology rebelled against such conformity anyway. "We were far too individualistic to accept that kind of system," recalled one French officer. "We did it among ourselves and we didn't like telling anyone anything." Whenever a new plan was floated, the Poles, having been in the castle longer than any other group, tended to insist that they had thought of it first. But over time the bonds of trust and familiarity strengthened between and within the different national groups, bringing a greater willingness to aid the escape plans of others, so long as that did not impede their own. Just like the allies in the wider war, prisoners were united but rivals, competing with one another while locked in battle with a common enemy.

In the intimate confines of Colditz, that enemy was becoming ever more familiar. On a battlefield, the foe is anonymous. In a prison, he has a face, a name, and a personality. At the top of the German chain of command stood the Kommandant himself, Oberstleutnant (Lieutenant Colonel) Max Schmidt, an army veteran who stuck to the rules and seldom intruded into the prisoners' lives. Schmidt left the daily running of the castle to his underlings, living a domestic existence with his wife in a private apartment inside the *Kommandantur,* and emerging only to make formal pronouncements or issue punishments. Eggers described him as an "imposing figure" with "cold grey eyes" and an "austere way of executing his authority, uncomfortable but effective."

Eggers's immediate boss, the senior camp officer, was Hauptmann (Captain) Paul Priem, another former schoolmaster but of a very different sort. Priem was a cheerful drunk, regarded by the prisoners as "the only German with a sense of humor," albeit of the thumpingly unsubtle variety. Eggers considered his immediate superior to be "altogether too easygoing," but liked him nonetheless: "A charming companion and a lively character, fond of battle, fond of life, fond of the bottle . . ." Like many alcoholics, Priem could switch in an instant from joviality to apoplectic fury.

Priem was a "belligerent supporter of Hitler," whereas Eggers and others in the German officers' mess had little time for fascism, including Kommandant Schmidt, who discouraged political discussion and never gave the Nazi salute. These differences of political opinion were reflected in contrasting attitudes toward the prisoners: hardliners maintained that escape attempts should be met with force, lethal if necessary; others sought to cultivate good relations with the inmates, on the grounds that they were fellow soldiers. The ideological cleavage within the German garrison, between the Nazis and the non-fascists, the enforcers and those inclined to leniency, would continue throughout the life of the camp. As Eggers noted: "We were not a harmonious team."

The German Non-Commissioned Officers, promoted through the enlisted ranks, acted as the main contacts between prisoners and guards; they were awarded nicknames that became, over time, permanent, and well known to their owners. The two sergeant majors were "Franz Josef" Rothenberger and "Mussolini" Gephard, who, like Il Duce, was both fat and fascist. Unteroffizier (Senior Corporal) Martin Schädlich, an indefatigable sleuth, was known as "*La Fouine*" (the weasel) to the French, and dubbed "Dixon Hawke" by the British, a reference to the fictional detective popular at the time. The canny Schädlich's diaries offer another often overlooked angle on Colditz, the view from the German NCOs' mess.

Nicknames were a mark of familiarity that could be cruel, affectionate, mocking, descriptive, or entirely arbitrary. Allocating the jailers monikers diminished their power, rendering them human, and frequently ridiculous. The nicknames for Colditz guards, collectively referred to as the "ferrets," included Big Bum, Ropey, Dopey, Pieface, Tiger, Cheese, Snuffler, Hiawatha, Eggs, Auntie, and Bastard.

Eggers was by far the most formidable of the German officers. Long before the prisoners began testing possible avenues out of the castle, he was exploring ways to keep them in, an approach that was systematic, scientific, and extremely effective. The British feared and distrusted him, particularly Pat Reid, who considered him "foxy, competent and a bit too smooth." Eggers liked to wander into the British barracks of an evening to speak English and reminisce about his time in Cheltenham; but, behind his smile, he was sniffing for clues. The animosity toward Eggers came with a nagging respect: "He was a thorn in our side because he was very good at his job," said Kenneth Lockwood, one of the original Laufen Six. "He thought he understood how the British mentality worked, and was rather slimy in that regard." The French nicknamed him "Tartuffe," after the character in Molière's play, the most famous hypocrite in French literature. Eggers believed the name derived from his "habit of suppressing all my hostile or unpleasant reactions beneath a somewhat strained and wavering grin." He took the nickname as a compliment.

For in addition to his intelligence and discipline, Eggers possessed an even temper, forged by years of being baited by schoolboys. Soon after the British arrived, he made an observation to the SBO, Guy German, that sounded like a challenge: "I will never allow you gentlemen the honor of getting me rattled." That resolution was assaulted on a daily basis over the next four years, and the German officer was ragged mercilessly. If escaping was the main arena of rivalry inside the camp, then trying to egg Eggers into losing his composure was a close second.

As the late-spring weather grew warmer, Eggers could sense anticipation heating up in the camp, a restlessness presaging more escapes. Yet Eggers felt a justified measure of pride: so far just one prisoner had gotten away and several attempts had been foiled. Security was improving all the time. The inmates included seasoned escape artists, with more arriving from other camps every week, but Eggers was confident: "The experts had to lay on absolute masterpieces to beat us."

3

The Bad Boys' Camp

The first British prisoner to get beyond the castle walls did so not through escape artistry, but by virtue of being exceptionally small. On May 10, a gang of French prisoners from other ranks was brought up from the town and put to work hauling old mattresses out of an attic and loading them onto the back of a truck in the courtyard. After a hasty negotiation, these French workers were persuaded to add Lieutenant Peter Allan to the load.

Allan was one of the Laufen Six, who had come to Colditz in November 1940 with Pat Reid. A cheerful Scotsman seldom seen without his kilt on, at five feet four inches tall Allan was one of the smallest prisoners in Colditz, and therefore also one of the most portable. He was stuffed into a mattress filled with rotting straw, sewn inside, and placed on the lorry, with two more palliasses on top of him. His escape equipment consisted of a fifty-Reichsmark note and a pair of white socks and shorts, which made him look a little like a member of the Hitler Youth.

As the vehicle rumbled out of the gate, in his dusty hiding place Allan struggled against the powerful urge to sneeze. The palliasses and the little Scotsman were offloaded, none too gently, in a barn outside the village. Allan climbed out, brushed himself down, and headed to the station, trying to look like a keen young Nazi out for a walk. There was still an hour before evening roll call. Allan, who spoke passable German, purchased a single ticket to Vienna, where he knew there was an American consulate. "I had no papers and no maps, but I thought if I went to see the Americans, who were not in the war, they might help me." That night, while Allan settled down to sleep in the station lavatory at

Regensburg, the Germans launched a full-scale manhunt. In the barn, they found the empty palliasse cover and an open window.

Eggers admitted defeat in his best idiomatic English: "The bird had flown."

As the days passed without word of Allan's capture, elation in the British quarters came tinged with national pride at having scored an equalizer with the French. Allan had gotten away with a "snap escape" involving no preparation whatsoever. How much more might be achieved with proper planning?

The British were still quietly celebrating two weeks later, when they were joined by a new arrival who would go on to become one of the most famous Colditz inmates, a young officer with a bullet hole in his side and the fury of thwarted ambition in his heart.

Airey Neave was ferociously competitive and, as such people often are, quite insecure. His ambition would eventually lead him to the summit of British politics, and an early death from a terrorist bomb. Neave was twenty-five years old, and looked younger, with piercing blue eyes, a boyish grin, and an infectious laugh. But he was also angrier than he seemed. Neave's war was not going the way he expected, and he was very cross about it. After Eton and Oxford, he had joined up in expectation of military honor, or at least a heroic early death, but instead ended up in an unglamorous searchlight battalion, shining beams into the night sky over London, an effect that officers in fighting regiments dismissed as "quite Christmassy." In France a few months later during the battle for Calais, a stray bullet (possibly British) bounced up from the pavement and hit him in the chest. "I felt the blood running down inside my clothes and trickling to my stomach." Mostly, he felt extreme irritation. The bullet had missed his heart by half an inch. He crawled a few yards and collapsed. About an hour later, "a huge man in German uniform and a Red Cross armband put me gently on a stretcher." Neave was taken prisoner having fired only one shot, at a spotter plane, and missed.

After attempting to escape from the prison camp at Thorn in Poland, he was transferred to Colditz. "The vast domain of princelings was heavily guarded," he wrote. "Barbed wire and machine guns bristled on the parapets . . . I felt the battlements close in, enfolding me."

This prison camp was quite different from the one Neave had known before. For a start, the officer who greeted him wore an orange polo-neck jumper, ragged khaki shorts, and a pair of wooden clogs. "I felt I was being ushered into a school for waifs and strays," he wrote, inhabited by "eccentric and unusual men." As he sat down in the long mess hall to a "Tudor feast" of black bread and stew drunk from tin bowls, the conversation around him revolved around escape. He felt his mood lift. Fired by "a sense of injustice [that] scars the spirit," and goaded by what he called his "hysterical impatience," Neave oscillated between ebullience and morosity. He wrote feelingly about the misery that sometimes threatened to engulf him. "The POW is to himself an object of pity," he wrote. "He feels he is forgotten, he broods over the causes of his capture, and to himself and his friends, he soon becomes a bore, endlessly relating the story of his last stand." Here he was among kindred, restive spirits. Planning escape could be an antidote to the depression that lurked beneath his bluster, and he knew it.

Neave arrived at the very moment the canteen tunnel was revived, thanks to a new weapon in the prisoners' arsenal: bribery. A few of the prison guards were prepared to swap eggs and coffee for the prisoners' chocolate and cigarettes, and one in particular had revealed himself to be an eager trader, ready to strike an altogether bigger bargain. From time to time, this sentry was posted at night to the small lawn outside the canteen window where the tunnel was intended to exit. A deal was agreed: in return for 700 Reichsmarks, after the evening roll call he would "look the other way" for ten minutes at exactly 9:50 p.m.

This was a considerable sum by any standards, and in Colditz, where real money was rare, it represented a small fortune. But if the expenditure meant getting a dozen men out in one attempt, it would be money well spent. This was to be a genuinely communal effort: a team of forgers and tailors set to work making civilian clothes, fake passes, and maps for the twelve designated escapers (ten British and two Poles, who spoke better German). The team would be led by Colonel Guy German himself, but Reid was the plan's prime mover and chief financier, collecting cash from wherever he could find it: brought in by new arrivals, hidden in parcels from home, or obtained by barter. Half the bribe would be paid to the venal sentry in advance, the rest dropped out of a window after the escape.

Neave agreed to act as a stooge, keeping watch from an upper window, and at 9:30 p.m. on May 29, he was at his post, observing the bribed sentry as he paced the lawn, bathed in the searchlights. The guard seemed oddly relaxed, thought Neave, "indifferent to the tension of that silent night." The same could not be said for the escapers, twelve sweaty and anxious men crammed into the tunnel and poised for a mass breakout.

Equally highly strung were Eggers and his posse of armed guards lurking just out of sight behind a buttress, and "quite as keyed up as the prisoners." Ten more guards stood ready in the guardroom. The apparently corruptible sentry had every reason to be calm, because he had reported the British approach to Eggers the moment it was made. Kommandant Schmidt had ruled that instead of shutting down the tunnel, the escapers must be caught *in flagrante*. This was an ambush.

"The tension among us was terrific," wrote Eggers, who worried that a trigger-happy guard might open fire. Still, he was enjoying himself, and described what ensued with the relish of a schoolmaster one step ahead of his unruly wards: "The stage was set. We waited in the wings for the actors. We blinked at every sound. Our eyes watered with the strain. Suddenly came a movement on the grass. A line appeared—a break. A patch of grass started to move, upward. A square of turf rose straight up out of the ground . . . then a man's hands and arms followed, pushing up the turf and frame. Then up came the British Captain Reid." Eggers pointed his flashlight into Reid's eyes and bellowed at him to raise his hands. Reid shouted to the men behind him to go back, but by this point the contingent from the guardhouse had burst into the canteen, guns at the ready.

"We came out and just roared with laughter," Reid later claimed. Neave, observing from the window, did not remember the denouement that way: "The tunnellers were led sadly away to solitary confinement." Four months of careful planning, hard digging, rising hope, had been expended for nothing, not to mention the loss of 350 Reichsmarks. The duplicitous German guard was rewarded with a medal, a promotion, and a week's leave. He was also allowed to keep the money already paid. "This was our first big success," crowed Eggers. "Due solely to the loyalty of one of our men." Eggers was promoted to Hauptmann, or Captain.

Two days later, after three weeks on the run, Peter Allan limped back into Colditz under guard, still wearing the shorts he had escaped in, now a grimy gray color. He could barely speak from exhaustion.

The little Scotsman had made it to Vienna and presented himself, ragged and half-starved, at the American consulate. "I'm an escaped British officer," he told an astonished consular official. "I've escaped from Colditz. My feet are worn out and I'm hungry. I don't want a passport. All I want is a twenty-mark note to get a meal, some beer and a railway ticket to take me to the Hungarian border. Please help me."

America had not yet joined the war, but many Americans were already supporting the Allies, and despite the risks some diplomats were prepared to lend assistance. This consular official was not one of them.

"No. You have made a mistake. Get out and forget you ever came here. This consulate exists under diplomatic privilege of the German government." Then he added, unpleasantly: "They'll get you in the end. They always do." Allan left the consulate, slept for an hour on a park bench, and then staggered into a police station and gave himself up.

Given that he had set out without papers, a companion, equipment, or a realistic plan, Allan had done well to remain at large for twenty-three days and get as far as Vienna. Moldering in solitary back at Colditz, he felt ashamed: "I let down the other escapers, because I hadn't succeeded." A shared sense of purpose could be an additional burden, as well as a solace. Peter Allan would not set foot outside the castle for another four years.

There was an unseasonal heatwave that year. In traditional fashion, the British immediately rushed to bathe in the sunshine, and just as quickly regretted it. "The courtyard every day was strewn with shining, sweaty bodies in various stages of redness, rawness and suntan." Sunburn added to the peevish mood. Incarceration was difficult in winter but even harder in summer, when the sun sparkled off the Mulde and heat shimmered in the lush valley below. Allan's ignominious return was followed by the disappearance, just two days later, of a second French officer, who had hidden during the Park Walk and then vanished over the wall. The Poles, by contrast, were having as little luck as the British: during the first six months of 1941, a dozen Polish officers launched at least seven escape attempts, including one from the solitary confinement cells. All came to nothing, although one officer managed to reach Nazi-occupied Poland before his recapture.

On June 25, returning from the park, a line of British officers passed a woman in a checked blouse walking in the other direction. Women were a rare sight in Colditz, though not unknown. The wives of German officers occasionally visited from the married quarters (a separate building beyond and outside the *Kommandantur*), and a handful of local women were employed in the laundry and kitchens. The woman was middle-aged and stocky, and wore a wide-brimmed hat and sensible shoes; but she was, at least, female, and was therefore greeted with admiring whistles, which she stoutly ignored. As she passed the end of the line, a wristwatch fell off her arm. An RAF officer picked it up: "Miss, you've dropped your watch." She appeared not to hear him and walked on, rounding the corner. The officer handed it to a guard and pointed out: "That young woman has dropped her watch." The guard ran after her, handed over the watch, and then did a double take. On closer inspection, the *Fräulein* turned out to be Lieutenant Émile Boulé, a bald forty-five-year-old French officer dolled up in a wig and skirt. The British considered this to be an example of gallantry gone awry, and found the episode most amusing. The French did not.

Colditz reflected, and in some ways exaggerated, the characteristics of British society. Many prisoners continued to observe the baked-in distinctions of status, rank, and class that pertained at home. Some officers, like Old Etonian Airey Neave, had been to major boarding schools and looked down on others from minor boarding schools, while a few had not been to boarding school at all, and were therefore patronized by those who had. Most of the time, national solidarity papered over minor gradations of birth and education, but as more British officers arrived, the informal clubs grew more exclusive, the snobberies and resentments more acute. Francis (Frank) Flinn, inevitably nicknamed "Errol" after the Hollywood film actor, was an RAF officer who had come up through the ranks and observed these class divisions with a wry eye: "There was a certain amount of [boarding] school chatter: 'He's a Wykehamist' . . . 'He's a Rugby man.'" Padre Platt claimed that in Colditz "there are none who regard themselves as being of different clay from the rest," but as the prison filled up, the different strata of British class began to emerge in ever more distinct seams.

The widest social division in the prison—and the only one of real significance—was between officers and orderlies: the men of rank forced into idleness by the rules of wartime imprisonment, and those who worked for them. The officer corps at Colditz was predominantly upper-middle or upper class; the orderlies were almost all working-class men with little formal learning. In the normal circumstances of military life, contact between private soldiers and officers was strictly regulated by tradition, rank, and obedience. Officers issued orders, which were conveyed to the troops via NCOs, and then obeyed. A batman might serve an officer for years without their ever getting to know each other. But in a prison camp the distance between officers and other ranks was less structured: they were now living together, albeit in separate quarters, an unfamiliar and unsettling experience for both. The informality of Colditz added to the erosion of traditional deference: saluting felt odd when wearing a dressing gown and clogs. To further complicate matters, the orderlies were officially employed by the Germans, not the British, and required to obey both. But, as in wider society, the old habits of obedience were starting to erode: some orderlies resented having to work for other prisoners, whatever their seniority in rank and status. Britain's class war was festering inside Colditz, and in the summer of 1941 it erupted into open conflict.

The grumbling began with an Irishman named Doherty, "a rebel who tried to stir things up with the other orderlies," according to one of their number, John Wilkins, a submariner who refused to join in the agitation. Led by Doherty, the orderlies began to complain about having to clear up after messy and demanding officers. The officers, in turn, felt that they were not being accorded proper respect. Padre Platt was particularly outraged at the threat to established social order. He complained that the orderlies monopolized the washbasins and toilets. Reid was equally affronted by the sedition among the other ranks: "Rooms were dirty, insolence was frequent, two of them regularly talked for our benefit about 'revolution' and 'parasites.'" As the weather grew hotter, the rebellion simmered, and then boiled over.

In mid-June, the orderlies went on strike, with the exception of Solly Goldman, who was in the sickbay and would never have joined such a rebellion, Wilkins, and two others. Guy German was still in solitary confinement after the failed canteen tunnel escape, and so it fell to the next officer in seniority, a pompous naval lieutenant commander, to try to subdue the "mutiny." He immediately assembled the disorderly orderlies and addressed them "as though speaking from the bridge with the authority of the Admiral behind him." The orderlies declared "they would take orders from no one but the Germans," and walked out. Doherty was banned from entering the officers' quarters, which he had refused to do anyway. It was a bizarre standoff, a direct challenge to the traditional master–servant, officer–other ranks relationship, which left the disgruntled officers taking turns to do "the work of laying and clearing tables, sweeping floors and so on." The rebel leader, Doherty, confronted the loyalist Wilkins. "He had a couple who would back him," Wilkins later recalled, "saying why should they work for the officers, they were prisoners the same as them. We nearly came to blows." Eventually, the mutiny fizzled out: some of the orderlies returned to work, while others, including the ringleader, were shipped out to Stalags and replacements brought in. But it left a residue of mistrust. For Eggers, the incident offered a fresh insight into the British class system, and an opportunity that might be exploited.

The French were almost equally conscious of class distinctions, but with added divisions along lines of politics and race. By the end of June, the Jewish-French contingent consisted of some eighty officers. Their number included Robert Blum, a classical pianist and the son of the former and future French prime minister Léon Blum, and Elie de Rothschild, a cavalry officer and scion of the banking dynasty. Some of the French Jews were confined in Colditz because they were well-born, but as Pat Reid pointed out, "most of the Jews were there because they were Jews"—which made what followed even more repugnant. Some senior French officers demanded that their Jewish compatriots be segregated from the gentiles and held in a separate part of the castle. Sensing a potential propaganda coup, the Germans were happy to oblige, and the French Jews were moved to an attic, in cramped quarters immediately dubbed "the Ghetto." Many of the British were astonished and appalled to discover that some of the French shared the anti-Semitism of the Germans. The French were already divided, as was France itself, between those impatient to join Charles de Gaulle and fight the Nazis, and officers who supported the collaborationist Vichy regime. In July, Anglo-French relations were further soured by news of the British attack on the Vichy French fleet at Mers-el-Kébir on the Algerian coast. The Vichyites displayed a large poster of Pétain in their quarters.

Airey Neave was particularly incensed by the banishment of the French Jews. "The behaviour of their fellow officers in a fascist prison camp seemed to me outrageous," he wrote. "Among those singled out for special persecution by the French officers of Aryan extraction was the son of Léon Blum." To demonstrate solidarity with the Jews, the British ostentatiously invited them to dinner in their mess. Neave gave the first political speech of his life to the assembled Jewish prisoners in the Ghetto, denouncing the racial discrimination. The future politician's address was "received with applause," and every week thereafter he attended "splendid suppers cooked by an expert Jewish chef." It had been an ugly episode. Even Eggers was embarrassed by the treatment of the Jews, but maintained, unconvincingly, that "they preferred to all be together."

The "Great Jewish Row" was still smoldering when an important new ingredient was added to the international mix with the arrival of 68 Dutchmen, most of them officers from the colonial forces of the Dutch East Indies, who marched into Colditz in perfect regimental order. Some 15,000 Dutch soldiers were captured during the German invasion of the Netherlands, but most had been set free after signing a pledge to take no further part in the war. The new arrivals had refused to do so.

The Dutch were Eggers's favorite kind of inmate. "They were model prisoners. They had no orderlies of their own, but kept their quarters clean themselves. Their discipline was faultless, their behaviour on parade exemplary. They dressed smartly at all times." The Dutch, in short, behaved as the British ought to. But, as Eggers soon discovered, the Dutchmen were just as *deutschfeindlich* as the other inmates, and dedicated escapers: highly organized, and particularly adept at picking locks. Many spoke German. Their uniforms were almost identical, in shape and design, to those of the Wehrmacht, a similarity that would prove exceptionally useful. The politeness was a front. "The Germans could never tell if anything was going on among the Dutch," wrote an admiring Pat Reid. "Their behaviour was always the same." Within days, the Dutch contingent was planning its first breakout under the leadership of Captain Machiel van den Heuvel, a stolid-seeming man with a special talent for looking bored and innocuous while planning acts of extreme skulduggery. Reid spotted in "Vandy" a kindred spirit.

One evening in late June, the stationmaster at nearby Grossbothen put in a telephone call to the Colditz switchboard to inquire if a prisoner was missing. A man had come into the station an hour earlier and attempted to buy a ticket for Leipzig with an out-of-date fifty-Reichsmark note. He was dressed in a smart civilian suit and wearing a monocle. "He can't be German," said the stationmaster.

Pierre Marie Jean-Baptiste Mairesse-Lebrun, French cavalry officer, aristocrat, Olympic show jumper, polo champion, holder of the Légion d'honneur and the Croix de Guerre, was by some distance the most elegant prisoner in Colditz. An exquisite figure with deep-set eyes, swept-back hair, and a consistently impeccable uniform, the Frenchman "gave the impression he was at his best in the Bois de Boulogne and the Champs Elysées," wrote Platt. The gorgeous Mairésse-Lebrun also felt he was out of place in Colditz and had no intention of staying there a moment longer than necessary. He had made his civilian suit out of an expensive pair of flannel pajamas sent from Paris. His cravat was Givenchy. The Frenchman haughtily declined to say how he had escaped from the castle (he had hidden in the rafters of another empty park building) and was sentenced to twenty-one days in solitary confinement.

Two weeks later Mairesse-Lebrun and a handful of other officers from the solitary cells were marched down to the enclosure in the park for their daily exercise, escorted by three German sentries, one officer, and an NCO. Even in gym kit the cavalry officer cut a dash: running shorts, short-sleeved shirt with crisp creases, a natty sleeveless leather jacket, gloves, and plimsolls with thick rubber soles. Under his shirt, wrapped in his cravat, he had thirty Reichsmarks, a packet of sugar, chocolate, soap, and a razor. Lieutenant Mairesse-Lebrun was not going to go on the run unshaven.

For an hour Mairesse-Lebrun and his compatriots played leapfrog, or *saute-mouton* (sheep jump), around the enclosure. Then Lieutenant Pierre Odry sauntered over to the urinating ditch dug next to the wire, before turning, bracing his back against the fence, and cupping his hands. Mairesse-Lebrun sprinted toward him and placed his foot in the stirrup, Odry heaved, and the Frenchman soared gracefully over the top of the wire, like a thoroughbred taking the final fence at the Grand Steeple-Chase de Paris. Ducking and zigzagging, he raced toward the park wall as the sentries opened fire. The guards had only three shots each, Mairesse-Lebrun calculated, so nine shots in all. Having reached the wall, he ran up and down "like a rabbit," while the guards blazed away from a distance of seventy yards and bullets pinged off the stonework. When the guards paused to reload, Mairesse-Lebrun clambered up and over the stone wall, and sprinted into the woods. Three days' walking, in the rain, brought him seventy miles to the town of Zwickau. There he stole a bicycle and set off down the wide *Autobahn* toward the Swiss border, "bare-chested in the sun, like a German on holiday." Troops streamed up the opposite side of the motorway, heading for the Eastern Front: "Operation Barbarossa," the German invasion of the Soviet Union, was underway. After five days of pedaling, the last fifty miles on wheel rims after his tires melted, Mairesse-Lebrun reached Singen, near where Alain Le Ray had crossed into Switzerland by train three months earlier. A German policeman stopped him and started a conversation, which Mairesse-Lebrun ended by knocking him out with the bicycle pump and haring into the woods. Hopelessly disoriented, he wandered among the trees until, in a clearing, he spotted a girl heading toward a chalet carrying a pail of milk.

"Don't be afraid," he told her. "I'm a French officer. Am I in Switzerland, or Germany?"

The milkmaid beamed. "But, monsieur, I am Swiss. You are in Switzerland."

Back in Mairesse-Lebrun's cell at Colditz, the Germans found his packed suitcase with a label attached: "If I succeed, I would be grateful if you would arrange for my personal possessions to be sent to the following address . . . May God help me!" In a remarkable gesture of wartime politesse, the Germans did as requested: Mairesse-Lebrun's elegant prison wardrobe arrived in Orange shortly after he did.

Eggers was impressed: "For sheer mad yet calculated daring, the successful escape of the French cavalry lieutenant, Pierre Mairesse-Lebrun, will not, I think, ever be beaten." An additional two feet of barbed wire was added to the top of the wire fence surrounding the exercise cage.

News of Mairesse-Lebrun's successful "home run" prompted fresh jubilation in the French quarters. Three Frenchmen had now escaped by acting alone, each following a plan of their own devising shared with few others. This pattern was not lost on Airey Neave.

The main weakness in the castle's security, he concluded, was not architectural but human. The successful Frenchmen had each, in different ways, fooled their jailers. They had not attempted to dig through solid rock. "Escapers," Neave concluded, "must pit their wits against a frailer element—the Germans themselves."

Everyone entering the inner courtyard of Colditz, German soldiers and workmen alike, was handed a numbered brass identity disc, which they then surrendered on leaving. Neave surmised that if he could obtain this rudimentary pass, and fashion a sufficiently credible German uniform, he might simply walk out of the front door. Beyond the inner courtyard were three more sentries: at the gateway to the outer courtyard, under the outer clock tower, and at a final gate leading to the moat bridge. Then it was just a matter of getting to the Swiss border, 400 miles away. He began to assemble his escape kit.

By the end of July, the prison population had swelled to over 500 officers, of whom roughly half were French, along with 150 Poles, 68 Dutchmen, and approximately the same number of British. The place was now over half-full, and humming with suppressed energy. That summer, escape attempts rose to a climax. "Hardly a day passed without an incident," wrote Reid. The British escape officer saw his role as that of a sports team manager, organizing his players in a competition that required rigorous training, the right equipment, and absolute dedication. Playing the game was all very well, and Reid never let the "jolly-hockey-sticks" tone lapse; but he also knew that unless the British recorded a win, and soon, then team morale might collapse entirely.

The Germans uncovered one Polish tunnel that started in the chapel, and another two meters deep out of the French quarters. Over the next four years, according to Eggers, at least twenty tunnels would be discovered under construction. Two officers, one British and one Polish, were caught trying to hide in an air raid shelter in the basement of the Terrace House on the way back from the park. Two Frenchmen almost reached Leisnig station before they were intercepted: the pair had cut through the barred window on an air shaft, climbed down four stories on bedsheet ropes, donned the yellow armbands worn by workmen, and walked out of the park gate. A Polish captain hacksawed through the bars of his solitary cell by the courtyard archway, swung down on his bedsheet, dropped twenty feet to the ground, and fractured his ankle; he limped all the way to the Swiss border before he was caught. Two British officers tried to slip out of the park wearing vests with swastikas of a type favored by the Hitler Youth, but were discovered when they failed to execute convincing *Heil Hitler* salutes.

British efforts were focused on what became known as the "toilet tunnel." The Long Room, where many British officers ate their meals, backed onto the lavatories on the second floor of the German garrison. At night, the only soldier on duty in that part of the *Kommandantur* was a telephonist, wearing earphones. If tunnelers could break through the eighteen-inch wall, they could wriggle into the German quarters dressed as workmen, and then walk out. Even though he considered it pointless, Neave took part in the tunneling "to avoid the tedium which may lead to madness." At lunchtime on July 31, twelve escapers assembled in the Long Room, wearing workers' overalls stitched from blankets, and climbed into the opening.

The Germans were once again waiting. The plan had been discovered from the outset, when the telephonist went to the toilet and heard scratching. "Let them tunnel," Hauptmann Priem had ordered. "It will keep them busy and happy." The Germans drilled a hole in the door opposite the lavatory entrance and posted a sentry (wearing noiseless felt slippers) to maintain surveillance.

Frank "Errol" Flinn was first out of the tunnel. He climbed over the cistern, opened the toilet door, and crept around the corner. "The next thing I knew was a pistol in my back." "*Hände hoch!*" demanded a grinning Priem. "This way, please, gentlemen." All twelve were marched into solitary confinement, and a mass of escape equipment was confiscated: fake papers, maps, compasses, food, money, and civilian clothes. The prisoners pooled specialized skills within national groups and, to a lesser extent, between them: how to pick locks, forge papers, sew credible civilian clothes and military uniforms. Pat Reid devised individual "escape kits" for British officers including maps traced from originals and some German money. "Officers had their specialities and turned out articles in quantity," wrote Reid. But the Germans were also sharing whatever they learned.

A pedagogical obsessive, forever offering instruction from beside a metaphorical blackboard, Reinhold Eggers treated escape prevention as a branch of logic: for every escape, successful or otherwise, there was a countermeasure; every gap in the castle's security could be filled in retrospectively, until the whole place was sealed tight; every item of escape equipment he uncovered, either fabricated inside the castle or smuggled in, offered another clue to the prisoners' methods. With pedantic precision, Eggers gathered the confiscated items in a locked room, and brought in the town photographer, Johannes Lange, to create a visual record of the various escape techniques: some prisoners even agreed to be photographed re-enacting their attempts. He made maps of tunnel routes and compiled his own annotated scrapbook for reference. This was the "Colditz Museum," the educational center for what Eggers called "the Colditz Escape Academy." It was also a propaganda tool, used to impress visiting German dignitaries with the garrison's success in keeping the most difficult prisoners confined.

Security was beefed up yet again, with extra sentries around the exercise area that the Germans called "the sheep pen," and a squad of Alsatian guard dogs housed in kennels on the south side of the moat. Prisoners on the Park Walk were forced to march with their overcoats open to prevent the concealment of escape equipment. A door was installed in the park wall, enabling guards to pass through quickly if an escape was attempted in that direction. There were additional and more irregular searches. A rapid deployment force, or "riot squad," was placed on standby, to be dispatched quickly to any part of the camp in the event of trouble.

Eggers avidly perused the pages of *Das Abwehrblatt* (*Security News*), an in-house journal for German prison guards that described escape attempts and the latest measures to foil them. "It was fascinating reading," wrote Eggers, who became one of the trade magazine's regular contributors. Studying the psychology of escape, he concluded that prisoners were also formulating a methodology. In selecting disguises, for example, they attempted to look "conspicuous in a normal way, rather than try to be nervously inconspicuous." Apprehending anyone who looked "normally conspicuous" was obviously going to be tricky. But where were escaped prisoners most likely to head? Leipzig was the nearest large city, with rail links in all directions. A full list of prisoners, with identification numbers and photographs, was dispatched to Leipzig police station. The castle solitary cells filled up with captured escapees, so additional space was commandeered in the town prison. Escapes were increasing in frequency, but not in success. "We were top dog," gloated Eggers in the summer of 1941.

The most valuable armament in war is knowledge, and into the escalating battle between prisoners and guards the Dutch contingent now introduced the equivalent of a secret weapon: how to get across the German border into Switzerland.

Lieutenant Hans Larive had been captured in Amsterdam and imprisoned for refusing to submit to German rule. In late 1940, he escaped from a transit camp before being recaptured on a train near Singen on the Swiss border. Suspected of espionage, Larive was taken to the local Gestapo headquarters and interrogated by an irate SS officer resembling an "enormous bull," who threatened to shoot him. Larive insisted he was not a spy but a Dutch naval officer with rights under the Geneva Convention. At this point the Bull's demeanor abruptly altered. He had once worked as a cook in an Amsterdam hotel. He liked Dutch people. He became chatty. Why, the German asked, had Larive tried to cross the frontier by train rather than on foot?

"I didn't know how to get through the defense line," replied Larive, who was not a spy but was skilled, nonetheless, in extracting useful information from the unwary.

"Defense line!" the Bull snorted. "What a crazy idea. You could have walked straight through."

Now positively garrulous, the SS officer unfolded a map. Germany would win the war by Christmas anyway, and this Dutchman would surely not attempt another escape. What harm could there be in demonstrating his superior geographical knowledge?

With a fat finger, the officer indicated a point on the map where Switzerland jutted 300 yards into German territory, the so-called Ramsen salient. The spot was easy to find, he explained, because there was a house nearby on the edge of a wood, with a sharp bend beyond it. A quarter of a mile farther along the road was a path to the left, leading straight into Switzerland. "There are no defenses at all."

Larive relayed this priceless nugget of information to the Dutch escape officer, Captain Machiel van den Heuvel. In a spirit of solidarity, "Vandy" shared the secret with the international escape committee. Larive's accidental discovery of the unguarded back door into Switzerland, gleaned from a foolishly talkative SS officer, would prove to be the single most valuable item of escape equipment in Colditz.

Escaping depended, in large part, on deception. If a successful escape could be concealed from the Germans, even for a few hours, the escapers stood a far better chance of getting away; if, on the other hand, prisoners could hide inside the castle, the Germans would eventually assume these individuals had escaped, giving them time to escape later without raising the alarm. Enormous ingenuity was devoted to convincing the Germans that prisoners had not escaped when they had, and to persuading them that there had been an escape when there had not. The roll call could be distorted in a variety of ways: an officer who had been counted at one end of the line might duck down behind the others and pop up at the other end; by contrast, one small officer might be hidden on the shoulders of another under a greatcoat, leaving the German count one short. The Poles had built a sliding panel between two rooms in their quarters; if they reported four men sick in bed and unable to attend roll call, a German guard was sent to check; he would see two men in beds in one room and then two in another, without realizing they were the same two, who had slipped through the dividing wall "like rabbits" and pulled the sheets over their heads while the German made his way from one room to the other. Such ruses did not always work, but they frequently served to confuse the Germans, requiring a lengthy recount and buying precious time for escapers to make a getaway. The Dutch even created two replica prisoners, with clay heads, long capes, and dangling boots, which could be held upright between two officers during roll calls. The two models were named "Max" and "Moritz," after the disobedient boys in the German verse-story by Wilhelm Busch. One

British officer remarked that the Dutch lined up "like a bunch of bandsmen from a toybox," and Eggers himself noted that they stood "motionless on parade, like dummies." That was because, on occasion, two of the Dutchmen were actually dummies.

On the afternoon of August 16, a Dutch officer named Gerrit Dames was leaning against the fence of the exercise cage watching his fellow countrymen play a Dutch version of rugby that involved a great deal of scrummaging. Calmly, he clipped a hole in the wire, wriggled through, and began walking toward the tree line. He was halfway up the slope before the sentries spotted him, blew their whistles, and unslung their rifles. "Run! Run!" Dames shouted, in the general direction of the woods, before putting his hands up. The prisoners were lined up and marched back to the castle, where a head count revealed that two were missing: clearly these must have gotten away ahead of Dames, and made it into the woods without being seen.

The two missing men were, at that point, shivering and half-naked, up to their necks in stagnant water in a drain in the middle of the exercise pen: they were Hans Larive, discoverer of the Singen route into Switzerland, and another Dutch naval officer, Francis Steinmetz.

During exercise sessions Van den Heuvel, the Dutch escape officer, had spotted a large wooden manhole cover in the middle of the pen, secured by two large bolts. The Dutch held a Bible reading clustered around the hole, undid the bolts, and levered it open: the drain led nowhere and smelled revolting, but it was ten feet deep and large enough to hide two men. The nuts and bolts were carefully measured and replicated out of painted glass. On August 16, the Dutch rugby players set a scrum over the drain, removed the manhole cover, and lowered Larive and Steinmetz into it, securing the lid with the fake nuts and bolts. In the dank darkness the two could hear the whistles and muffled shouting as Dames staged the planned diversion. Seven hours later, in deep darkness, they emerged. "We pushed the wooden cover upwards and broke the glass dummy bolt, collected the broken glass and inserted the real bolt. We left the manhole ready for use another time." At dawn they reached Leisnig station and bought tickets for Dresden.

Back at the castle, something like panic was running through the German garrison. Larive and Steinmetz had vanished, along with five other Dutch officers. Two had already hidden in the drain two days earlier before making a getaway, their disappearance carefully concealed, while three more were still hiding inside the castle. The Germans launched another manhunt.

From Dresden, Larive and Steinmetz traveled on to Nuremberg, posing as immigrant workers. The trickiest moment came when they hid in a graveyard, only to discover this was a popular trysting place for local youths. They decided to join in, "making loud smacking noises to imitate passionate kisses." Two days later, they crossed the border into Switzerland, at the point revealed to Larive by the SS "Bull." Four months later, they were debriefed in London by British intelligence and then, to their astonishment, introduced to the exiled Queen Wilhelmina of Holland, "a small, dumpy woman, sixty-one years old, and badly dressed," but the living embodiment of Dutch resistance to Nazi rule. "We gave her the message of loyalty of her officers who were in Colditz," wrote Steinmetz. "After the audience, we turned into the next bar and had a stiff drink."

The two Dutchmen who had used the same exit route two days earlier were caught, as were the three hiding in the castle, but two more managed to get away via the drain a month later. "We were faced with an unknown breach in our defences," wrote Eggers, his confidence badly dented. It took four months before the hole was finally discovered. "One of our more observant sentries noticed a crowd of prisoners concentrated, for no obvious purpose, around a manhole cover in the sheep pen." Inside were one Polish and one British officer, the Dutch having generously extended the route to the other nations. The manhole was permanently sealed in concrete, but the Dutch had vaulted into the lead on the escape scoreboard. "Four Dutch officers had got right away in six weeks," wrote Eggers, disappointed that the Dutch contingent, apparently so tidy and courteous, had revealed themselves to be just as bent on escape as the rest of his captives. In the schoolmaster's traditional mantra: they had let Eggers down; they had let the school down; but most of all, they had let themselves down.

4

Goon-Baiting

Airey Neave, a young man in a frantic hurry, added the finishing touches to his costume. In exchange for a month's supply of Red Cross chocolate, he had obtained a khaki Polish tunic, approximately the same shape as a German uniform, which he painted using scenery paint intended for the backdrop of trees in a theatrical production. A Polish tailor obligingly sewed on dark green cloth epaulettes and silver breast pocket insignia made from tin. Neave added RAF trousers, a Czech forage cap dyed green, white piping, and a cardboard eagle and swastika. The outfit was completed with a pair of jackboots, bought from a Polish orderly, and a wooden painted bayonet scabbard attached to a cardboard belt.

Neave was rushing it; he did not look like a German soldier; he looked like an extra from the chorus of a Gilbert and Sullivan comic opera.

The homemade uniform was more pea-green than field gray and gave off a faintly luminous sheen under lights. Pat Reid, the escape officer, was not impressed by this outfit, but gave permission for the escape to go ahead. A visiting German worker was bribed with cigarettes into surrendering his brass identity disc. Neave gathered a map of the Swiss border traced on silk, a forged identity card, a little money, and a tiny compass; these were sealed into an object he could not bring himself to name but described as "a mysterious cigar-shaped container about two and a half inches long," which fitted snugly into the rectum of the future Conservative MP for Abingdon. This object, known as an "arse-creeper," would become an indispensable addition to every escape kit, a way to hide valuables from all but the most intrusive searches, and an inexhaustible source of scatological humor.

On August 23, a warm night, Neave came on evening parade wearing a British greatcoat over his disguise and a considerable quantity of escape equipment up his bottom. As soon as the roll call ended, the coat was whisked from his back, Neave clapped on the cap, fell in behind the German guard detail, and strode toward the gate in as brisk and military a fashion as the situation allowed.

"I have a message for the Kommandant from Hauptmann Priem," he said, proffering his brass identity disc. The guard let him out of the inner courtyard. Neave strode on, but after barely twenty paces a loud voice called "*Halt.*" He turned. In the full glare of the arc lights, his cap "shone like an emerald." In seconds he was surrounded by guards. The officer in command was livid: "This is an insult to the German army. You will be shot." The Germans appeared offended less by the escape bid than the absurd costume it had been attempted in, which they "seemed to regard as an insult to the uniform." Kommandant Schmidt himself arrived a few moments later, surveyed this figure from a "Christmas pantomime" clad in a "burlesque German uniform," and sniffed: "What impertinence. Take him away to the cells."

For probably the first time in his life, Neave was an object of derision. Lange was brought up from the town to photograph this strange military elf in his green outfit. The guards came to snigger and gawp, as if at "a newly captured animal." The uniform was placed in the museum. At evening roll call, a vastly amused Hauptmann Priem offered up a clunking joke, which was translated into French, Polish, and Dutch: "Gefreiter [Corporal] Neave is to be sent to the Russian Front." Neave could hear the laughter from his cell.

The episode left Neave mortified. The battle within Colditz was partly about status and dignity, and he had gifted an easy victory to the Germans, so often the targets of mockery themselves. "I had reduced escaping to a ridiculous farce, a music hall turn," he reflected. And yet for the twenty seconds between leaving the courtyard and the sentry's shout, he had experienced "an exquisite unburdening of the soul," a rush of "intense pleasure," and a transitory moment of pure, unalloyed freedom. "It was like a drug, and highly addictive," he later wrote. Neave was hooked.

When they looked back after the war, Colditz inmates felt a collective obligation to make the experience of imprisonment sound exciting, even fun. There were undoubtedly episodes of high exhilaration, and moments of humor, such as Neave's absurdly failed escape. Mostly, however, the life of a prisoner in Colditz was spectacularly, soul-crushingly, and sometimes almost unbearably boring. Unlike prisoners from the other ranks, officers did not even have the distraction of work to take their minds off captivity. There was nothing to do, which meant that most did very little. Some read books or sought to improve or entertain themselves in other ways, including theatrical productions and music concerts. Some, like Reid and Neave, spent every waking hour formulating and refining escape plans, while others played cards, wrote letters, dreamed of home, surreptitiously masturbated, and cooked up new recipes using Red Cross supplies.

A disproportionate amount of time was spent thinking about food, one of the few aspects of their lives susceptible to adaptation and invention. The German kitchens at Colditz provided the bulk of prison nourishment, highly variable in both quantity and quality: one-fifth of a loaf of black bread (*Roggenbrot*) a day, or five thin slices, small amounts of sugar, margarine, and dripping, or fat, which some believed to have come from horses, thin soup at midday, a strictly limited ration of potatoes. This was supplemented by food parcels, which offered more imaginative culinary possibilities. Most men ate together in self-selected "messes"; planning and cooking the evening meal became a major preoccupation and an important diversion. Orderlies cooked for the senior officers, but the more junior officers took turns to cook for one another. Eventually, Red Cross parcels came to include such delicacies as peanut butter, rice pudding, chocolate, sausages, Fray Bentos bully beef from Argentina, tinned milk, and cheese. But most supplies were basic. A typical evening meal might consist of a slice of Spam or other tinned meat mashed up with some potatoes, flavored with a Marmite cube, bulked up with ground biscuits, and then heated in a mess tin. "The Hun rations by themselves were quite inadequate, the Red Cross supplies bridged the gap from a nutritional point of view and most certainly saved us from malnutrition," said one ex-prisoner. As the war ground on, the inmates of Colditz would become far better nourished than their captors.

The frustration of imprisonment found expression in various ways, most obviously "goon-baiting," the practice of goading their German captors to a point just short of explosion. The origin of the word "goon," a catchall term for the guards, remains unclear: it may derive from the "gony-bird," a sailors' nickname for the lumbering, ungainly albatross; the "goons" were thick-witted characters in the *Popeye* comic strip; the comedian and war veteran Spike Milligan named his post-war radio comedy *The Goon Show*. The aim of goon-baiting was to make the guards uneasy and baffled, and therefore look foolish; if a goon lost his temper, or "lost face," the prisoners scored a small but valuable moral victory. Eggers knew that the prisoners were trying "to upset us in every possible way." Pushed too far, however, a guard might resort to violence.

Each nation had different methods of irritating the guards. The Poles simply pretended the Germans were not there, and if accidentally touched by a guard went through an elaborate process of self-cleaning, as if brushed by a leper. The French developed a way of singing on parade, in counterpoint, without moving their lips:

Où sont les Allemands?
Dans la merde!
Qu'on les y enfonce?
Jusqu'aux oreilles!

Where are the Germans?
In the shit!
Push them down?
Up to the ears!

But the British elevated goon-baiting to an art. Many of the officers had been to boarding school and were well versed in a contest of psychological one-upmanship that was both highly sophisticated and completely puerile. Competitive goon-baiting frequently occurred during roll calls, and might take the form of catcalling, whistling, loud farting, speaking in English the Germans could not follow, and deliberately interrupting the count, so it had to be restarted. More extreme techniques included knitting on parade, cutting their hair in strange shapes, and staring at a German officer's fly buttons until he became self-conscious and felt obliged to check them. The high windows above the courtyard offered opportunities for throwing things at the guards and then ducking back inside without being spotted: water bombs, snowballs, burning newspapers, and occasionally packets of excrement. The confrontations were usually jocular, but sometimes deliberately threatening. Insubordination could shade into sabotage. Any leftover food from the prisoners was used for pig swill down in the village: on one occasion this was found to contain broken razor blades.

Another technique was simply to behave oddly: playing imaginary snooker, for example, or walking a nonexistent dog. In one celebrated POW prank, prisoners took to pushing small pebbles around the prison yard with their noses. There was no aim to the game, other than to destabilize the guards and make them ban a wholly pointless and benign activity, which they did.

Clothing was another way to express resistance. Eggers was outraged at the way British officers turned up for morning *Appell* "in pyjamas, unshaven, slopping about in clogs and slippers, smoking, reading books, wearing the first assortment of garments that came to hand when they got out of bed." Many were still clad in remnants of the uniforms they had been captured in. The Scots wore kilts. On days of national importance by contrast, such as the King's birthday, the prisoners made a point of turning out in "unrecognizably smart" uniforms with every button and buckle gleaming.

"Indiscipline was the order of the day, often amounting to plain personal insolence, or at least studied off-handedness," wrote Eggers, who never got over the contrast between the politeness of Cheltenham's citizenry and the extreme rudeness of their compatriots in Colditz. "I cannot see that this kind of attitude to us served any purpose, beyond allowing prisoners to work off their repressions."

Most senior British officers tolerated goon-baiting as high jinks and letting off steam, but some, including Padre Platt, saw it as demeaning, infantile behavior that reinforced the German sense of superiority and gave the authorities an easy excuse to impose collective punishments, such as suspending exercise privileges. The lampooning of the guards was tremendously silly, but it served as a psychological prop, enabling powerless men to humiliate and needle their captors. Guards tended to be older, allowing the younger prisoners to imagine they were back at boarding school, ragging the teachers. Goon-baiting released pressure, for anxiety was steadily rising in the sealed confines of Colditz, and cracks were appearing, along fault lines of nation, race, and class.

The prisoners reacted to the mental and physical trauma of captivity in very different ways: anger, resistance, and courage, but also despondency, guilt, and acquiescence. Some found ways to amuse and educate themselves. Some kept calm and carried on, discovering a sort of peace in enemy custody. Some became frantic. Some lost their minds.

One of the many unconscious defense mechanisms was to behave as if there was nothing inherently odd about being locked up in a gloomy medieval castle with hundreds of other bored, predominantly middle-class men. In fact, of course, there was nothing remotely normal about Colditz, a place of isolation without women, work, children, news, money, liberty, or a foreseeable future. After less than a year in existence, Oflag IV-C was already one of the strangest places in the world, pervaded by a unique sadness that the men tried to ignore. Sometimes, at night, an eerie lupine howling could be heard rising from the French quarters, a keening, wordless lament picked up by one voice after another, echoing from the windows and reverberating around the castle walls. "After these outbursts, the French said, they all felt much better." The indefatigably positive Pat Reid claimed the maxim of the camp should be "Never a dull moment," but that said more about him than it did about Colditz. A more accurate motto would have been: "Dull in the extreme but interspersed with moments of extreme excitement and paralyzing fear."

In August 1941, the Poles organized the first "Colditz Olympic Games." Men might be able to survive, at least for a time, without women, pubs, or freedom. But they could not live without sport, a central element of masculine identity, then as now, a way to keep fit but also an opportunity to compete, emote, and bond. There were games of rugby, hockey, boxing, cricket, and an form of volleyball. Soccer was the most popular sport, and competition was fierce. Sport, wrote one prisoner, "acted as a balm to utter boredom": played hard, watched avidly, and then discussed afterward, endlessly. Whether the prisoners were participating or spectating, sport made the sluggish time pass more quickly. The YMCA shipped out equipment, via the Red Cross, including bats and balls. The Olympics saw the different nations competing at soccer, boxing, and even chess, and offered another reflection of national character: "The Poles were deadly serious; the French exuberant; the Dutch were solemn; the Belgians followed the French, and the Brits just laughed." Typically, the British cheered the worst competitors loudest, and came last in every event.

The inner courtyard of Colditz, dark, cramped, and cobbled, was ill-suited to any existing type of sport, and so a new one was devised. Eton created the "Wall Game"; rugby was invented at Rugby; and in the strange boarding school atmosphere of the camp, the prisoners devised "stoolball," a game of extreme violence dictated by the architecture and atmosphere of Colditz, played there and nowhere else. A cross between rugby and cage-fighting, stoolball was conducted as follows: one man from each team sat on a stool at either end of the courtyard, and the opposing squads with up to thirty players each then competed to knock him off his perch while carrying the ball, using any means possible. Biting and kicking were not permitted. Pretty much anything else was. Padding was optional. "There was a half-time when everybody was too tired to continue." This was less a sport than an exercise in testosterone-release: "If you wanted to thump someone, then you'd play them in stoolball." The two teams fought up and down the courtyard, under the perplexed gaze of the guards, slipping and crashing over the uneven stones, and frequently sustaining fairly serious injuries. "The Germans were convinced that the players were insane."

In September, a fresh batch of prisoners arrived in the camp, including two who were different from any of the others, and would be treated in contrasting ways, for entirely different reasons: one was Winston Churchill's communist nephew, and the other was Indian.

Birendranath Mazumdar was a doctor, and a very good one. The son of a distinguished surgeon from the city of Gaya in northeast India, he was a Brahmin born into the high noon of the British Raj, well educated, with elegant manners and fastidious tastes. Round-faced and soft-voiced, Mazumdar spoke English with a refined accent, as well as Bengali, Hindi, Urdu, French, and German. He never smoked without gloves on. He wrote in green ink on thick azure blue notepaper. The family owned a large farm at Ranchi and a pharmacy. As a boy, his devout mother had insisted he undergo *Upanayana,* the Hindu "sacred thread" ceremony, a rite of passage requiring fasting and isolation. His more anglicized father, whose patients included officers of the British East India Company, encouraged the young Biren to read aloud from *The Times* every evening. The boy was educated at elite schools modeled on the English education system and brought up to observe a code of honor that was Victorian British in tone: "Duty, loyalty, morality, sincerity: stick to these principles and you won't go far wrong," his father had told him. The Mazumdars had prospered under the Raj, but Biren grew up to become a committed Indian nationalist, fiercely opposed to British rule in India. "I had seen in my country the superiority of the British, the oppression." He was a supporter of both Mahatma Gandhi, the leader of the Indian independence movement, and the radical nationalist Subhas Chandra Bose.

Mazumdar sounded and behaved like an Englishman, but to many Englishmen he did not look like one. Among Indians, he was a figure of respect, even grandeur, an educated, high-caste

Hindu from a rich family; but to the majority of white men, he was just another Indian. In 1931, he left Gaya for London, intent on becoming a Fellow of the Royal College of Surgeons. "To succeed, you are going to have to be ten percent better than the others," he was told by the pioneering surgeon Gordon Gordon-Taylor. The young Indian doctor was proud, funny, ambitious, occasionally obstreperous, solemn, and conflicted: the product of two distinct, entwined, overlapping, and increasingly incompatible cultures.

Despite his opposition to the British Empire, when war was declared Birendranath Mazumdar came to its defense. Some 2.5 million Indians served on the Allied side during the war, mostly as uniformed soldiers of the British Indian Army. Mazumdar, however, being resident in London and British-trained, joined the British Army, which was still almost wholly white. In September 1939, he volunteered for the Royal Army Medical Corps, swore an oath of allegiance to King George VI, and was dispatched to France with the rank of captain, the only non-white officer in the corps and the only Indian officer in the British Army. He was posted to the 17th Base Hospital at Étaples as general medical officer. In May 1940, with German forces closing in, Mazumdar led a convoy of forty ambulances carrying 500 wounded soldiers toward Boulogne-sur-Mer in the hope of joining the evacuation. Outside the village of Neufchâtel-en-Bray, their path was blocked by twenty Panzers, which opened fire. Two of the ambulances were hit. Mazumdar helped to pull the survivors from the burning vehicles, then tied a khaki handkerchief to his baton, held it above his head, and walked toward the German tanks. The Panzer commander was most polite, and spoke perfect English: "I'm sorry. I'm afraid you won't reach Boulogne. And please, don't try to escape." These were words Mazumdar would hear repeatedly over the coming years.

The prisoners were marched 100 miles to Nijmegen on the Dutch border with Germany, and then crammed onto a flotilla of filthy coal barges with hundreds of other captives. For two days they were slowly hauled down the canals into Germany, with human excrement slopping around their feet. Many of his fellow captives were infested with lice and already suffering from dysentery. Another two-day march brought them to Kassel prison camp, where Mazumdar's belongings were confiscated, including his gold cigarette case and lighter, Parker pen and pencil, medical bag, and typewriter. A German officer ordered him to have his head shaved before delousing. Mazumdar refused, pointing out that in Hindu culture "you only shave your head when your father or mother dies. I am not going to shave my head under any condition." A shouting match ensued, which ended with Mazumdar being dragged off to the barber and then the solitary cells.

Mazumdar was not remotely cowed by this experience, and over the following year he was in constant conflict with his German captors: he complained of inadequate medical supplies and insufficient food; he demanded fresh milk and vegetables for his patients; he pointed out that the prisoners were inadequately clothed, with "torn trousers and soleless boots." Tuberculosis was rife. "You are an Indian," the Germans told him. "Why should you care if a few Tommies die?" But Mazumdar was persistent, and "relations with the German authorities went from bad to worse." He was shuttled from one camp to another, more than a dozen in all, a difficult customer, and an anomaly. Mazumdar's attentive medical care and willingness to confront the Germans ought to have endeared him to his fellow inmates, but he was always a creature apart, treated with suspicion, and occasionally outright discrimination. "I was the sole Indian in whichever camp I went to," he wrote. "All the other prisoners were English or Dutch. I had read so many books of the First World War and the camaraderie. That was absolutely missing here." When the Red Cross parcels arrived, Mazumdar was left without. "They had the food but they wouldn't share it. These were so-called educated people. I couldn't believe my eyes." The other prisoners called him "Jumbo," a nickname he detested but could not shift. This was probably a reference to Jumbo, the Victorian circus elephant that was once the star attraction at the London Zoo. The prisoners may have assumed that Jumbo was an Indian elephant, and hence attached the name to the sole Indian prisoner. In fact, Jumbo was an African elephant, but in the eyes of certain white people, elephants, like Indians, were all the same.

In Nazi ideology all non-whites were subhuman *Untermenschen,* but for political reasons Indians occupied an anomalous position in the fascist racial hierarchy: they were to be tolerated, even courted, if they aided the Nazi cause. The growing nationalist movement in India posed a direct threat to British power. From the German standpoint, Mazumdar was not just an oddity but an opportunity. Several thousand soldiers of the British Indian Army were captured during the fighting in North Africa. If these prisoners, and other Indians resident in Germany, could be persuaded to throw in their lot with the Nazis, that might simultaneously undermine British rule in India, boost Germany's military forces, and deliver an important propaganda victory. Mazumdar had made no secret of his nationalist sympathies, and so the Germans set about trying to persuade the only Indian officer in the British Army to switch sides.

Soon after arriving in Kassel camp, Mazumdar was summoned to the Kommandant's office, where a "completely bald" German officer and a young Indian man were waiting. The German came straight to the point and asked Mazumdar to make a radio broadcast encouraging other Indians to join a new military unit to fight the British and hasten the end of the Raj: "You can have a good life if you join us and join your countrymen." The fascist William Joyce, known as "Lord Haw-Haw," was already making regular broadcasts to Britain from Berlin, predicting Nazi victory and calling on Britons to surrender. This well-spoken Indian might fulfill a similar role in India, by urging his fellow countrymen to rise up against the British. Mazumdar flatly refused. "I cannot do it."

Now the young Indian chimed in. On the desk he spread out photographs of bomb-damaged London. "The war is virtually over," he said. "Germany has won the war and it is foolish for you to undergo the hardships of a POW camp when you could be living in comfort and freedom. You only have to agree to broadcast for the Germans." Again, Mazumdar refused, and was marched out of the Kommandant's office.

In the summer of 1941, at Marienberg camp, he was interviewed by a young German officer: "Have you changed your mind?" he asked. "Will you speak on the wireless?" Mazumdar again declined. "Will you at least go to Berlin?" Mazumdar shook his head. "Well, you are going anyway." Mazumdar replied archly that if he was forced to travel, as an officer he should have an orderly to carry his suitcase. "Forced at the point of two revolvers to carry my own luggage," he was marched onto a train and taken to an office block in Berlin, where the officer was waiting with another, more senior.

"Have you changed your mind about making a broadcast?"

"No, and what is more you are ascribing to me an importance that I do not possess, and do not even claim."

The officer changed tack. "When were you last with a woman?"

Mazumdar was outraged. "If you think my honor can be bought with a woman you are very wrong."

Now the other man spoke up: "This man is *deutschfeindlich*."

"Well, you are the best judges of that," snapped Mazumdar.

Back at the camp, an irate German officer ranted at him: "You have troubled us and bothered us wherever you have been. You are a traitor to your country." When Mazumdar opened his mouth to protest, the officer punched him in the face. The red tab denoting an anti-German attitude was added to his file, and Mazumdar was on his way to Colditz.

The Indian doctor arrived on September 26 in the middle of the night, the castle rearing up above him bathed in searchlights, a vision that "would fit naturally in the pages of a Bram Stoker novel." He turned to the sentry, and asked in German: "Where am I?" The man simply put his finger to his lips.

Birendranath Mazumdar was taken to an empty room, and locked inside. "I didn't know where I was. All I heard was the click of the key as the door shut. I was, to say the least, miserable and lost."

A few days earlier another singular prisoner, a short dark-haired man in his mid-twenties, had been brought to the castle by car, escorted by two German officers.

Giles Romilly was a civilian, a journalist, and a communist, who had been captured while covering the disastrous Norway campaign for the *Daily Express*. Romilly was confined to Colditz for one reason only: his mother was the younger sister of Clementine Churchill, Winston Churchill's wife. In German eyes this family connection made him a prisoner of special significance, and a potentially valuable asset. Had he not been Churchill's nephew, Romilly would almost certainly have been repatriated to Britain; instead, he was retained as a useful pawn, less a prisoner than a hostage who could be swapped, held for ransom, or used to extract concessions from Britain's prime minister.

This calculation was based on a false premise. Churchill barely knew Romilly, whom he referred to vaguely as "Nelly's Boy," and what he did know was unlikely to endear his nephew to him. Giles and his equally rebellious brother, Esmond, had distributed communist leaflets while schoolboys at Wellington and set up a radical newspaper "to champion the forces of progress against the forces of reaction on every front." Giles declared himself a pacifist and refused to join the Officer Training Corps. In 1934, the *Daily Mail* published an article about the communist Romilly brothers under the headline "Red Menace in Public Schools! Moscow Attempts to Corrupt Boys." Giles reported from Spain during the Civil War, while his brother fought for the International Brigades against Franco's Nationalists. In 1937, the Soviet intelligence officer Walter Krivitsky defected to Britain and revealed to MI5 that the Soviets had recruited a young British aristocrat as a spy. Krivitsky could not recall the man's name, but knew he had been sent to Spain by his Russian spymasters under the cover of journalism with orders to assassinate General Franco. The British security service became convinced that this boarding school–educated communist would-be assassin must be Giles Romilly, and placed him under surveillance. MI5's hunch was wrong: the man recruited by Soviet intelligence was Kim Philby, who would go on to become the most infamous spy in British history.

Romilly was a communist renegade, a suspected Soviet agent, and an embarrassment to his aristocratic family. But even if he had been none of those things, Winston Churchill would never have attached special value to a prisoner just because he happened to be a relative by marriage. The prime minister was far too politically astute for such favoritism. The Germans did not understand this and remained convinced that certain highborn or well-connected prisoners were of greater worth than others and should therefore be more closely guarded.

Romilly was the first of what the Germans came to refer to as the *Prominente*—the prominent ones—individuals who, by virtue of birth or social standing, were gathered in Colditz and held under the tightest security. The Nazis regarded these VIP prisoners as a kidnapper treats a captive: objects of value to be traded or ransomed, carefully safeguarded, and, if no longer useful, dispensed with. They were the trump cards of the POW population, and on no account could they be allowed to escape.

The other prisoners observed Romilly's arrival, a man "with a boyish face and light blue eyes, as unlike his illustrious uncle as one could get." He was locked in a cell at the end of a long stone passage, on the opposite side of the courtyard from the British quarters. "The sensation of enclosure was overpowering," he wrote; down in the courtyard, "a motley collection of people were shuffling round the cobbles like figures in Van Gogh's asylum drawing." The window was barred, the outside frame painted white so that the guards could immediately identify which one contained the most prized prisoner in Colditz. He was kept under twenty-four-hour surveillance. Though Romilly was allowed to mix with other prisoners during the day, his whereabouts were checked and noted every hour, and he was locked away at night, with a sentry permanently stationed in the corridor and changed every two hours. The guards watched him through a spyhole in the door. He was not permitted to leave the inner courtyard for the Park Walk. "These precautions, from the start, seemed ominous," he wrote.

These extreme security measures were motivated by fear. The orders from the Wehrmacht High Command were explicit: "Kommandant and Security Officer answer for Romilly's security with their heads" and should take "any and every exceptional measure" to ensure he did not escape. Eggers believed this command had come from Hitler himself. Romilly was an additional "security headache," and one that posed a direct threat to the jailers themselves. A photo of Romilly was posted in the guardroom, and every guard was expected to familiarize himself with his appearance. The sentries lived in fear that he might escape on their watch, and so two or three times a night the guard would enter his cell to pull back the blanket and check he had not magically vanished. A prized specimen in his own customized cage, Romilly was the only Colditz prisoner to merit his own codename: "Emil." The guard on duty outside his door was known as an *Emil-Beobachter*, an Emil-watcher.

Initially, Romilly reacted with fury to this unique form of incarceration, hurling his boots at the door and pasting paper over the spyhole. But gradually he adapted. He received better food than the other inmates, and was allowed his own gramophone. At night, the sound of Mozart's Haffner symphony could be heard wafting from his cell, as a small, lonely figure in an old dressing gown gazed out from behind the bars. Padre Platt noted Romilly's changing demeanor as the months passed: "There is a restless look in his eyes, and a droop of discontent at the corners of his mouth." Romilly enjoyed a more comfortable existence than other inmates, but it was also, he reflected, a "privileged nightmare." The founder member of an elite club, he would eventually be joined by other *Prominente*, accorded an exclusive form of incarceration because, as Romilly put it, they had been "singled out as 'specially special.'" They were also uniquely vulnerable, protected for only as long as they remained valuable. These men were bargaining chips, and at some point they would be cashed in.

5

Ballet Nonsense

Anyone who has not experienced imprisonment might imagine that inactivity and lack of responsibility are also, in contrast to war itself, relaxing. The reverse is closer to the truth. Prisons are always places of intense nervous strain, and in Colditz, with its peculiar human mixture, men of action consigned to a life of inaction, the internal pressure was more acute than in any other camp. Romilly felt this "powerful and unrelieved tension from the aggressive, extrovert spirit as it beat outward, found no space, beat inward again . . . at times it seemed as if the tension was so powerful it must crack the walls of the castle."

Every snippet of news from the outside world was avidly devoured and minutely dissected. The prisoners craved amusement, intellectual stimulation, and above all entertainment, and so they manufactured their own. One of the more bizarre by-products of the POW camps was an efflorescence of dramatic talent, and a uniquely dark and bawdy sense of humor: Denholm Elliott (*Indiana Jones* and *Defence of the Realm*), Clive Dunn (*Dad's Army*), and Donald Pleasence (Blofeld in the James Bond film *You Only Live Twice*) were all wartime prisoners. Talbot Rothwell, an RAF officer shot down in 1941 and held at Stalag Luft III, went on to write twenty of the *Carry On* films.

The theater at Colditz was the focus of prison entertainment, the setting for performances of all sorts, including concerts, plays, and pantomimes. As well as a Polish choir, musical groups proliferated, playing instruments provided by the German authorities: a Dutch Hawaiian band, a British jazz ensemble, a French chamber group, and an international orchestra. A large, ornate room on the third floor of the *Saalhaus,* beside the main gate, the theater was a place of faded grandeur and incongruous artistic pretension; built in 1876, it boasted a sprung floor, a stage, and a grand piano. The smoke-stained walls were decorated with the names of great German writers, along with Shakespeare and Rossini, surrounded by fluffy painted clouds to denote genius transported up to heaven. The Germans regarded the prisoners' use of the theater as a privilege, not a right, and one that could be withdrawn as punishment. Even so, they not only tolerated dramatic and musical entertainments but encouraged them, and frequently attended: producers were allowed to order makeup and stage paint from Berlin and borrow tools for building the sets, having solemnly given their "parole" that these would not be used for escaping. That pledge was never violated, despite the prisoners' willingness to steal anything and everything else they could lay their hands on.

Over the years of its existence as a camp, Colditz saw a rich variety of performances: Shakespeare, comedy-revues, plays by Noël Coward and George Bernard Shaw, and others written by the prisoners themselves. Enormous effort went into productions that ran for just a few days. Some were genuinely terrible, and almost all were hugely popular. "Prisoners of war are perhaps easier to please than other theatregoers," observed Giles Romilly, after watching a performance of *The Importance of Being Earnest* by Oscar Wilde. "Helped by a most convincing Lady Bracknell, the play had a very long run of two nights, to packed houses of nearly 150 people."

Late in 1941, the British drama community of Colditz decided to put on a Christmas show, a revue entitled *Ballet Nonsense,* as in bally nonsense, a series of sketches, skits, and musical numbers performed to the accompaniment of the Colditz band, led by Jimmy Yule, a skilled jazz musician. The revue was a perfect distillation of amateur British comedy, a potpourri of off-color jokes, puns, lavatorial humor, slapstick, satire, and farce: one scene was set in the Rose and Crown pub, another in a school. The *pièce de résistance* was a choreographed display by the *corps de ballet,* led by *prima ballerina* Pat Reid, "consisting of the toughest-looking, heaviest-moustached officers available, who performed miracles of energetic grace and unsophisticated

elegance attired in frilly crepe paper ballet skirts and brassieres."
As one of the "leading ladies" observed, "The only trouble with
our female parts was that our dresses were made out of paper
and during the winter it was exceedingly cold." As they clomped
and pirouetted across the boards of Colditz theater, the troupe
sang lustily:

Ballet Nonsense, Ballet Nonsense,
Everything's just mad today.
Ballet Nonsense, Ballet Nonsense,
Everything will be OK . . .

Airey Neave, a man not hitherto noted for an interest in
drama, threw himself into the preparations for *Ballet Nonsense,*
and contributed a sketch entitled "The Mystery of Wombat College" featuring an unpleasant headmaster called Dr. Calomel
(calomel being a form of mercury chloride used to relieve consti-
pation). Neave cast himself as Calomel, with a mortarboard, a
drawn-on mustache in the manner of Groucho Marx, and jokes
that made sense only if you had been to Eton. Even Neave admitted it was a "wretched little piece"; indeed, he regarded the entire theatrical effort as "pathetic," an exercise in distracting
prisoners from their grim reality: "No amount of ingenuity can
conceal its futility," he wrote. Yet, in truth, he regarded the
Christmas show as anything but pointless, and rehearsed his part
with gusto. Jimmy Yule described *Ballet Nonsense* as "escap-
ism." And escape was exactly what Neave had in mind.

On his way to the solitary confinement cells in the town following his humiliating failed escape, Neave had spotted a small
wicket gate on the bridge, leading down into the moat and
toward the woods on the other side of the park. That discovery
coincided with another: staring at the wall of the *Saalhaus* beside
the main gate, Pat Reid noticed a window, just below the level of
the theater floor, for which there did not appear to be a corresponding room. This, he worked out, must connect with the so-
called witches' walk, a corridor running across the top of the
main gate and leading to the attic of the German guardhouse.
Sure enough, by prying up the boards of the stage and breaking

through the ceiling below, Reid gained access to a narrow passageway with a locked door at the end that, when picked, led to the walkway; from this a spiral staircase descended to the guardhouse. Between them, Reid and Neave developed a simple escape plan: two prisoners dressed as German officers would walk brazenly through the guardhouse and out of the door, before slipping through the wicket gate and away into the woods. On his last attempt, Neave had been challenged leaving the prisoners' courtyard; this time, he would be emerging, attired as a German officer, from the guardhouse itself.

This would be a joint Anglo-Dutch operation: the escapers would leave in twos, on successive nights, an Englishman paired with a Dutchman. The first attempt would take place on the closing night of *Ballet Nonsense,* immediately after the curtain came down. Neave was fantastically overexcited: "The thought of disappearing under the stage in the costume of Dr. Calomel and then reappearing in German uniform outside the guardhouse delighted me." His partner would be Tony Luteyn, a lieutenant in the Royal Netherlands East Indies Army who spoke excellent German.

Neave was not going to make the same mistake twice. This time, his disguise would be the very best Colditz could fabricate. Two Dutch greatcoats, so similar in shape and color to those of the Wehrmacht, were modified with green collars made from baize, badges, buttons painted gray, buckles from melted lead piping, epaulettes fashioned from linoleum cut out of the bathroom floor, and belts and pistol holsters of polished cardboard. Two British service caps were remodeled in the German style, with high shiny peaks made from varnished black paper. Once outside, they would be posing as Dutch immigrant workers; beneath the disguise they would wear laborers' overalls. Luteyn had a Dutch passport, but Neave needed an entire set of false papers. One night, he broke into the interrogation room, where prison documentation was stored. There, using the German typewriter, he typed out an *Ausweis* (travel permit) permitting the Dutch electrician "De Never" to travel from Leipzig to Ulm to install a factory electrical system. He also typed up a passport, using Luteyn's as a model, with a photo taken from the German files.

By opening night, the elaborate preparations were still incomplete. The escape was delayed.

Ballet Nonsense opened to a packed theater. Reinhold Eggers attended with officers of the German staff and declared: "The pantomime was a great success . . . the cream of the show was a German schoolteacher's address to his pupils on the subject of Nazism." Eggers never came close to understanding the British sense of humor: he had no inkling that the ridiculous schoolteacher played by Neave was a send-up of Eggers himself as a caricature Hitler. Hauptmann Priem allowed the show to run for an additional night, and attended the closing performance.

The only dissenting voice amid the critical acclaim was that of Jock Platt. Ever alert to sin, the Methodist padre thought he had detected the illicit flutter of sexuality, onstage, backstage, and in the audience. Men dressed up as women could only incite sexual thoughts, which in turn would encourage masturbation or, worse, homosexuality. *Ballet Nonsense* was camp theater, in both senses. "It was primarily the production of sex-starved, virile young men whose minds, perforce, inclined towards abuse as an antidote," Platt wrote in his diary. Neave's Calomel sketch, the padre feared, was "redolent of a master's perverted interest in small boys." The spectacle of men in paper tutus, however heavy their mustaches, could only encourage impure desires, he feared, among prisoners "perverted with longing in a battle no young man should have to fight." While some of those onstage were obviously men dressed as implausible women, others had gone to considerable lengths to achieve a simulacrum of femininity. "The leading ladies were incredibly convincing" and inevitably became the objects of desire, imaginary, sometimes confused, and occasionally candid. "It was very hard to keep your hands off them," said Luteyn, who played the ukulele in the band.

British attitudes to sex have never been straightforward, but in Colditz they achieved a uniquely torturous complexity.

The prisoners' repressed sexual urges were coped with in ways both obvious and innovative. One frustrated inventor came up with the "lecherscope," a homemade telescope that could be used to ogle young women down in the town, some of whom obligingly, and perhaps knowingly, undressed in front of their windows or sunbathed in the open. One doctor in Colditz even prescribed a treatment for heterosexual longings: "If one felt the absence of feminine company, there were always two or three among the French who were prepared to give a vivid account of the pleasures of a high-class brothel in Paris." Another source of stimulation was obtained accidentally when one officer, in an idle moment, wrote to the American film star Ginger Rogers. His letter was published on the front page of the Los Angeles *Observer*, prompting a flood of responses from aspirant Hollywood film actresses to the inmates of Colditz. Padre Platt noted that every letter from an American starlet invariably included "a pretty photograph, showing her in a devastatingly attractive bathing costume." These were plastered all over the British quarters.

The prisoners tried to make light of their sexual frustrations, mocking them or pretending they did not exist. Yet enforced celibacy was an additional cruelty, the more burdensome for being a taboo subject. Peter Storie-Pugh, a medical student before the war, worked in the sickbay and noted how many men were suffering the prolonged effects of sexual repression. But over time sexual longings tended to diminish, particularly in periods of hunger. "If you had the choice between the most beautiful woman in the world and a cheese roll, you'd choose the cheese roll," said one orderly. The pain of wondering what was happening to wives and lovers back at home was exacerbated by a deeper anxiety: some wondered, secretly, if imprisonment might render them impotent, castrated by Colditz.

As in other camps, formal dances were held in which men, inevitably and exclusively, danced with men. Lieutenant Jimmy Atkinson, a Scottish soldier at Laufen camp, even invented a Highland reel with minimal body contact in which men danced by clasping each other's hands at a suitably chaste distance. A letter sent by Atkinson to his mother describing the "Reel of the 51st Highland Division" was intercepted by the Abwehr, the German military intelligence service, which spent the rest of the war trying to decipher what was assumed to be a secret message hidden in its complex instructions.

On October 7, 1941, the first and only Colditz prison wedding took place. Soon after capture, Elie de Rothschild, scion of the French banking dynasty, wrote to his childhood sweetheart Liliane Fould-Springer. She replied encouragingly. He proposed by letter, she accepted (despite her mother's doubts about the wisdom of taking the name Rothschild in Nazi-occupied France), and they married, at long distance. He took his vows in the Jewish attic in Colditz. She made hers the following April, 1,200 miles away in Cannes, with a photograph of the groom on the table in front of her and an empty chair at her side. The marriage was not consummated until 1945.

Since there were no women available as sexual partners, that left only men.

Sexual attraction between men was an unmentionable subject in Colditz, which the British dealt with by the time-honored method of not talking about it. The proportion of men likely to engage in homosexual activity increases sharply when there is no alternative. During daylight hours the castle was so crammed with milling prisoners that, as one observed, "it would be easier to have a homosexual relationship on a Tube train." But nighttime, when the castle's hidden corners were accessible, was a different matter. A few French officers made no secret of their inclinations. "*Quels sont les garçons?*" some demanded on arrival. Which ones are the boys? That relaxed approach was not shared by the moral guardians of the British contingent.

For Padre Platt, sexual deviancy (as he saw it) was not merely a problem of discipline, but eternal damnation. He first became alarmed in the spring of 1941: "Since the beginning of March homosexualism has occupied an increasingly large place in contemporary prison humour," he noted anxiously. Books by Oscar Wilde and Frank Harris, purveyors of "perverse sexualism," were being surreptitiously passed around. Ever vigilant for onanistic tendencies among his captive flock, the padre recorded that "jocular references to masturbation are freer than is usual among healthy minded adults." Two officers were found to be discussing the ancient Greek taste for sex with young boys. "They foresaw themselves as the founders of a Platonic cult"; Platt knew that Plato was the slippery classical slope to unnatural vice. Flirtatious graffiti began appearing on the walls: "Don Donaldson will kiss Hugh Bruce if he (Hugh Bruce) is here at his next birthday." Then, shortly before Christmas, the padre heard rumors that "a small mutual masturbation group hold what they hope are secret sessions." In April he recorded the arrival of a young officer liable to turn the heads of those "susceptible to homosexual inclination": Platt did not explain how he knew this unnamed man might have such an effect, which raises the possibility that the padre was not immune to such proclivities himself. Those who wondered whether the padre's interest in this subject might be more than pastoral pointed out that he was one of the few who could have enjoyed an "undisturbed relationship" since he shared a room, known as the Priests' Hole, with just one other chaplain. Whatever his own leanings, Platt decided it was his religious duty to intervene. Telling grown men to keep their hands off themselves and each other was, he admitted, "as difficult a task as has yet come my way." He fully expected that the group would "tell me to mind my own business! But this happens to be my business!" Whether Padre Platt ever intruded into this delicate matter remains a mystery. The mutual masturbation group was never directly alluded to again in his diary, leading some to imagine that it had miraculously ceased following the intervention of God's representative.

It was simply easier to pretend that same-sex relationships did not happen, or at most to concede, as did one senior officer, that "there was probably an element of homosexual feeling at times but never practicing." This is, of course, nonsense. The men of Colditz probably practiced exactly as much, if not more, than one would expect, but as in the wider world where homosexuality was still illegal, they did so in secrecy, in closets and in perpetual fear of being caught.

As autumn turned to winter, and the snows began to fall on Colditz, Reinhold Eggers could again sense something brewing. It was too quiet. In October, his suspicions were confirmed when a cracked beam in the French quarters led to an alarming discov-

ery: the attic floors above were buckling under the weight of
newly excavated debris, including "bricks, dressed stone, mortar, even pieces of virgin porphyry rock." Clearly the French
were digging, and through the very fabric of the castle foundations, "not only a long tunnel, but a tunnel a long time building." Placing a permanent guard inside the French quarters was
against prison regulations, and would immediately have alerted
the tunnelers to his suspicions. Like every good hunter, Eggers
waited and watched, hoping that the ceiling did not give way
before he discovered the source of the spoil.

The war hung in the balance. Hitler's invasion of Russia in
June 1941 had brought the Soviet Union into the conflict on the
Allied side. In December came news of the Japanese attack on
Pearl Harbor, and war between the United States and the Axis
powers. But Rommel's forces were still advancing in North Africa and the U-boat wolf packs continued to savage Allied shipping. Eggers remained confident of victory, but noted that, for
the first time, German rations had been reduced while Red Cross
parcels continued to arrive: "The prisoners' food supply was in
some ways better than ours." The Poles had distilled a savage
species of vodka from raisins and prunes. "Where did they get
the yeast?" wondered Eggers; "from our sentries obviously." On
New Year's Eve, as a special concession, the prisoners were allowed to stay up until 1:30 in the morning. They sang "Auld
Lang Syne" in the courtyard, threw snowballs, and then belted
out national anthems until many were in patriotic tears, especially the Poles. Then 200 prisoners formed a vast conga and
paraded through the snow and up and down the staircases, "on
a tour of all the quarters of the Schloss." The festivities, frantic
in their gaiety, threatened to get out of hand, but instead of calling out the riot squad, Eggers observed from a doorway, smiling,
and then said quietly: "Now you have had your songs, it is time
to return to quarters." The prisoners trooped upstairs, acquies-
cent, tired, and a little let down, as everyone almost always is at
New Year's. Even Pat Reid, who loathed Eggers, was forced to
admit that he had handled a potentially ugly situation with "ad-
mirable tact."

Eggers had a lot on his mind that Christmas, what with an

undiscovered tunnel, dwindling German rations, corruptible sentries, and a war as yet unwon. But the German officer totted up the escape tally with some satisfaction. A total of 104 prisoners had tried to abscond in forty-nine attempts, but only fifteen had gotten away. The French were in the lead with ten "home runs," followed by the Dutch with four, and the Poles with one. The British and Belgians came last, with not a single success. Some thirty-five British prisoners had tried to break out, but only two had managed to get beyond the castle walls and not one had made a clean break.

On January 5, 1942, the Colditz orchestra played Beethoven's First Symphony for a combined audience of prisoners and guards, an altogether more soothing and dignified production than *Ballet Nonsense*. Tony Luteyn played the double bass; Airey Neave waited in the wings. After the crowd had drifted away into the cold night, a much smaller ensemble gathered onstage and levered up the boards; then two costumed members of the company, one British and one Dutch, performed a double disappearing act without an audience.

1942

6

Le Métro

The girl gave him a long look, coy but suspicious. It was midmorning in the snowy Leipzig park, and the young blond woman had perched beside him on the bench. She was within touching distance, the first female he had seen up close for more than a year. Airey Neave tried to return her gaze neutrally and buried his chin deeper into the collar of his worker's jacket, an adapted French officer's blouson with the insignia removed. She was evidently poor, around eighteen years old, with a tattered overcoat and a short, tight skirt that barely covered her knees. She continued to stare at him intensely. "Her prominent blue eyes had a ruthlessness." His heart was thumping. Beside him, he could feel Tony Luteyn tensing.

"Guten Morgen," she said, a note of inquiry in her voice.

Neave did not reply. His German was too rudimentary to risk a conversation. The silence froze between them. The girl pouted, irritated.

Luteyn rose, and with studied nonchalance began to amble off.

Neave now got to his feet.

"You are unsociable, my friend," the girl said sharply. Again, he left her words hanging and turned away. "I felt her blue eyes watching, deep with suspicion and annoyance."

Neave fought the urge to run, feeling the familiar downward lurch of "dismay and embarrassment." There had been so many moments of near disaster in the previous twelve hours, and now he was about to be caught and shipped back to Colditz because a pretty young woman in a park had tried to flirt with him.

The first part of the theater escape had gone eerily smoothly.

In their fake uniforms, Neave and Luteyn descended the stone spiral staircase, past the officers' mess and into the guardroom corridor. Through a half-open door Neave glimpsed German uniforms and heard the sound of a radio playing organ music. The whiteness of the snow as they emerged from the guardhouse was momentarily dazzling. Under the arch to the outer court-yard, the sentry saluted without interest. They walked on, through the second arch. Two German sergeants emerged from the *Kommandantur,* and fell in behind. Trying to appear relaxed, Neave had laced his fingers in the small of his back, a posture adopted by British officers but never by German ones. "March with your hands at your sides, you bloody fool," hissed Luteyn.

On the bridge, Luteyn opened the wicket gate for the senior officer. The sergeants walked past them and continued over the bridge. Across the dry moat, the path led to the married quarters and then down into the valley. A corporal appeared from the op-posite direction. The soldier seemed to shoot them a quizzical look as he passed, shoulder to shoulder. "Why do you not salute your senior officer?" snapped Luteyn, in crisp parade-ground German. The startled soldier raised his hand and mumbled an apology. It was snowing hard when they reached the park wall, twelve feet high and topped with ice. "It took us thirty-five min-utes to get over it," Neave recalled. The sounds of barking floated across the snow. "There was a dog patrol somewhere in the park." Finally, Luteyn managed to haul himself onto the wall and pulled Neave up after him. They landed heavily on the other side. "I was bruised and shaken and frightened," wrote Neave. But he was out of Colditz.

After a long, cold trudge through the darkness, they reached Leisnig before dawn, bought two workmen's tickets for Leipzig, and boarded the 5:45 train with a crowd of laborers. Their civil-ian disguises consisted of RAF trousers, old French jackets, and ski caps made of blankets. For sustenance they carried chocolate, raisins, vitamin tablets, and meat cubes. Each had sixty Reichs-marks. Neave dozed in the smoky fug of the third-class compart-ment, until woken by Luteyn with a sharp kick in the shins. He had been mumbling in his sleep, in English. Luteyn was a "strong and buoyant character," and exceptionally self-disciplined. The Dutchman was finding Neave's slapdash approach rather trying.

At Leipzig, they shuffled into the waiting room. The train to Ulm did not depart until 10:30 that evening. Neave discreetly studied the other travelers. They seemed "shabby and worn"; he thought he could detect the grim toll of war in their lined faces. Suddenly famished, Neave unwrapped a bar of chocolate and bit off a chunk. "A woman with fierce, hysterical eyes gazed at the chocolate as if she had seen a ghost." She angrily nudged her neighbor and pointed. Such a delicacy was almost unknown by this time in war-rationed Germany, let alone in the thick slabs provided by the Red Cross. Luteyn was also gaping at Neave in consternation. "I had committed a terrible blunder." Too quickly, he stuffed the chocolate bar back in his pocket. They rose and shuffled awkwardly out of the waiting room, stalked by the stares of the other passengers.

For several hours they wandered the ancient streets of Leipzig, once a great center of commerce and culture that had been home to a thriving Jewish community before the rise of Hitler. The Jews had been expelled. Many of the shops were boarded up. In a small park, a handful of people meandered among the scabby flowerbeds. It was bitterly cold. Neave sat heavily on the bench and hugged himself, the anxiety of the night washing through him. "I was a detached spectator." At first, he did not notice that a girl was sitting alongside him, observing him through penetrating blue eyes.

Neave followed Luteyn to the park exit, as casually as he could, blood drumming. Then they ran.

The next twenty-four hours passed in a succession of incongruous scenes. Refuge in a stuffy cinema where they watched newsreel of Rommel's victories in Africa, and then sang "We Are Marching on England" along with the audience; the SS officer in a spotless uniform on the evening train, who summoned them to his carriage and demanded: "Are you Jews?" "Certainly not," said Luteyn. "We are Dutch"; changing trains at Regensburg, where, in the ticket hall, "a man and a girl smelling of spiced sausages and garlic lay near us in a close embrace"; the snow-wrapped Bavarian countryside slipping past the misted window as they trundled south.

When Luteyn asked for two one-way tickets to Singen, the woman in the Ulm ticket office summoned a railway policeman in a blue uniform, who inspected their papers, shrugged, and sent them to the local Labor Office to register themselves with the town authorities. They were accompanied by another policeman with a revolver, who ushered them into the building: "Second floor," he said. "Room 22." He would wait. It was impossible to tell if the policeman was suspicious, or merely passing the time. Trying to appear casual, they sauntered to the top floor, then rushed down some back stairs to the basement, out through the coal store, into the back garden and over a little fence. Neave and Luteyn ran, in the direction of the Swiss border, still 100 miles to the south.

Back at Colditz, four officers were found to be missing; two more escaped via the theater the following night. Eggers was publicly calm, and privately enraged. The smug British and the unreadable Dutch did not even try to disguise the escapers' identities. "How very damnably sure they were of themselves and their mysterious bolthole," Eggers raged. The railway police at Ulm reported that two Dutch electrical workers had appeared by train, and then vanished. When two more arrived by the same route, the second Anglo-Dutch pair, they were immediately arrested. "We clawed back a point," wrote Eggers. But Neave and Luteyn had not been found and nor, more important, had their escape route. The Germans began, systematically, to pull the castle apart.

On the evening of January 8, three days after their escape, Neave and Luteyn, armed with spades, stood on the road to Singen, just three miles short of the Swiss border. Barring their way were two teenage members of the Hitler Youth, carrying truncheons. "What are your names and where are you going?" they demanded.

Neave later asked Luteyn what went through his mind at that moment.

"For me to kill one with my spade and you the other," the Dutchman replied. "What did you intend to do?"

"Exactly the same."

Earlier that day, the two men had found an empty beekeeper's hut in the woods. "Weather conditions were terrible and the temperature was minus 17," wrote Neave. Exhausted and hungry, Neave was starting to hallucinate and suffering bouts of snow blindness. An hour before, they had been stopped by a band of suspicious woodcutters, but had broken away and outrun them, before collapsing in the snow. Neave was beginning to falter. "My breath came painfully, and my head began to swim. I could not look at the whiteness around me without pain." The sound of distant barking showed that the woodcutters had alerted the border authorities. "We were being hunted by dogs," wrote Neave. They slept until nightfall, ate their few remaining raisins, and then set out once more, carrying the beekeeper's spades and white jackets as a rudimentary disguise.

But now the two uniformed Hitler Youths stood menacingly between them and freedom.

"We have been told to look for two British prisoners who have escaped and are thought to be trying to cross the border tonight."

"They won't get far," said Luteyn, "it is much too cold for prisoners of war."

Luckily for the Hitler Youth, this entirely illogical observation somehow seemed to allay their suspicions. They cycled away, having narrowly escaped being brained by two desperate men with spades.

At around three in the morning, Neave and Luteyn crossed the railway line, and headed southwest into the woods, in what they hoped was the direction of the Ramsen salient. To the east they heard voices, and through a gap in the trees they glimpsed the frontier huts. For fifty yards, the road ran parallel to the border, with a guard post at either end. Crouching in the roadside ditch, they held their breath as a German sentry clumped past. Beside the road, to the west, lay a field of unbroken snow. The temperature was dropping fast. The sentry's footsteps died away.

"Do you agree to cross now?" whispered Luteyn.

"This is the moment."

They scrambled across the road and plunged into the snow field. "We continued crawling, ploughing on hands and knees through the deep snow. Our white coats helped to camouflage us. After what seemed an eternity we rose to our feet, and surged forward into Switzerland." Or so they hoped. After 200 yards of wading through snowdrifts, both were thoroughly disoriented, and close to collapse. Even the phlegmatic Luteyn was babbling to himself in Dutch. A single light flickered to the east. Neave felt himself begin to "flounder, helpless and distraught." The soft snow beneath their ice-caked boots gave way to the hard surface of a paved road. A church clock struck five. A row of small farmhouses and then the silhouette of a clock tower rose out of the darkness. "A single question tortured us. Were we in Switzerland?" The village street was empty. The place seemed deserted. But then a solitary figure strolled into view, a gun over his shoulder. "My heart was beating so I could hardly breathe," wrote Neave. The night guard spotted them and unslung his rifle. He wore a long green coat, a pointed hat, and, Neave saw with a wild surge of relief, a broad smile. "With shouts of joy we flung ourselves upon him."

The three men clasped one another and "danced in the snow, pirouetting first one way and then the other. The guard shouted merrily, as if he was the most delighted man in the world." In the freezing dawn on an empty street in Switzerland, two escaped prisoners, famished, drained, and half-blind, and a Swiss guard they had encountered thirty seconds earlier, performed a strange dance of liberty.

Morale in the British quarters soared, in Padre Platt's words, "like a hydrogen-inflated balloon." As the days passed and it became clear that Neave and Luteyn had gotten away, an almost spiritual wave of optimism gripped the rest of the British prisoners, "like the dove released from the ark which has found land," an olive branch of hope.

It took Eggers less than a week to discover how the doves had escaped. He had long suspected the theater might be a "weak spot," and that something other than entertainment was taking place there. One of the boards on the steps to the stage was pried up; a small German soldier wriggled underneath and found the knotted bedsheets used to climb into the space below. Access to the theater was suspended; the hole was filled with concrete; the door leading to the spiral staircase was double-bolted; and the Kommandant presented Eggers with a congratulatory bottle of champagne.

But Eggers was too anxious to enjoy his reward. The escape route used by Neave and Luteyn had been ingenious, but it was a minor subplot compared to whatever the French were planning. Examination of the excavated spoil making the attic beams sag revealed fresh mud, suggesting that the tunnelers had somehow penetrated into the earth outside or beneath the castle. In the northwest side of the courtyard, at night, sounds of digging were clearly audible, but repeated searches failed to identify where the noise was coming from. Moreover, materials clearly intended for the construction of a large tunnel were being systematically pilfered from the rest of the castle: metal bedframes, electrical cables, 300 planks from unused beds stored in an attic. "Something is brewing," Unteroffizier Schädlich noted in his diary, after a large iron wall bracket was pried off the wall of the *Saalhaus*. "So many things are disappearing." The undiscovered tunnel was the talk of the German guardroom and Eggers was being ribbed by his fellow officers: "Can't find the hole, eh?" they mocked. "Is this the Channel Tunnel?" To make matters worse, Berlin had been informed, and the authorities were increasingly jumpy that this undiscovered tunnel might be used to exfiltrate the camp's most important prisoner. They took to calling in the middle of the night: "Is Romilly there?" Gestapo security experts arrived to offer advice on the search. Eggers resented the intrusion. "This was our world," he wrote. "We knew more about it than anybody else. Something just had to be done." Deep beneath their feet, a gargantuan hole was being dug. Unless it was found, and quickly, then dozens, if not hundreds, of prisoners could escape, and that, as Eggers and his Kommandant knew well, would mean a ticket to the Eastern Front, almost certainly one-way.

The Great French Tunnel, or Le Métro as it became known, was the most ambitious construction project yet undertaken by the prisoners of Colditz. It was started in March 1941 at the top of the clock tower, eighty-five feet above the courtyard; ten months and fifty feet of subterranean digging later, the tunnel was just a few feet from the face of the sheer ravine on the north side of the castle. The workings for the clock, which had long since ceased to tell the time, were housed in a small room on top of the tower; from this, two long shafts or sleeves, just sixteen inches wide and originally housing the weights and ropes that powered the mechanism, ran all the way down to ground level. A group of nine French officers, calling themselves La Société Anonyme du Tunnel (The Tunnel Company Limited), first broke into the attic above the clock, and then climbed down the shafts, one floor at a time, using improvised ladders. From the ground floor, they sunk a shaft through an arched brick roof into the wine cellar in the basement, using the steel axles of the clock mechanism as drills, the tips tempered and hardened in a make-shift forge. The principal tunneler was a muscular Foreign Legionnaire called Bernard Cazaumayou, nicknamed "La Taupe," the mole. Having penetrated the *Kellerhaus,* in August 1941, they began burrowing through the foundations under the dividing wall with the chapel, hoping to find a crypt with an exit to the outside. The hole was carefully disguised with the original stones and sprinkled with dust, since the Germans continued to use the cellar—a fact that did not inhibit the tunnelers from occasionally refreshing themselves with its contents, before refilling the bottles with water and reinserting the corks. "There was not the slightest trace of our having helped ourselves," recalled Cazaumayou. "Even the number of bottles remained unchanged." Some of the rocks were so large they had to be cracked apart, by alternately heating them with fat lamps and then pouring on cold water. Frank "Errol" Flinn managed to steal a large crowbar from a visiting German workman, which he presented to the French tunnelers, making their job considerably easier and earning him a place on the escape team. The ground beneath the chapel was solid rock, the floor held up by medieval oak joists, each over a foot thick. One by one, they were severed, using miniature saws made from kitchen knives with teeth cut into them. "It was dark, cramped, hellish work," said Cazaumayou. "If I had known how difficult it would be, I would never have started." Above, the French choir sang lustily to cover the noise. An elaborate system of stooges warned of any approaching guards. The French chaplain pretended to take the confessions of three officers while they rigged up an electric light system to the tunnel by diverting cables from the fuse box in the sacristy. The French had demanded the chapel remain open because "they needed the spiritual consolation of choir practice and religious instruction." Eggers's sense of fair play was outraged when he later discovered this had been a ruse to work on the tunnel. It was, he huffed, "the very grossest abuse of our concession to culture and religious worship."

The spoil was laboriously hauled up the shafts in sacks made from mattress covers and bound with electrical wire: some 1,200 cubic meters of earth, rubble, stones, and shards of wood, distributed across the attics. By September, they had cut through twelve joists. It was a gamble whether the ceilings would collapse under the weight of debris before the chapel floor gave way. Cazaumayou and his diggers finally reached the outer wall of the castle, seven feet thick and impenetrable without a power drill or explosives. There was no choice but to go under the foundations, a job that would require the labor of many more hands. The limited company was expanded to include thirty-one French officers and a single Englishman, burrowing in three shifts. A shaft was sunk fifteen feet beneath the wall, before resuming its horizontal trajectory. By mid-January 1942, the tunnel, lined with wooden boards stripped from around the castle, had extended under the catwalk on the terrace to beyond the wire, and was now separated from the cliff face by just a few yards of soft earth.

The company now opted to float. It was agreed that all the French prisoners would escape, the tunnelers first, in an order of precedence decided by drawing lots, followed, after a half-hour interval, by all the rest, in pairs, each man equipped with civilian disguise, money, maps, and false papers. One by one, this small army of escapees would climb down the face of the precipice on a sheet rope to the valley below, cross the stream at the bottom, and then disperse. The mass breakout was set for January 17.

Eggers went into overdrive, hunting for the hidden tunnel as if his life depended on it, which it probably did. A natural bureaucrat, he set up a "Private Search Committee" to assess the problem from every angle: the other members of this secret panel were two trusted NCOs, the diarist Unteroffizier Martin "Dixon Hawke" Schädlich and Stabsfeldwebel Ernst "Mussolini" Gephard, the best ferrets in the garrison. Eggers did not tell his senior officers what he was doing. "The Kommandant and Security Officer were panicking," he concluded, and there was no point in feeding their paranoia. Eggers suspected that some of his colleagues actually wanted the tunnel to succeed, so they could argue for a more draconian regime. Just as the prisoners had an escape committee, so the Germans now had an equally secret anti-escape board.

Eggers's private committee came up with a plan: to focus on unoccupied parts of the castle; to collate any relevant observations, "however casual," made by the prisoners; and to explore "every conceivable place where an exit could have been made."

The collective noun for ferrets is a "business," and the German hunters had never been busier. By mid-January, they had meticulously searched the cellars, attics, chapel, and theater. "Still no tunnel," Eggers fretted. "Our minds wandered round the rooms, floors, landings, corridors, buttresses and entrances that we knew so well. Suddenly I thought of the clock tower." On the morning of January 15, Stabsfeldwebel Gephard, accompanied by Willi Pönert, the camp electrician, shone a flashlight down one of the narrow shafts. Then he dropped a pebble, which made an oddly hollow sound. Gephard picked up one of the redundant clock weights, a lump of metal weighing forty pounds, and dropped it into the hole. A terrible crash resounded as it smashed through the boarding erected by the French to hide the tunnel entrance. "We were onto something," recalled Gephard. Too stout to climb into the shaft himself, he summoned the electrician's apprentice, a skinny teenager, strapped a fire hose around the boy's waist, and lowered him slowly into the hole. Some forty feet down, the apprentice appeared dangling above the heads of three startled French officers who had been stitching sacks of rubble when the clock weight smashed down: "There's someone here!" yelled the terrified boy, who was swiftly hauled back up the chute. "He looked pretty shattered," wrote Gephard. Eggers was summoned with the riot squad, and the three cornered Frenchmen took evasive action: using a wooden beam from the chapel floor as a ram, they battered a hole through the wall into a washroom on the second floor.

Count Philippe de Liedekerke, an aristocratic army major descended from the kings of Belgium, was quietly reading his book in the bath when a brick shot out of the wall and landed on his stomach. "Iron bars flayed the opening." The count barely had time to leap out and grab his towel before a body scrambled through the hole, followed by two more. Liedekerke was a remarkably brave man, a member of the Belgian Resistance who would later escape, join Britain's SOE, and parachute into Nazi-occupied Belgium three times; but for sheer shock, nothing quite compared to having three sweaty, dusty, half-naked Frenchmen jump into his morning bath.

Eggers was astonished, and deeply impressed, by the feat of engineering he now uncovered: a tunnel that extended for forty-four meters, from the top of the castle to within a few feet of the ravine, complete with an electrical early-warning system of flashing lights, a pumped ventilation system using tins joined together as pipes, and a track and trolley to remove debris. "I crawled to the end and right out to the working face. Over my head, I could hear the sentries marching up and down. We were only just in time." The members of his Private Search Committee were rewarded with additional leave. Eggers again wheeled out his colloquial English in celebration: "We were all cock-a-hoop." The next day, Gauleiter Martin Mutschmann, the Nazi potentate of Saxony, paid a visit to the castle and was shown the tunnel by a triumphant Kommandant Schmidt. Some 1,200 cubic meters of rubble, rocks, and earth had to be laboriously carted out of the attics.

"We succeeded in building a tunnel forty-four meters long in the space of two hundred and fifty days," said Cazaumayou. "A superhuman effort dashed at the last moment." The French, plunged in gloom, suspected treachery. How had the Germans known where to look, just two days before the breakout? Eggers later insisted the discovery of the tunnel was the result of methodical hard work, intuition, and good fortune, "one of those lucky chances that happen occasionally if one follows a sound principle for long enough." He denied receiving a tip-off. But there was something too convenient about the timing; the "sudden" German decision to look in exactly the right place smelled of betrayal.

Every schoolteacher needs a class sneak. From the start, Eggers was on the hunt for stool pigeons, that particularly loathsome species of spy who agrees to supply information while posing as a loyal member of his community. At the height of the confrontation between the British officers and their orderlies, Eggers noticed that one private soldier was complaining bitterly in letters home that "he was sick of acting as servant to officers." When no one was within earshot, Eggers sidled up to him.

"I could send you away," he offered. "But I should want some information in exchange."

The reply was blunt. "Captain Eggers, I may not like it here, but I am still British."

That approach failed, but others were more successful. Eggers liked to think of himself as a man of honor, and in his memoirs he played down the morally dubious task of recruiting moles. "There were only two traitors," he insisted, "and they came forward on their own initiative. Information was offered voluntarily." He did not identify these turncoats by name and claimed that "attempts to get information from prisoners were hardly ever successful." Eggers was writing after the war, at a time when revealing his spies inside the camp would have done him little good and great harm to them. Internal treachery did not sit comfortably with the post-war Colditz mythology and was therefore glossed over, but it occurred nonetheless, among all nations: prisoners willing to supply information for material gain, hoping to win their freedom, for ideological reasons, or opportunists taking out an insurance policy should the war end in German victory. The families of Polish prisoners were living under brutal Nazi occupation; cooperation might ensure their safety. Some of the Poles were *Volksdeutsche,* ethnically German in origin, and therefore considered more pro-German than the rest. The French contingent, deeply divided between adherents of the pro-German Vichy government and supporters of de Gaulle, was ripe for infiltration. According to Airey Neave, "Frenchmen trained in German propaganda were introduced but had to be removed as they were threatened with lynching and in some cases were actually injured. It was suspected that in some cases escapes were given away by French informers." Even the ranks of the British military included some Nazi sympathizers. Finding such people and bribing, blackmailing, or otherwise inducing them to betray their fellow prisoners was the aspect of his job Eggers liked least, but he was extremely skilled at it.

The Poles first began to suspect a traitor in April 1941 at a time when their escape attempts were failing, one after the other. Four Polish officers had hatched a plan to escape via the canteen, but in the end only three had made the attempt when one was taken ill at the last moment. "Only three?" said one of the guards, who picked up the escapers before they were even out of the inner courtyard. "Where is the fourth?" The French had already ostracized one officer believed to be a mole, who was quietly removed by the Germans. Some in the French camp remained convinced that the secret of Le Métro had been passed to Eggers, either as an act of deliberate treachery or inadvertently through "incautious remarks." Suspicion focused on a group of officers recently moved from Colditz to another camp. Mistrust is contagious. The British could not point to any specific incident that suggested betrayal, though several of their tunnels had also been discovered with notable ease. Doubt began to circulate, like a fine poisonous miasma, around a prisoner with unconventional political views, a short temper, and a skin that was not white.

Birendranath Mazumdar never fit in, because he was never allowed to. Two days after arriving, the Indian doctor was summoned to see Guy German, the SBO.

"You're still in the King's army," snapped the colonel.

In his confusion, Mazumdar had forgotten to salute.

German's manner was unfriendly: "Where have you been and what have you done since you were captured?"

Mazumdar was dismayed: "What have I been doing? What has been done to me?"

The SBO delivered a lecture, or a warning, instructing Mazumdar to "on no account fraternize with the Germans." The clear implication was that, as an Indian nationalist, he would be tempted to make common cause with his captors. Mazumdar fought to control his anger. "I was not impressed. I disliked him at once."

Mazumdar was allocated a top bunk at the back of the uppermost attic in the British quarters, which meant that if he needed to urinate in the night, he tended to wake his roommates by clattering in clogs across the wooden floor, and had to endure a flurry of curses. "What the hell is the matter with you, Mazumdar?" As an Indian, "Jumbo" was assumed to be able to make curries, though he had seldom cooked a meal in his life. He once accidentally added a tin labeled "Mincemeat" to his curry, thinking it must be minced meat rather than the sweet fruit filling used in baking; the resulting concoction was inedible, and fiercely mocked. Mazumdar was never allowed to forget his "mince pie curry." Word soon spread that though the Indian doctor "may have been anti-German, as indeed we all were at the time, he was certainly anti-the British Raj." He naturally gravitated toward the only other person of color in the castle, a half-Indonesian officer in the Dutch East Indies army, named Eduard Engles. That alliance of outsiders only seemed to compound his unpopularity with some British officers.

Mazumdar was excluded from the camp's primary topic of conversation. "I heard about escape plans from the French and the Dutch, but not from the British," he recalled. When the Indian doctor approached Colonel German and said that he would like to be considered a candidate in future escape attempts, the suggestion was greeted "with derision." "You? Escaping from here? With your brown skin?" It was hard enough to evade capture in Germany with a white face, said the SBO, let alone a distinctive brown one. This was possibly true. But it was also highly discriminatory, another measure of his alienation. Though a better physician than the German camp doctor, as an officer he was not permitted to work. Prevented from practicing medicine, with no one to vouch for him and few friends, Mazumdar retreated into himself, which made him appear even more alien and dubious in the eyes of those determined to see evidence of treachery. "I found myself lost, and I used to keep to myself," he recalled. "Colditz seemed disjointed. It was everybody for himself." One day, a French officer took him aside: "You know the British officers are calling you a spy. They've asked us to keep away from you." Mazumdar was mortified. The high-caste Indian had become untouchable.

7

Clutty of MI9

Late in 1940, Dodo Barry received an extremely odd letter from her husband, Rupert, one of the first British officers sent to Colditz. The opening line read: "Am so glad to hear you are going to buy a puppy. The first dog in each three litters you will find the best." Dodo was not buying a puppy, let alone three from different litters. At first, she assumed her husband must have gone mad in captivity. What was he on about? She didn't even like dogs. She did, however, like crosswords, and on closer examination she grasped that Rupert was using a simple code: read every third word. This was not a letter about dogs.

Because in addition to stool pigeons, real and imaginary, the castle was home to another, more commendable sort of spy, the type gathering secret information and sending it back to Britain. The prisoners might be locked away from the world, yet as captives inside enemy territory they had access to some important (or at least interesting) intelligence, and with a steady stream of new arrivals, newly captured officers or men transferred from other camps, that stock of useful knowledge was growing steadily: observations on German troop movements, defensive capabilities, bomb damage, the location of potential targets, civilian and prisoner morale, food supplies, and so on. In order to pass on this information, the prisoners needed a method of communicating with London without the Germans knowing. Letters in and out of the castle were carefully screened for secret messages, and heavily censored. References to names and places were systematically erased. Letters home had to be written in pencil, on glossy paper forms to prevent the use of secret ink. The only way to send secrets to London was by code, and if such a secret cipher could be agreed upon, then London could write back.

Once she had spotted the code, it took Dodo just a few minutes to read Rupert Barry's message: "Get From War Office American Passport Visa Ex Sweden." She rushed to London and explained to an official that her husband was planning to escape via Scandinavia and wanted a fake American passport with a visa for Sweden. He did not get one. But a few weeks later Barry received two letters from Christine Silverman, a maiden aunt living in Leeds he had not heard from in years; using the same third-word code, these letters indicated that two parcels would shortly be arriving in Colditz from the Prisoners' Welfare Fund, containing a set of handkerchiefs and a pack of sugared almonds in different colors. Following his "aunt's" instructions, Barry dissolved the yellow almonds in water and then added the handkerchief with a green border: there, before his eyes, like a developing photograph, emerged the details of the "HK" or "5-6-O code," the cipher for communications to and from British prisoners. The code was both simple and hard to crack (see Appendix), and it remained unbroken for the rest of the war. Some of the intelligence supplied by POWs was already out of date when it arrived, but the psychological value of this link between the War Office and the camps was immense: by means of coded letters, the prisoners could send information, make requests, and receive orders, in ways the Germans strongly suspected, but never discovered. With a reliable method of communication, the distance between Colditz and London no longer seemed so great, the impotence of imprisonment less oppressive. The men might be prisoners, disarmed and detained, but they were still fighting the war. Back in London, the War Office had begun to view the POW population in a different light: not as non-combatants irrelevant to the wider war, but as potential military assets.

Auntie Christine in Leeds was, in reality, part of a new branch of British intelligence dedicated to aiding POWs and servicemen shot down or lost in enemy territory. It operated under various cover names, including The Lisbon Book Fund, The Welsh Provident Society, The Licensed Victuallers Sports Association, The

British Local Ladies' Comforts Society, and The Jigsaw Puzzle Club. But its official name was MI9, the youngest addition to the Military Intelligence family that already included MI5 and MI6. Originally housed in a single room at the Metropole Hotel in London, this new, top-secret unit expanded rapidly, and at the start of 1942 it recruited the only person in Britain with first-hand knowledge of escaping from Colditz.

Airey Neave was initiated into the bizarre rituals of the secret world as soon as he arrived in Switzerland. At the British legation in Berne he was told: "MI9 have asked for you" (it was the first time he had heard the name), and instructed to go to Geneva, where a man reading the *Journal de Genève* would be waiting at the station bookstall. Sure enough, a "slender Englishman in a pinstripe suit" introduced himself as "Robert." This was Nicholas Elliott of MI6, an espionage veteran with a taste for the absurd who managed the escape routes out of Switzerland. Elliott took Neave to a hotel-brothel for a party, and then handed over false papers identifying him as a Czech refugee: an odd choice of nationality, since Neave could not even pronounce the name on his identity card. Having crossed the border into France, he and another British escaper were met by an elderly man wearing worker's overalls and smoking a clay pipe. "Good morning, gentlemen," said the Frenchman. "I am Louis Simon, formerly of the Ritz Hotel, London." The ex-waiter introduced them to a "young, sad-faced Frenchwoman," who transferred them to a black marketeer in Marseille, who handed them on to the "Pat Line," an escape route across the Pyrenees run by Pat O'Leary, a doctor who, despite his name, was Belgian. From neutral Spain, Neave was bused to Gibraltar with two dozen other escaped soldiers of every Allied nation, where they boarded a troopship bound for Britain.

Two weeks later Neave was sitting down to lunch in Rules restaurant in Covent Garden with a middle-aged man in tartan trousers. Colonel Norman Crockatt, a former head of the London Stock Exchange and now chief of MI9, had a straightforward philosophy: by training military personnel to avoid capture and aiding escapes from the camps, MI9 would tie up enemy resources, boost the morale of prisoners and civilians alike, and bolster the war effort. Soldiers, sailors, and airmen must cultivate "escape-mindedness," and treat evading capture, or escaping if caught, as a patriotic obligation. Every prisoner freed from captivity was another man back in uniform. Crockatt came straight to the point: Would Neave join his team at MI9? "You are one of the very few who has had such experience." Neave accepted without hesitation: "I have become used to the atmosphere of escape and would do anything to help the people over there."

MI9 was one of the smallest and most secretive corners of British intelligence, and one of the oddest. It was run by Crockatt, but its presiding genius was Christopher Clayton Hutton, the most prodigious inventor of escape equipment in history. War has a way of finding useful employment for people who, in peacetime, would be dismissed as cranks and misfits. "Clutty" was such a person. Balding, bespectacled, and violently allergic to military discipline, he did more to aid the war effort than most generals, while working from a large underground bunker in the middle of a field to avoid being disturbed. His fascination with escapology started in 1913 when, at the age of nineteen and working in his uncle's Birmingham sawmill, he met Harry Houdini. Hutton bet the American illusionist he would not be able to escape from a sealed wooden packing case. Houdini won the wager, but only by secretly bribing the mill workers to secure the lid of the box with false nails. This was a eureka moment for the young Clutty, but it would take another twenty-seven years, two world wars, and failed stints as a journalist, film publicist, and soldier before he discovered his life's calling: inventing escape and evasion devices for MI9, a task he undertook with quite staggering energy and ingenuity.

Clutty started by creating escape kits for downed airmen, before graduating to the even trickier task of smuggling gadgets into POW camps to help prisoners escape, using every corner of his exceptionally fertile brain.

Maps of enemy territory were his first priority, and Clutty made maps as they had never been made before: maps printed on silk with permanent ink that could be folded into a tiny size and hidden inside a chess piece or boot heel; maps on edible tissue paper made out of mulberry leaves, which did not rustle when a prisoner was searched, could be soaked without disintegrating, and screwed up into a ball and then flattened again without losing shape; maps sewn into uniform linings or concealed in books, gramophone records, cigarette tins, and playing cards. He invented a compass from a magnetized razor blade: when this was hung on a thread, the G in Gillette pointed north. He hid miniature compasses inside food, tins, bars of soap, collar studs, pencil stubs, and buttons that unscrewed the wrong way (based on the impeccable theory that the logical German mind would never imagine something might unscrew clockwise). He worked out methods to conceal money inside board games, hide hacksaw blades in parcel twine or a screwdriver in a cricket bat handle, and fit hairbrushes with hidden compartments to conceal money and other contraband. Food tins in parcels were pierced top and bottom by the Germans and the contents inspected before being handed over: Clutty invented a tin with a double skin, a thin compartment between the inner and outer layers to hide maps, money, and even diagrams of enemy aircraft should an escaped pilot contrive to steal one. His inventions for downed airmen included shoes with false heels containing emergency supplies such as food and Benzedrine tablets (a type of amphetamine to fight off fatigue), and flying boots that turned into civilian shoes and a warm leather waistcoat when the leggings were detached. Some prisoners arrived at Colditz already secretly equipped with a mass of gear to help them get out again.

Disguise was essential, and so Clutty put his strange mind to thinking about costumes. POWs were entitled to receive new uniforms, so he designed a reversible uniform with a dark lining that, when turned inside out, resembled an ordinary civilian jacket. After consulting the Wool Association to find the right material, he drew cutting marks with invisible ink on what appeared to be ordinary blankets; on receipt, a tailor in the prison community would develop the ink, cut out the shapes, and sew a replica uniform of the Wehrmacht or Luftwaffe. With the application of dyes, sent separately, these were virtually indistinguishable from the real things.

Crockatt allowed Clutty freedom to experiment, which was

just as well since the inventor was quite incapable of doing what he was told. "This officer is eccentric," said Crockatt, with pride. "He cannot be expected to comply with ordinary service discipline." This frequently got him into trouble. A blowpipe for French Resistance fighters to shoot poisoned gramophone needles into the faces of SS officers was rejected as highly unsporting. He was arrested on Ilkley Moor while testing a miniature radio hidden in a cigarette packet. His driving was so erratic that he was given a driver who was warned, before taking the job, that her passenger was mad.

The actor Desmond Llewelyn was a prisoner in the officers' camp at Laufen, and doubtless handled some of these extraordinary escape gizmos; Llewelyn would go on to play "Q," MI6's irascible inventor, in seventeen James Bond films, a fictionalized version of Clutty himself.

Red Cross parcels were never used to smuggle escape equipment, since this would have violated the neutrality of the system and potentially imperiled the source of rations so vital to prisoner welfare. Instead, MI9 inserted escape aids into packets sent by family members, or under cover of various bogus charitable organizations at fake addresses. These parcels were known as "phony," "explosive," or "naughty." The Germans even permitted signed receipts to be sent back for such packages, enabling MI9 to gauge which illicit equipment was getting through. Coded letters were used to alert inmates to what was arriving, when, and how, although the system was imperfect: after discovering a map concealed inside a gramophone record, the British destroyed most of their music collection before learning that records containing contraband had a dot in a specific place on the label.

Clutty tirelessly bullied British firms into helping him: John Waddington of Leeds allowed real cash to be included with the Monopoly money in sets sent to prisoners; Wills, the tobacco company of Bristol, agreed to produce customized tins to conceal escape kits; John Bartholomew and Sons, the Edinburgh mapmakers, mass-produced microscopic charts on a variety of surfaces. MI9's productivity was prodigious. Blunt Brothers, a small instrument factory on the Old Kent Road in London, was at one point churning out 5,000 mini-compasses a week. Of the

35,000 Allied troops who made their way to safety from captivity or after being shot down, about half were carrying one of Hutton's maps.

Christopher Clayton Hutton's bizarre achievements prove that war is not solely a matter of bombs, bullets, and battlefield bravery; they also serve who work out how to hide a compass inside a walnut.

The most important map of all came not from a British mapmaker, but a German one. The escape committee surmised that over the centuries of its construction, the builders of Colditz must surely have drawn up a plan of the castle, room by room, floor by floor. A coded letter was sent to London requesting that a search be made for such a record, since it might reveal "old drainage systems and possible bricked-up cavities in the massive walls." MI9 scoured the nation's libraries and eventually located, in the bowels of the British Museum, Cornelius Gurlitt's nineteenth-century description of the castle, including a detailed floor plan based on a 1696 inventory drawn up during the reign of Augustus the Strong. This showed every seventeenth-century room, staircase, window, cupboard, and cubbyhole, many of which had since been walled over. The map was copied and dispatched to Colditz, concealed in a parcel that was not merely naughty, but priceless.

Parcels from Britain occasionally included unexpected luxuries. Pat Reid was delighted to receive two boxes of Upmann Havana cigars from some university friends. Each of the fifty cigars was kept fresh in an aluminum tube with a screw top. The tube made the perfect arse-creeper, much more durable than the cardboard toothbrush cases used hitherto, and sufficiently roomy to accommodate, in Reid's words, "a button compass, 100 Reichsmarks in various denominations, a route map from Colditz to Singen, a workman's pass, and a leave permit on foolscap paper." There was poetic justice in the choice of brand: Hermann and Albert Upmann had used H. Upmann Cigars Ltd as a cover for running a German intelligence network in Cuba during the last war. But the real clue lay in the name, since "up man" was precisely their intended destination. This was the kind of joke Clutty liked.

It is impossible to quantify how much contraband was successfully smuggled into Colditz and how many escapes were fostered by Clutty's inventiveness, but during the early part of the war money, maps, and gadgets flowed into the prison almost undetected. Before being handed over to the addressees at the parcels office on the ground floor of the inner courtyard, packages sent from abroad were inspected, but not rigorously. In the army-run camps, newly arriving prisoners were seldom properly searched.

But early in 1942 the indefatigable Eggers smelled a large and pungent rat. Given the worldwide shortage of paper, some of the hardcovers on books sent to the prisoners seemed oddly thick. Those arriving from the Prisoners' Leisure Hour Fund in Lisbon were particularly fat. Slicing open the boards, the Germans found 100-mark notes, maps of the Swiss, Dutch, Belgian, and Yugoslav borders, and even, in the case of one particularly hefty tome, a hacksaw. "We were a little late before we discovered what was going on under our very noses," wrote Eggers, who rapidly made up for lost time. Hardback books were banned. Food packets were opened before being handed over, and the contents of tins emptied into bowls so the interiors could be probed. Incoming objects were minutely examined, leading to some surprising discoveries: "A German 20-mark note inside a prune," marveled Unteroffizier Schädlich. Every arriving prisoner was strip-searched, his clothing and possessions pulled apart. One new prisoner brought with him a chess set, which Eggers found to contain "1,000 Reichsmarks, three compasses and seven maps." Every parcel that did not emanate from the Red Cross was now thoroughly searched before being handed over. Finally an X-ray machine from Leipzig was installed in the parcels office. "We subjected every incoming object without exception to its penetrating gaze," wrote Eggers, and it yielded swift results: a set of badminton racquets with hollow handles containing sawblades, maps, and money. Clutty's methods of concealment grew ever more ingenious.

That second winter in Colditz was cold, with temperatures dropping to minus thirty. At the end of January, a coal shortage cut off the hot-water supply for a fortnight. Freezing and filthy, the prisoners found their moods oscillated, sometimes abruptly, between defiance and resignation. The elation following the successful British escape was swiftly eclipsed by the discovery of the French tunnel: "The whole camp felt the loss and were inwardly seething." The anger was compounded when Kommandant Schmidt announced that the cost of repairs to the chapel floor would be docked from the officers' wages. Hauptmann Priem, increasingly drunken and erratic, was "helped upstairs" to the meaningless role of deputy Kommandant; Eggers took his place as senior duty officer. "It fell to me now to bear the maximum brunt of contact with the 'bad boys,'" he wrote. Whenever Eggers entered the inner courtyard, he was met with "howls and catcalls," or worse. For a representative of the Master Race, Eggers was exceedingly thin-skinned. "I was naturally upset to have aroused so much hatred, but as this arose from my job I took it as a measure of my success." Eggers had microphones installed at thirty-foot intervals around the prisoners' quarters. The "ferrets" were issued rubber-soled shoes, in order to creep silently around the buildings at night. Use of the chapel was suspended. The Park Walk was restricted. At the end of January, Guy German was moved to another camp on the grounds that he was "totally committed to promoting the escape of officers and also to collusion with disruptive and non-cooperative practices amongst the POWs." German was replaced as senior officer by Colonel David Stayner, a more diplomatic figure, gray-haired and grave. In the eyes of the prisoners the tightened security measures were really petty punishments, humiliating regulations imposed out of spite, of which none was more irksome than the saluting rule.

Under the terms of the Geneva Convention prisoners were obliged to salute senior German officers. The Bavarian camp doctor was particularly insistent on this formality, and the solitary cells were crammed with prisoners who had declined to salute him, or had done so in an impudent way. One evening in late January, at evening roll call, a twenty-two-year-old Belgian officer, Lieutenant Verkest, slouched past with his hands pointedly dug into his pockets. Eggers told him to salute. Verkest refused. At the resulting court-martial, the Belgian was found guilty of disobeying a direct order, but when it emerged during his testimony that Verkest had organized the Belgian contingent, now thirty-three strong, in a mass refusal to salute, the charge was increased to mutiny, carrying the death sentence. A casual act of insolence had escalated into a lethal confrontation. The entire company of prisoners united in outraged protest. When the doctor appeared in the courtyard soon afterward, he was greeted with a chorus of jeers from the window, and insulting shouts of *"Tierarzt!"* ("Horse doctor!"). The riot squad appeared with bayonets fixed and cleared the yard. The death sentence was later commuted by Hitler himself, with a laconic note on Verkest's file—"sentence sufficient"—but the so-called Saluting War was a measure of how raw tempers were becoming on both sides.

Upsurges of rebellion were sporadic and, like escaping, at least partly seasonal—more acute in summer, less fierce in winter; at times the escape-planning and goon-baiting evaporated, replaced by a sour acquiescence.

The specter of depression stalked Colditz, seldom openly discussed but ever-present. Morale ebbed and flowed, dependent on war news, or an escape attempt, the latest theatrical entertainment, or merely a victory at stoolball. Spirits might rise with the arrival of a Red Cross parcel, or plunge again when the hot water stopped or an escape failed, as fickle and changeable as the weather. Prisoners with wives or girlfriends longed for contact but dreaded a "Dear John" letter breaking off the relationship. The POWs wondered and imagined what was happening at home; but, unlike civilian prisoners, their sentences had no visible end, and no chalking off the passing days would bring liberation closer. Civilians, one prisoner reflected, "could never imagine what it is like to get up in the morning to face a long empty day with nothing whatever to do except what you do to yourself." Crammed into a warren of small rooms, the prisoners were seldom more than a few feet away from one another; the air felt musty, the conversation stale; minor disagreements could flare quickly into angry confrontation; tempers were short, and attention spans shorter. Some were undoubtedly experiencing what would today be diagnosed as post-traumatic stress disorder. A few of the afflicted spent hours in front of their cupboards, arranging and rearranging the few possessions inside, an obsessive activity Reid described as "locker-pottering." As time wore on, the symptoms of psychological damage grew more dramatic. "It was a mental battle to keep sane," said Jimmy Yule, the jazz band leader.

The prisoners were not alone in suffering under the psychological burden of Colditz life. The jailers of Colditz were also bored, cramped, homesick, and uncertain. On February 8, the body of a young German soldier was discovered in the park. He had shot himself in the head with a revolver. No one ever discovered why.

The captives, including the doctors and priests, tended to regard depression in much the same way that homesickness was treated in all-male boarding schools: a sign of weakness best ignored, since "mollycoddling," it was believed, would only make the unhappiness worse. "The stiff upper lip is a great thing to hide behind," one inmate remarked. Yet the POWs monitored one another carefully for signs of serious mental disturbance. Eggers was similarly alert. "We didn't want them to go mad," he wrote.

For all his pedantry and guile, Eggers was a humane man, and he had noticed that Frank "Errol" Flinn was starting to behave quite oddly. The RAF officer repeatedly tried, and failed, to escape. "I wanted to get back to flying," he said simply. "I had not had enough of the war." He had been sent to Colditz after escaping from Thorn camp and trying to steal a Heinkel bomber; then he had been caught emerging from the "toilet tunnel" back in July; he contributed "Frank's crowbar" to the French tunnel, and that, too, had come to nothing; he had tried to hide inside a sack of outgoing packages in the parcels office, only to be caught before he was out of the room; on his way to solitary in the town cells, he had tried to break away from the guards yet again. On April 3, Eggers launched a raid on the British quarters that took everyone by surprise, and found Flinn hard at work on a new tunnel; he was out of solitary on a three-day break between twenty-eight-day sentences for his earlier escape attempts. A further sentence was added. "This brought his total to 170 days," noted Reid, the longest tally of any prisoner so far. "If you confine any animal, more and more it fights to get out," he said. Flinn was losing weight (Red Cross parcels were not permitted in solitary) and suffering from acute asthma. He developed his own survival strategies: "Always make your bed in the morning, think of the next thing you can do, keep your brain alive." In an effort to keep fit he did yoga exercises, a spiritual and physical discipline then almost unheard of in Britain.

Not having been to boarding school, a sergeant-pilot until he was commissioned as an officer in 1939, Flinn was always a figure apart. At first, he found enforced solitude a trial, then a matter of indifference, and finally an unhealthy habit. "Solitary confinement did you a lot of good," he wrote. "It was a holiday in some respects from the continual noise, people escaping, guns going off occasionally." Seclusion, he decided, offered "trains of thought that you could work on." But the tracks led in unexpected directions. "I was a Roman Catholic. In solitary, theology and things like that enter your mind. You can get a new look on religion. I changed my religion and had my own philosophy: I decided God is a self-regulating intelligence who works for the good of the whole." Every time he emerged from the cells, gaunt and intense, Flinn seemed a little more eccentric, a little more paranoid. He was convinced he had been betrayed.

In the five months following Neave's "home run," there were twenty-two attempted escapes by Colditz prisoners, some involving international cooperation. Only one was successful: a Belgian officer broke out after being transferred to a military hospital, and eventually managed to swim to a British ship moored off Algeciras in Spain and stow away in the cargo hold. Every other attempt foundered. Two Dutchmen were picked up trying to walk out disguised as workmen. A French officer was found half-suffocated in a cart carrying excavated tunnel rubble from the attics. An international tunnel under construction was discovered beneath a bed in the sickbay. A Dutchman was found hiding under a pile of leaves in the park. Poking around for gaps in the castle fabric, the Dutch located a hollow buttress adjoining their quarters, the shaft for an ancient long-drop toilet, once used by Elector Frederick the Wise, that ended six feet below ground level. A tunnel running horizontally from the bottom toward the ravine was just fifteen yards from completion when Eggers raided it, hauling out two diggers and a huge stash of escape equipment. "The treasure was immense," he crowed, and included the two Dutch dummies, Max and Moritz, used to cover for escaped prisoners during parades. Eggers never revealed how he had learned of the tunnel's existence.

Staring out at a blizzard one evening, Pat Reid noticed that four feet of fallen snow had piled up on the flat roof running between the second floor of the British quarters and a buttress on the wall of the *Kommandantur*. He cut through the bars on a window using a saw made from serrated razor blades, lowered himself onto the roof, and then burrowed a tunnel through the drift, "shaped like an arch, one foot nine inches high," wide enough to wriggle through unseen by the guard below. He had just completed gouging a hole through the wall into the German quarters when Unteroffizier Schädlich suddenly appeared, revolver drawn. Reid half jumped, half fell into the snow of the courtyard and scrambled away. Yet another escape had been stymied.

The more philosophical prisoners put the run of failures down to bad luck. Eggers credited his own ingenuity. Others detected something more sinister.

One evening, Colonel Bronisław Kowalczewski, the senior Polish officer, ordered his compatriots to attend an emergency meeting, in full uniform. The forty-eight Polish officers assembled in the Polish Long Room, including Ryszard Bednarski, a young army lieutenant.

Bednarski, a forester by trade, was something of a celebrity among his compatriots. In April 1941, he simulated illness and escaped while being transferred from Colditz to a military hospital. The officer who escaped with him was swiftly recaptured, but Bednarski managed to reach Kraków and remained at large for some weeks before being caught by the Gestapo. After "many beatings," he was sent back to Colditz, and a hero's welcome.

The Polish adjutant called the men to attention. Colonel Kowalczewski ordered the lieutenant to step forward. "Second

Lieutenant Bednarski, you are a spy and a traitor, unfit to wear the uniform and insignia of Poland."

A brief court-martial commenced. Bednarski was accused of conspiring with the Germans. It was claimed he had been allowed to escape in order to infiltrate the Polish underground Resistance in Kraków, before being brought back to the castle to continue betraying his fellow prisoners by revealing their escape plans. One Polish officer claimed that, while in military hospital, he had seen a document proving Bednarski was in league with the Abwehr, German military intelligence.

The verdict of this ad hoc tribunal was never in doubt. Some favored summary punishment, arguing that Bednarski should be taken to the top floor of the Polish quarters and thrown out of a window: an execution disguised as suicide. Instead, with solemn fury, the adjutant ripped off Bednarski's epaulettes and ordered him to leave the room. After a sleepless night of terror, expecting to be lynched at any moment, the trembling man was marched into the courtyard for the morning parade. "Forty-seven officers present," barked Colonel Kowalczewski. "And one traitor." Bednarski was removed by the guards and escorted from the prison the same day.

The episode is mysterious. Eggers insisted that only one of the recently failed escapes had been foiled thanks to an informer. He confirmed that Bednarski had fallen into Gestapo hands in Poland, but claimed that far from betraying his comrades, the young man had returned with "valuable information" about the Polish underground escape networks "from which his fellow prisoners were able to benefit." His removal from Colditz was not evidence of his collaboration, said Eggers, but to protect him from those who wrongly accused him. A few days after Bednarski was drummed out of the Polish army and almost murdered by his compatriots, the Germans took the unprecedented step of announcing during roll call that the man "had disclosed no POW secrets to the German staff." In his diary, Schädlich recorded that Bednarski had merely sought to "ingratiate himself" with the Germans "so that he can escape more easily." Frank Flinn was convinced Bednarski had revealed his escape plans to Eggers, but some in the Polish community voiced sympathy for a man who, if he had collaborated with the Germans, must have done so under duress: "The Germans had some hold over his family," said Anthony Karpf, a Polish cadet officer in Colditz. "It is difficult to judge what a man does in that situation."

Ryszard Bednarski may have been a ruthless traitor who betrayed countless fellow prisoners in Colditz. But it is possible that he was entirely innocent.

Some years after the war, a former Colditz inmate recognized Bednarski on a street in Warsaw, publicly denounced him, and then informed the Polish authorities that this notorious war criminal was at large in the city. By the time police arrived at Bednarski's apartment, he had killed himself.

8

Seeking for a Path

Birendranath Mazumdar was summoned to Kommandant Schmidt's office. There stood a young, smiling, dark-skinned Indian, of medium height. Another Indian in Colditz was surprising enough, but what made the encounter even odder was his outfit: the man was dressed in the field gray uniform of the German Wehrmacht. Only the badge was different: a leaping tiger, set against the orange, white, and green flag of the Indian National Congress, the organization leading the struggle for independence from Britain.

The young man spoke in English: "I bring a message from Subhas Chandra Bose. He wishes you to come to Berlin."

Subhas Chandra Bose, Indian nationalist and Nazi collaborator, soldier and politician, was, and remains, one of the most controversial figures in twentieth-century history. In many Indian eyes, he was a patriotic freedom fighter; in most British ones, a traitor and a quisling.

Bose's early life mirrored that of Mazumdar, seventeen years his junior: the son of a wealthy Bengali family, educated in Britain, he was intellectual, cultured, charismatic, and fiercely opposed to British rule in India. He had risen to become president of the Indian National Congress, but, unlike Mahatma Gandhi, Bose was ready to use violence to hasten independence. His followers called him "Netaji," or "revered leader." The British considered him a dangerous subversive, and in 1940 he was placed under house arrest in Calcutta. A year later, with the help of the Abwehr, he escaped disguised as an Afghan insurance salesman. German agents spirited him to Peshawar and across Afghanistan to the Soviet Union, where he assumed a new identity as an Italian nobleman, Count Orlando Mazzotta. From there, the Germans laid on a secret plane to bring him to Berlin.

Once inside the Third Reich, with German backing, Bose set about recruiting his fellow Indians to fight against Britain: he founded the Free India Centre, set up a radio station broadcasting anti-British, pro-Axis propaganda to India, and formed the Free Indian Legion, also known as the Tiger Legion, an all-Indian infantry force of volunteers made up of expatriates and POWs recruited from the camps. Its soldiers swore an oath of allegiance to both Adolf Hitler and Subhas Chandra Bose. By 1942, the Tiger Legion was 1,000 strong.

Word quickly spread through Colditz that Mazumdar was being taken to meet the Indian quisling raising an army to fight the British in the Far East. The other prisoners were scornful: "Goodbye, Jumbo. Have a good war in Burma." Most assumed that the Indian doctor had already switched sides, confirming their suspicions of disloyalty. "We never expected to see him again," said one. On the morning of his departure, Mazumdar was cleaning his teeth in the washrooms when someone remarked loudly: "That bloody Mazumdar is a spy. He's going to Berlin."

The voice belonged to Captain Harry Elliott, one of the first British officers sent to Colditz. Mazumdar turned in a cold fury.

"Harry, did I hear you say I am a spy? I give you five minutes to withdraw this accusation."

The two men squared up. Elliott was a Guardsman, six feet two inches tall; he looked down at the Indian doctor, five feet seven in his socks, and laughed. "My blood tingled from my feet to my head," Mazumdar later wrote. "I gave him such a hook, right on the jaw, and he fell flat." Astride Elliott's chest, punching him repeatedly, Mazumdar shouted: "I'll kill you. You don't know what I've gone through." He was dragged off by the other officers, panting and pale with rage, and brought before Colonel Stayner for assaulting a senior officer. "I told him the reason," said Mazumdar. "But he didn't believe me."

On June 23, Mazumdar was taken to Berlin in a first-class train compartment. At the station, he was picked up in a chauffeur-driven Mercedes and driven to the Free India Centre on Lichtenstein Allee in the *Tiergarten* area of Berlin. A dozen well-dressed Indian men were smoking and talking in the lobby. To his astonishment, they greeted him by name. A minute later he was shown into a large room. A balding, bespectacled figure wearing a civilian suit rose from behind the desk and extended a hand. An admirer of Bose since childhood, Mazumdar was suddenly star-struck dumb.

In a soft, authoritative voice, Bose made his pitch. "Join my Legion," he said. "Come and fight for the freedom of India, our Motherland."

When Mazumdar said nothing, he carried on. "I am an example of someone who has always struggled for my country's freedom. Join me."

Mazumdar pointed out that he had pledged an oath of allegiance to the King: "I have given my word of honor and cannot go back on this."

Bose smiled. "Let us have some lunch."

Over a leisurely meal in Bose's private quarters, served by a waiter in white gloves, the Indian nationalist leader kept up the pressure. They spoke Bengali, occasionally slipping into English. Bose described meeting Hitler at the Reich Chancellery a few weeks earlier; the Führer had offered a German U-boat to take him to Bangkok, "from where the Indian revolution could be directed."

"I am not in full agreement with the Nazi philosophy," Bose told Mazumdar. "And I candidly told them so. But I hope to gain India's independence through Nazi help." He said he had recruited hundreds of Indians from the British Indian Army, but as yet not one King's Commissioned Officer from the British Army. Mazumdar could be the first.

"I have been fighting the British for the last fifteen years," Bose said earnestly. "I know what it is like to be a prisoner, as you do, so I sympathize with your circumstances."

They talked through the afternoon, and long into the evening. Mazumdar was flattered that this great man should try to recruit him, but he was also insistent: "I am opposed to the British rule in India—I have seen the results—but I have sworn an oath of allegiance to Britain."

At 2 a.m., the meeting finally broke up. "Think it over," said Bose, as they parted. "We will meet again in the morning."

Despite clean sheets and the most comfortable bed he had known for two years, Mazumdar slept little, torn by the choice he now faced: the opportunity to fight for Indian independence under a magnetic leader and win his freedom, not just from the confines of Colditz but the racial prejudice that redoubled the misery of imprisonment; and on the other hand his vow of loyalty to Britain, his ingrained sense of duty, and his father's admonition that a gentleman's word is his bond.

The next morning, Mazumdar sensed Bose was losing patience. "What is your decision?"

Mazumdar replied that while he strongly sympathized with Bose's position, and opposed the British, he was not ready to join the Tiger Legion. "The answer is no."

Bose pressed a button on the desk, and rose to his feet. "I have chosen my way, and you have chosen yours. Goodbye and good luck." As Mazumdar left the room, Bose called out: "When you change your mind, we will be here . . ."

In contrast to his first-class outbound journey, Mazumdar returned in grimy third class. "There was no doubt in my mind that I had done the right thing," he reflected. The other British officers must accept him now.

But back in Colditz, he faced fresh mockery.

"Didn't he want you after all?" they jeered.

"Oh yes, he wanted me all right, and I would very much have liked to accept his offer to join him. He's such a wonderful man. But then I couldn't, could I?"

"Why ever not?"

"Because I hold a British commission, and I therefore owe my loyalty to the King, whatever my political views and private feelings might be."

He explained what had happened to Colonel Stayner: "They asked me to join them and cooperate with the Germans. I told them I can't do it." The SBO seemed unimpressed.

"Look, Colonel, I'm going to escape one day," Mazumdar continued.

"Well, don't expect us to give you anything, maps or money."

"It's what I expected, sir," Mazumdar said quietly. "You will hear from me."

Mazumdar's decision to reject Bose's offer did not change the way he was seen by other officers. Instead, it widened the gulf. He had turned down an opportunity to escape, a prospect they spent their days and nights plotting and imagining; he merely had to say the word, and he could walk free at any time, because he was of a different race. Mazumdar was more alone than ever: no one shared his predicament; no other prisoner had made a choice to remain locked in Colditz. Most of the other prisoners were distant, and sometimes actively hostile. "I was the sole Indian. It was impossible even to converse in my mother tongue. In ordinary times, this is no handicap, but prison life with its restrictions and whatnot makes it doubly so." Mazumdar sounded oddly English in his understatement: only an Englishman would refer to the grim privations of Colditz as "whatnot." At night, on a scratchy mattress in an uncomfortable bunk, he wrote poems in Bengali, searching for a way out of his dilemma.

> In the darkened light the awakened soul
> Seeking for a path
> Which direction to take
> Disturbed, he starts to think
> What to do
> He then realizes the need for a companion
> The question is where to find one
> They are so precious.
> At last he pleads with the Gods to find him one.

Colditz was riddled with hiding places, where escape equipment and money could be securely hidden until needed: in wall cavities, under floorboards, in ceilings. The "ferrets" launched repeated raids in search of contraband, and were often successful, recovering stockpiles of food, maps, money, files, compasses, pliers, batteries, drills, keys, screwdrivers, rope, fake uniforms, and counterfeit documents. Sometimes the work of concealment combined with goon-baiting: Unteroffizier Schädlich, the indefatigable ferret, found that the floorboards in a corner of the

British quarters had been "neatly cut." He levered them up, and found a piece of paper underneath with the words "*Leck mich im Arsch,*" "Kiss my arse" (the original name of Mozart's Canon for Six Voices in B-flat major). Each successful search augmented the collection of confiscated escape artifacts in Colditz Museum, but Eggers was worried: Where were these things coming from? The X-ray machine was working efficiently and every incoming parcel was carefully searched; the quantity of "naughty" packages seemed to have dwindled away, yet somehow objects, including tools of considerable size such as hammers and a soldering iron, were still being smuggled in. Eggers blamed corrupt guards willing to trade cigarettes and Red Cross luxuries for banned items. An undercover civilian police inspector was introduced to the castle disguised as a German corporal, to try to find the culprits: "The whole charade turned out to be useless." The guard contingent was replaced. But the contraband was still getting through.

Only years later did Eggers find out how: a half-Egyptian, Algerian-born French officer with a scar on his cheek from a sword slash, a red silk scarf around his neck, and an uncanny talent for burglary. Despite his villainous appearance, Lieutenant Frédéric "Scarface" Guigues was a man of education, who had studied engineering at the elite École des Arts et Métiers in Paris. He was the best lock-picker in Colditz.

The system for receiving, guarding, and then distributing incoming packages followed a set pattern. The locked door to the parcels office from the courtyard was manned by a sentry, with two further internal doors, each locked. When parcels arrived, they were registered and kept in the office overnight, inspected and X-rayed the following day, and then allocated to the recipient in person. The only way to ensure the delivery of contraband was to get to a parcel *before* it was handed over, remove the hidden item, and replace it with an innocuous replica. This in turn required access to the parcels office without being detected, a task made even harder when the outer door was fitted with a cruciform lock, the latest development in German lock technology. Made by Zeiss Ikon, the key was in the shape of a cross, with each groove on the four edges precision-cut to one-thousandth of an inch and corresponding to a set of pins, which in turn rotated a circular drum to open the mortice bolt. The Germans believed it could not be picked, which was an enormous advantage, because it could.

After months of experimentation, Guigues fashioned his own blank cruciform key using a spindle stolen from the mechanism of the tower clock. Next, during the distraction caused by a visiting German general, his team managed to extract the lock itself, measure the exact size of the grooves, and then reinstall it. Using a tiny saw made from a razor blade, Guigues carved the notches into his homemade cross-key, which he hid inside a hollowed bedpost, concealed behind a knot made of cork. Getting into the parcels office required a team of seventeen decoys, lookouts, and assistants to divert the sentry's attention just long enough for Guigues to enter and lock the door behind him. Picking the ancient lever-locks on the internal doors was comparatively easy. The French could now order specific items in coded letters to friends and family in France, and collect them at night, before the parcels were opened: two packages of tools weighing five kilograms apiece, cash, alcohol in two-liter tins, paint, documents, and finally the parts for constructing two radios, powered by a small generator with a hand crank sealed up in a tin of ham. Whenever a new "explosive" parcel arrived, often containing tins marked *"sanglier en sauce,"* wild boar in sauce, Frédo Guigues would sneak in, remove the contraband, and "defuse" the package.

Eggers never discovered how the prisoners were getting into the parcels depot, but his suspicions were sharply raised when, one morning, the prison cat was found on one side of the internal locked doors, and her kittens on the other. A second cruciform lock was fitted on the inner door, and an electric alarm system connected to the outer door. Astonishingly, during one of his nocturnal visits, Guigues managed to intercept the wiring, and rig up an additional circuit with a switch in the floor above. The alarm could now be activated and deactivated as necessary. The French also suspected that someone else was breaking in and secretly inspecting the parcels. A German guard from Alsace-Lorraine, the disputed area of France annexed by Germany in

1940, had been observed hanging around the office late at night. As a German-Alsatian he was already a collaborator in French eyes. Guigues installed one of his men in the parcels office, a tough young officer named Yves Desmarchelier. Sure enough, the suspect guard entered and began rifling parcels. Sensing a movement behind him, he turned and saw the prisoner watching him from behind a pile of sacks. A desperate fight ensued. As Desmarchelier's hands closed around his throat, the soldier gasped, in French, "Don't be a fool!" These were his last words. "He was a traitor," said Desmarchelier. The man's body was found the next morning, strung up from the rafters by a hangman's noose. Eggers was baffled. Why would this man have chosen to kill himself inside the parcels office? "We had no option but to assume suicide," he wrote.

The French were willing to order and extract items for the other nations, and eventually the Dutch and British were inducted into the secret, and the arcane art of cruciform lockpicking. British burglary duties were in the supple hands of an ebullient twenty-four-year-old Australian fighter pilot from Townsville, Queensland, named "Bush" Parker, an amateur magician and card sharp whose party trick was to place a matchstick on his sleeve "and when he let it go it used to jump a couple of feet in the air." No one ever worked out how he did this. Parker claimed to be able to open any lock in the castle, using a set of homemade picks and a tube of toothpaste to hold the lock open when the tumblers lifted.

"Free access to the parcels office," wrote Pat Reid, was "an inestimable boon," but in May 1942 a British officer almost destroyed the system. Frank "Errol" Flinn had recently been released from solitary. One morning, without warning and in full view of the courtyard, he rushed up to the outer door of the parcels office, and began trying to pick it, completely ineffectively and with considerable violence, using a wire hook. The German sentries did not immediately spot him, but Guigues did, in horror: if the Germans thought the lock was vulnerable or damaged, they would change it, and the arduous process of making another key would have to start again from scratch. The Englishman was "strong as a devil but undergoing some sort of psychological crisis," wrote Guigues. He signaled to an accomplice on the first floor of the French quarters to activate the alarm. "Seconds later," wrote Reid, "a squad of Goons rushed into the courtyard and carried Flinn off" to begin yet another stint in the cells. At first some of the Germans believed Flinn's erratic behavior was contrived: "he pretends to be 'mental,'" wrote Schädlich in his diary. "Colonel Stayner is doing his best to make us believe that this 'illness' is genuine." But Reid was convinced that this was no act: "Sadly, by this time, Flinn was 'going round the bend.'" The most solitary man in Colditz was becoming a liability.

Michael Sinclair arrived in Colditz in March 1942, with a plan already formulated that would grow into an obsession: to get to Poland, reunite with the formidable British woman Resistance fighter he had come to see as a surrogate mother, and then, with her help, get away.

A year earlier, three bedraggled and exhausted British soldiers knocked on the door of an innocuous two-roomed apartment on Chmielna Street in Warsaw. The trio had escaped from the prison camp in Poznań in central Poland by hiding in a handcart filled with rubbish. They had planned to cross the frontier into Russia, but the declaration of war between Germany and the Soviet Union rendered this impossible, so instead they had walked back to Warsaw, passed from one Resistance cell to another until, like so many other British escapers, they wound up at the Chmielna Street apartment.

The leader of the fugitive band was Sinclair, a red-haired twenty-three-year-old lieutenant in the 60th King's Royal Rifles. Until the retreat from Dunkirk, Sinclair's life had followed exactly the pattern that he, and everyone else, expected of it: the son of an army officer, he had played cricket for Winchester at Lord's, acted in every school play, studied languages at Cambridge with distinction, won a golf blue, prayed hard in church every Sunday, and joined his father's regiment. But then he had been captured, and Sinclair's vision of his own destiny had suddenly fallen apart. Out of uniform, without the structure of family, regiment, and religion, Sinclair had no idea who he was. His need to escape was not simply urgent and all-consuming, but pathological. "For Mike Sinclair, there was God—then the 60th, and that was it. His only aim in life was to get back to his Regiment."

The door was opened by Mrs. Janina Markowska, who ushered them into her back room where "an excellent lunch" had been laid on, the first decent food they had eaten for a month.

Mrs. Markowska lived with a husband twenty years her senior, a retired Polish civil servant she referred to, "with ill-disguised contempt," as "Daddy." Like so many Warsaw residents she spent her days scavenging for what little food could be found in shops or on the black market. In one of the unpredictable roundups that were a feature of daily life under Nazi occupation, she had been taken in for questioning, "before being released as a harmless old lady." Mrs. Markowska might have been a perfectly ordinary Polish housewife, except that she spoke English, with a strong Scottish accent.

Mrs. Markowska was really Jane Walker, an agent of British intelligence, a senior figure in the Polish underground army, and the coordinator of the "Anglo-Polish Society," a secret Resistance network sheltering escaped British POWs and smuggling them to safety.

Jane Walker was born in Dalmeny, west of Edinburgh, in 1874. As a teenager she moved with her family to Berlin, where her father was appointed military attaché at the British embassy. Intelligent and restless, she drifted into the world of intelligence, becoming a "King's Messenger," a Foreign Office courier carrying secret communications. Before the First World War, she conveyed dozens of messages on behalf of the British government between Germany and Switzerland. Speaking fluent German, French, and Polish, she worked for a time in Vienna as governess to a branch of the Habsburg royal family. In 1920, she married, settled in Warsaw, and became, to all outward appearances, wholly Polish. But as one escaping POW put it, she remained "British to the core, a great patriot of the old-fashioned kind, breathing with her every breath fire, slaughter, and defiance of Britain's enemies. She was tyrannical, obstinate, and intolerant. She was also capable of great affection, sympathy, and unselfishness." Her apartment was a haven for fugitive British soldiers, whom she then farmed out to safehouses around the city, moving them every few days. This feat of logistics was achieved in coordination with the Polish Underground State, the political and military organization of the Polish Resistance. Unlike other occupied countries, Poland never formally surrendered. While the Polish government-in-exile established its headquarters in London, the parallel Underground State was formed in Poland itself, with a secret parliament, executive, judiciary, and army, and even an education department, a propaganda wing, and social services.

Between September 1940 and May 1942, the Anglo-Polish Society escape network took in sixty-five British servicemen on the run and managed to smuggle fifty-two of them to safety: on ships to neutral Sweden, through the Balkans to neutral Turkey, via Hungary, Romania, or Yugoslavia, or into Germany and then out again through Switzerland. "Intense and overbearing," Mrs. Markowska treated her "Tommies" with stern fondness, as the children she had never had, providing food, shelter, patriotic pep talks, and even medical attention from a doctor prepared to risk treating escaped prisoners. She liked to lay on "more or less formal dinners" for her guests, with numerous toasts to the British royal family. The POWs feared, revered, and adored her. "In dark and dangerous days," wrote one escaper, "we loved her." They called her "Mrs. M."

Jane Walker's escape network was funded by selling ladies' stockings on the Warsaw black market, while the Polish Resistance furnished false papers, additional money, and guides. The work was spectacularly dangerous. The Gestapo knew an underground escape route for Allied soldiers was in operation, and devoted considerable efforts to destroying it. The average life expectancy of a courier for the Secret State was just a few months. Mrs. M knew that if caught by the Gestapo she would be tortured and executed, and she treated that knowledge with sublime insouciance. Whenever she was asked why she remained in Poland rather than return to the safety of her native land, she would fix the questioner with a shriveling look and a statement of what was, to Mrs. M, patently obvious: "A British woman does not like to run away."

Michael Sinclair and his two companions were now under the care of this particularly ferocious mother hen. "Thus began our strange sojourn in Poland's capital, temporary guests of those many brave and generous people who willingly accepted all the risk involved to help us on our way . . . Mrs. M was to become a mother to us."

Getting the soldiers home would be difficult, she warned, but Mrs. M promised to find a way. "We have contacts with underground organizations, official and unofficial," she said. The fugitives were split up and billeted among the members of Mrs. M's network. Sinclair struck up an immediate rapport with the Polish family who took him in, moved by their friendship, hospitality, and staggering bravery. One safehouse was near the Jewish ghetto, and at night the "rattle of machine guns" could be heard as the SS went about its genocidal work. One evening, Sinclair listened to the BBC on Mrs. M's illegal wireless and heard "a message of encouragement and hope." Every day he remained in Warsaw, Sinclair's loathing for the Nazis increased, along with his admiration for the Polish Resistance and the Scotswoman determined to fight them.

By late summer, Mrs. M had a plan. "You will go by train to Kraków, where a guide will meet you and take you through the mountains to Slovakia, then you will be driven south by car to the Hungarian border. You will take the train to Budapest, where you will be met by friends." These would then arrange safe onward passage through Yugoslavia and Bulgaria to neutral Turkey, where they could contact the British embassy. At the end of August 1941, after a fond farewell to Mrs. M, Sinclair set off, accompanied by Ronnie Littledale, with whom he had escaped from Poznań. Her prediction that this would be a "long and intricate journey" proved an understatement. After a grueling slog, by rail and on foot, they finally arrived in Budapest in October. A month later, furnished with false papers by the anti-Nazi Resistance, they boarded a train to Belgrade and, on November 16, Sinclair and Littledale reached the Bulgarian frontier. Then disaster struck. An observant border official spotted a mistake in their fake Yugoslav papers. They were arrested, handed over to the German police in Sofia, shipped to Vienna, and brutally interrogated by the Gestapo. After two months in a military prison, the two men were hauled out and loaded onto a train for Dresden, under armed guard. Somewhere on the outskirts of Prague, Sinclair squeezed through a lavatory window and threw himself out of the moving train. He had hobbled only a few hundred yards on a twisted ankle before he was recaptured, and sent to Colditz.

Sinclair's arrival injected new energy into the escapers' community. His single-minded pursuit of liberty came tinged with bloodlust. Freedom offered the possibility of vengeance, an opportunity to continue the fight not just for king and country, but for Mrs. M and her Polish network. "He seemed to be on a personal crusade between himself and the whole of Hitler's occupied Europe," said Pat Reid, who was impressed, and slightly awed, by Sinclair's unwavering resolve. Even Frank Flinn, the record holder for time spent in solitary confinement, seemed tame by comparison in his determination to get out of Colditz. Sinclair spent hours staring furiously over the castle ramparts, smoking his pipe, dreaming of escape, monitoring and memorizing the guards' movements, rehearsing details, searching for gaps in the walls around him. An opportunity came just a few weeks after his arrival. In June, he was sent to Leipzig for a sinus operation. He climbed out of a hospital window and got as far as Cologne, where, by sheer misfortune, an intensive manhunt was underway for an RAF bombing crew who had parachuted into nearby woods after their plane was shot down. Sinclair was captured and taken to a nearby camp; he promptly escaped, and was just as swiftly recaptured, and bundled back inside Colditz to resume his vigil at the window. "Poor Mike absolutely loathed every minute of this life, and had no other interest except in trying to escape," wrote a fellow inmate. "He would never admit defeat."

The kaleidoscope of the Colditz population changed continually, with new arrivals and departures. The POW administration was unpredictable in its decisions; the prisoners never knew when they might be moved to another camp, or why, creating another layer of uncertainty. Two-thirds of the Polish contingent were removed in May, leaving behind some forty officers, "mostly hardened escaper types," in Reid's estimation. Thirty-one of the French officers, including many of the Jews, were marched off to another camp at Lübeck, and others were brought in. The British population gradually expanded with the addition of officers who had tried to escape from other camps. As they were marched in, the new inmates were greeted with loud cheering from the windows, and sometimes a hail of water bombs. One of the nastier traditions of the British boarding school was the ritual humiliation of "new bugs" by older boys. This, too, had its counterpart in Colditz. Pat Reid described the reception given to sixteen naval officers from Lamsdorf. On their first day in Colditz, the new arrivals were summoned to a bogus medical examination in the British quarters, where an officer dressed in a fake German uniform and posing as the camp doctor, complete with stethoscope, ordered them to drop their trousers, before loudly declaring, in German, that they were all infested with venereal crabs. A "medical assistant" in a lab coat, barely able to contain his mirth, then daubed their testicles with a blue "woad" made up of scenery paint and "high smelling lavatory disinfectant." Reid described this incident as "having fun at the new boys' expense," but it was straightforward bullying, a brutal assertion of power of the sort that English boarding-school boys have always inflicted on one another.

In July, Oberstleutnant Schmidt reached the age of seventy and retired, to be replaced by a Kommandant of a different stamp. Oberst (Colonel) Edgar Glaesche was "very much a new broom," wrote Eggers. Punctilious in observing the Geneva Convention but a strict disciplinarian fresh from the Eastern Front, Glaesche came determined to make a clean sweep, as new brooms tend to. He demanded and expected respect, and got nothing of the sort. The new Kommandant had a squint; inevitably, the rowdier prisoners crossed their eyes whenever he appeared. "The halo of his authority was quite simply ignored," noted Eggers. "He had no idea of what he was letting himself in for."

Escape attempts continued at a rate of almost two a week through July and August, some promising, some wild, and almost all fruitless, the punctuation marks of life in captivity. Whenever anyone vanished, there was a slow rising of hope as the hours and days passed, to be dashed when the escaper was brought back. One Englishman jumped over the wall of the exercise yard beside the town cells and reached Chemnitz on a stolen bicycle before he was apprehended. Buoyed by Mike Sinclair's account of Mrs. M's Anglo-Polish escape network, some resolved to try to get to Poland rather than attempt the Swiss border crossing. The Dutch and British both tried to break into the main sewer but were caught in the act. A half-built Polish tunnel was discovered, containing tools and a homemade typewriter. A Frenchman tried to walk out of the park disguised as a painter. Among the new regulations imposed by Kommandant Glaesche was a limit on personal property. Guards arrived with boxes to remove surplus items into storage. RAF officer Dominic Bruce, one of the smaller prisoners in Colditz, was packed into a Canadian Red Cross tea chest labeled "surplus items," equipped with a forty-foot bedsheet rope and knife. He was loaded onto a lorry with the rest of the excess luggage, and carried to a third-floor room in the German *Kommandantur*. That night he emerged, climbed through a window, and descended the wall into the moat, leaving behind a note in German inside the empty box: "The air in Colditz no longer agrees with me. Goodbye." He stole a bicycle, and got as far as the port of Danzig, where he was intercepted before he could stow away on a ship.

That summer, the British recorded just one victory. In June, RAF officer Brian Paddon was transferred from Colditz to the camp at Thorn, where he was due to face a court-martial for insulting a guard. He joined a work party heading to the fields, hid behind a haystack, and then made his way to the Baltic coast and stowed away in the coal hold of a Swedish merchant vessel. Once the ship set sail, he persuaded the captain to take him to Gävle, 100 miles north of Stockholm, where the British consul arranged for him to fly back to the U.K. Paddon's escape was exceptional, an important morale booster when news filtered back to Colditz, but it had started when he was already far beyond the prison walls.

Kommandant Glaesche's raft of new security measures included roll calls in the middle of the night, body searches, a new system of passwords, and sudden, unexpected raids in search of contraband: "Books, papers, toilet requisites, cupboards, tables, chairs, and stools upturned, beds shifted, bedding removed, floorboards torn up." The new Kommandant reduced the alcohol intake in the German mess, installed a new alarm system with trip wires in the park, and ordered the construction of wire mesh catwalks and a wooden watchtower twelve meters high from which the sentries could survey the terraces. A machine gun emplacement was installed overlooking the inner courtyard, and a photographer to monitor and record what was taking place below. "Nearly every hour, guard parties are patrolling the castle or carrying out checks," noted Schädlich. The prisoners were constantly watched, while continually watching their jailers. The system of "stooging" never let up: the men stood at windows, apparently reading or casually smoking, while discreetly observing what was going on below, and passing a signal if the Germans appeared: a hat removed, a book closed. "The moment our search parties got anywhere near, their excellent warning systems took over and all we were met with was a dirty grin on the faces of the POWs," wrote Gephard. The unrelenting mutual surveillance, the searches, the ebb and flow of hope and despondency, created a unique atmosphere, a tension that increasingly erupted into near-rioting, horseplay that swiftly got out of hand.

In June, a fire was deliberately started at the bottom of the British staircase. It was quickly extinguished, but the acrid stench lingered in the stairwell and corridors for days. "How empty of amusement life must be for grown men to welcome fire as a diversion," Padre Platt reflected. A water fight in the hot courtyard reached such ferocity that the riot squad was summoned. The German officer in command was met with a chorus of barracking from the windows. A soldier pulled his trigger, and the bullet ricocheted into the neck of a French lieutenant watching from a window. He recovered but with a paralyzed left hand. A few weeks later, Glaesche ordered a roll call for the French alone as a punishment, at 1 a.m., and then another half an hour later. The other nations stood at the windows, baying their disrespect: "This took the form of loud animal and bird noises, a cockerel here, a cow there, mixed with wailing sirens." The uproar grew steadily louder. The guards lined up, rifles aimed at the upper floors. Suddenly they opened fire, and a volley of bullets smashed into the windowpanes. Eggers later claimed the order to fire had been accidental. No one was hurt, but friction was growing. "Indiscipline, almost mutiny, could be felt everywhere," wrote Eggers. But then occasionally, just as suddenly, the anger seemed to dissipate. "Sometimes the resistance collapsed," observed Giles Romilly, the prisoner singled out for "special treatment." "There were periods when the old looked old, the young did not look fit, and the ardours of defiance, never an unforced growth, failed to leap out. The Germans would find that they had quiet parades, and would patter secure along our files, almost like nannies."

There was desperation beneath the confrontational hilarity. Sometimes the mental pressure was visible and dramatic, as with Frank Flinn; more frequently it was hidden. A Canadian airman, among the first inmates to enter Colditz, became obsessed with releasing his wife from their marriage, and tried to cut his wrists. During roll call he went "demonstrably off his rocker," a friend recalled, "crying and pleading with the guards to shoot him." Finally, he slit his throat with a broken bottle, and was removed to a psychiatric hospital. In a mark of how deep the sexual frustration ran, another officer tried to castrate himself. Most wore their sadness in secrecy, or vigorously repressed it. "I suddenly realized I was going round the bend," wrote one officer. "I took myself, metaphorically, off into the corner of the room, and gave myself a good dressing down." But even the most optimistic felt their spirits start to sag as the months passed. Pat Reid stood down as escape officer; he needed to imagine the possibility of liberty again.

9

Dogsbody

In the middle of August, a new prisoner with an awkward walk and a distinctive air of authority entered the castle and sent a ripple of excitement through the camp.

Wing Commander Douglas Bader would become the most famous prisoner in Colditz. He was already the most celebrated fighting soldier, on either side, of the entire war. Fame had come to him suddenly, by way of an appalling accident, leading to a lifetime of acute pain. In later years, he raised millions for disability charities. He was supremely brave, able to inspire others to feats of courage they never dreamed possible, but he was also arrogant, domineering, selfish, and spectacularly rude, particularly to those he considered of lower status. Many of his closest comrades adored him. The war had made him into a hero. But it also made him insufferable.

Bader was the neglected child of a distant mother and a father who had died, of wounds sustained in the trenches, when his son was twelve years old. He grew up angry and bullied. At boarding school, he was once beaten up by Laurence Olivier, after he bowled out the future actor in a cricket match. He masked his loneliness with bluster, aggression, and exhibitionism.

In 1928 he joined the RAF and two years later he was commissioned pilot officer. In defiance of regulations, he took to performing competitive aerobatic stunts in his Bristol Bulldog biplane. In December 1931, on a dare, he attempted a slow roll over Woodley Aerodrome near Reading. Flying in too low, his left wing clipped the ground, and the plane somersaulted. Pulled from the wreckage, Bader would have died at the scene if a civilian had not held on to the severed femoral artery in his right leg.

By another stroke of good fortune, he was brought to the hospital just in time to catch pioneering surgeon Leonard Joyce before he went home for the day. Writing up the incident in his logbook, Bader was laconic: "Crashed slow-rolling near ground. Bad show." He did not mention that Joyce had amputated both of his legs, one above and one below the knee.

With the use of two prosthetic legs (slightly longer than the original ones, to make him taller), Bader was able to drive a modified car, play golf and cricket, swim, and even dance. But, to his fury, the RAF would not let him fly. He took a desk job with an oil company.

Bader never stopped lobbying the RAF to put him back in a cockpit, insisting he could pilot a plane just as effectively with prosthetic legs. "By God, I'll sit on their doorsteps until I get in," he vowed. With the war, the authorities relented, and he returned to the air. During the Battle of France and the Battle of Britain, he distinguished himself as a fighter pilot of reckless skill and supreme courage. He argued in favor of deploying mass fighter formations and developed techniques for ambushing enemy planes using the sun and altitude. In the space of two years, using the call sign "Dogsbody" (from his initials, DB), he shot down twenty enemy planes and shared in four more aerial victories and six "probables." He was awarded the Distinguished Service Order and Bar, and then the Distinguished Flying Cross.

In the aerial war, so many were indebted to so few; and few were owed so much by so many as Douglas Bader. But he might have remained just another fighter pilot, had the War Office not spotted a golden propaganda opportunity. The tale of Britain's double-amputee flying ace was exactly the sort of story to uplift and inspire the public in the darkest days of the war, so in a meticulously executed public relations campaign the Air Ministry set about turning Bader into a legend, by planting a series of newspaper stories. The *Daily Mail* interviewed the pilot's mother, who declared: "I wish I could tell you adequately the story of how he had to face life again without two legs . . . It was amazing to watch the gradual return of his sunny disposition." (A description of Bader's temperament so wildly at odds with reality that it reinforces how little she really knew him.) The *Daily Mir-*

ror hailed "The Greatest Hero of them All . . . Britain's most amazing RAF Fighter Command Pilot." By early 1941, he was the country's first officially sanctioned poster boy, photographed alongside his Spitfire, a square-jawed, pugnacious warrior, pipe in fist, the very incarnation of determination to overcome the odds, on earth and in the air. Newspapers competed to describe his daredevil escapades. Bader lapped up the attention. He was unconditionally adored by the public, and deeply resented by colleagues familiar with the man behind this hastily assembled myth. One of his fellow pilots observed: "He was a show-off, the most pompous chap I've ever met." Few glimpsed "the other Bader, quiet and alone." He treated the ground crew with withering superiority, and they detested him. Some put his fearlessness down to a complete absence of imagination. Bader was living evidence that it is possible to be courageous, famous, disabled, and quite unpleasant, all at the same time.

On August 9, 1941, Bader's 616 Squadron was flying an offensive sortie over the coast of France when he spotted a dozen Messerschmitt 109s flying in formation below him. "Dogsbody attacking," he radioed. "Plenty for all. Take 'em as they come."

He dived, shot down one German plane, and was opening fire on a second when he felt a tremendous impact and turned to see that the rear fuselage, tail, and fin of his Spitfire had been torn away. Bader believed he must have collided in the air with a German fighter. More likely he was the victim of "friendly fire" from another fighter, though he never admitted this. He jettisoned the cockpit canopy and released his harness pin. But as the rushing air started to suck him out of the stricken plane, his prosthetic right leg became trapped under the joystick. Spinning toward earth at 400 miles per hour, battered in the slipstream and losing consciousness, he pulled the ripcord of his parachute. The violent jerk as it opened snapped the leather strap holding his leg in place, and Bader floated free.

A German patrol picked up the one-legged parachutist with two broken ribs minutes after he landed, and took him to a hospital in Saint-Omer. The damaged prosthetic limb was found in a nearby field.

British prisoners of war herded into captivity by German troops in Dieppe, 1942.

Colditz in 1910: a mighty Gothic castle towering over a sleepy eastern German village.

Pat Reid, the irrepressible escaper who fashioned the myth of Colditz in his own image.

Peter Allan, the diminutive Scotsman who escaped hidden inside a mattress, with Hauptmann Paul Priem, the drunken senior camp officer.

Dutch prisoners being marched across Colditz bridge on arrival in July 1941.

Hauptmann Reinhold Eggers, the chief German chronicler of Colditz: civilized, punctilious, and anglophilic.

An aerial photo taken shortly before the war shows the tantalizing proximity of the castle to the town of Colditz. Prisoners were held in the inner courtyard to the left, while the courtyard on the right was the *Kommandantur,* or German barracks. Prisoners arrived via the main gatehouse, after crossing the bridge over the moat, seen lower right.

French cavalry officer Pierre Mairesse-Lebrun, the athletic aristocrat who leaped the perimeter fence in July 1941.

French lieutenant Alain Le Ray, the first POW to achieve a successful "home run" in April 1941.

Frédéric Guigues, the scar-faced French lock-picker, drawn by camp artist John Watton.

Airey Neave in his fake German uniform, a "strange military elf in his green outfit."

The inner courtyard of the prison, where during daylight hours the prisoners mingled, played sports, smoked, gossiped, and planned escapes.

Roll call: prisoners were assembled to be laboriously counted in the courtyard at least three times a day.

Dutch officers with "Max," fourth from right, one of two dummies used to confuse the count during roll call and buy time following an escape.

Giles Romilly, the communist nephew of Winston Churchill and the first of the *Prominente,* or special prisoners.

Doctor Birendranath Mazumdar, right, the only Indian prisoner in Colditz, nicknamed "Jumbo" by the other prisoners.

The celebrated flying ace and double-amputee Douglas Bader hauls his tin legs into the cockpit of a Spitfire.

Michael Alexander, the captured commando who escaped execution by pretending to be the nephew of a British general.

Volleyball in the inner courtyard.

The Park Walk: the daily march down to the exercise enclosure,
"a formal affair with a touch of menace."

"Stoolball," a game of extreme violence invented in Colditz, a cross between rugby and cage-fighting.

Senior Allied officers watch the first "Colditz Olympic Games." Guy German, the first Senior British Officer, is seated far right.

The hot summer of 1942: "The courtyard every day was strewn with shining, sweaty bodies in various stages of redness, rawness and suntan."

The German officer Eggers, second from left, attends a theater performance in 1943, flanked by British officers.

The Man Who Came to Dinner, performed in 1944: Colditz theater was the focus of prison entertainment of all sorts, including concerts, plays, and pantomimes.

Set design for Charlie Hopetoun's production of *Gas Light* at the prison theater, drawn by Lieutenant Roger Marchand, alias "Madame Décor."

Ballet Nonsense, Christmas, 1941. Neave in mortarboard and gown, back row, four from left; Mazumdar in Indian garb, back row, fifth from right; Jimmy Yule at the piano; Tony Luteyn, far left on double bass.

"The leading ladies were incredibly convincing" and inevitably became the objects of desire.

Max Schmidt, the first Kommandant, an "imposing figure" with "cold grey eyes."

Senior Corporal Martin Schädlich, an indefatigable sleuth nicknamed "Dixon Hawke" after a popular fictional detective.

Edgar Glaesche, Schmidt's successor, who demanded respect and got nothing of the sort.

The last Kommandant of Colditz, Gerhard Prawitt, a "typical Prussian martinet."

Two Belgian escapers brought back to the castle at gunpoint.

"Other ranks": private soldiers who worked as servants for the officer POWs. Solly Goldman, second from right.

Bader, the castle's most famous and difficult inmate, with his long-suffering batman Alex Ross at his feet.

Menu for an Anglo-French dinner party in June 1943, featuring delicacies from the Red Cross parcels, including prunes and cheese.

The famous pilot was treated with elaborate courtesy by his German captors: in an act of bizarre gallantry, they informed the British that Bader's artificial right leg was no longer fit for purpose and invited the RAF to send a replacement. Sure enough, with Reichsmarschall Hermann Goering's official approval, the unimaginatively named "Operation Leg" was launched on August 19, when an RAF bomber was given safe conduct over Saint-Omer and dropped a new prosthesis by parachute on the nearest Luftwaffe base in occupied France, along with stump socks, powder, tobacco, and chocolate.

With two operative legs, Bader immediately tried to escape. He climbed out of the hospital window, lowered himself to the ground with a bedsheet rope, and hobbled off. He was captured a few hours later, hiding in a garden. Transferred to Lübeck camp, he escaped again, and was recaptured. Yet another attempt, from Stalag VIII-B at Lamsdorf, also ended in failure. Bader's prosthetic limbs impeded his escape efforts, but so did his fame. Each camp Kommandant was "deluged with requests from local bigwigs who wanted a chance to see him." A German poster was printed, describing his distinctive, stiff-legged gait, in case he should escape again. He was a captive of his own notoriety. Bader was about as *deutschfeindlich* as it was possible to be, an incorrigible prisoner and a valuable propaganda prize: Germany's highest-security prisoner-of-war camp was the obvious place to put him.

This, then, was the warrior-celebrity saluted by the admiring German sentries as he clumped into Colditz on August 18, 1942: a man with legs of tin, a heart of oak, and feet of clay.

The cobbled slope up from the moat was too steep for Bader's rigid legs, and so he was pulled along by his batman, a diminutive, bespectacled Scottish medical orderly from Renfrewshire named Alex Ross, who also carried Bader's luggage and spare legs. Both had been imprisoned in Lamsdorf. "He asked if I would go with him to Colditz but warned me it was a 'bad boys' camp," Ross recalled. Compared to other prisons he had known, Colditz struck Ross as "a bloody good place." "What I didn't realize was that being Bader's orderly was a 24-hours-a-day job.

I soon realized why none of the other orderlies wanted to work for him; you had to be at his beck and call all the time. I know he was a very brave man, but he could also be a monster."

Ross's jobs included serving Bader breakfast in bed every morning. He would then carry the officer on his back down two flights of winding stairs for his bath, and back up again afterward. "He was no lightweight," said Ross. "He would have his arms round my neck, hanging on, and would dig the stumps of his legs hard into me in order to hold on. And I did that every day of the week." Bader liked to refer to his batman-steed as *Das Ross,* an old German word for a horse or charger of the sort a knight might ride into battle.

At Colditz, Bader appointed himself to a number of prominent positions: orchestra conductor, goalie in games of stoolball, and goon-baiter-in-chief. He successfully campaigned to be allowed to take long walks outside the castle walls, insisting there was not enough space in the courtyard to exercise the muscles in what remained of his legs. Twice a week Bader set off on his "parole walks," under guard, and used the opportunity to trade with local farmers, swapping Red Cross chocolate for fresh eggs and other luxuries. His artificial legs were regularly repaired and serviced by the Colditz town blacksmith. Despite these marks of respect, Bader treated his captors with profanity-laden contempt, "unmercifully baiting the Germans on every possible occasion." He blew pipe smoke in the sentries' faces, refused to salute any German of lower rank than him, led the chorus in anti-German chanting, and instituted a system of organized tuneless whistling whenever the guards were marching past, to throw them out of step. Once, when Ross was carrying him upstairs after his bath, they encountered a German general and two colonels coming the other way. "Don't stop for these bastards," Bader shouted, digging his stumps into his orderly. "They looked quite shocked but stepped back to let us go by. He just glared at them."

As ever, Bader provoked contrasting feelings. Many younger officers were inspired and amused by his restless defiance: "Douglas provided the fun." The more impolite he was to the Germans, the greater their respect. "A strange and unpredictable character, his was the most magnetic personality in the prison," said one fellow officer. Even Eggers was a little daunted by this celebrity inmate. Others found him intensely irritating, pointing out that by goading the Germans he provoked collective punishments that adversely affected everyone in the camp. His rudeness was legendary. "I don't think all the time I knew him he said 'please' or 'thank you,'" recalled Ross. Bader never offered his batman any of the eggs he obtained on his countryside walks. "I think if he had handed me one, I would have fainted."

Bader's tin legs obviously made him ineligible for escapes requiring physical agility, such as tunneling or climbing across roofs. Nonetheless he demanded a place on every escape plan. When the escape committee refused, he raged: "Do you realize that the government at home would rather have me back than all the rest of you put together?" This assertion, though supremely arrogant, was probably true. At one point, the committee sent a secret message to London suggesting that "a splendid propaganda coup could be achieved by landing a light aircraft on the *Autobahn* near Colditz and so rescuing Douglas Bader." MI9 did not dismiss this barmy idea out of hand. The government wanted Bader back in Britain, and many in Colditz would have been happy to see him go.

The morning roll call on September 10 revealed that no fewer than ten prisoners were missing. Chaos ensued. Two British officers were found in the Dutch lines. Eggers checked the Dutch contingent against their photographs and found three had vanished. To add to the pandemonium, a British officer tossed a bucket of water out of a window as the recount was taking place. One of the British, formally identified under one name, turned out to be someone else completely. Four "ghosts" were found hiding in the attics. Once the confusion had died down, it emerged that six prisoners—three Dutch, one British, one Canadian, and an Australian—had gotten away. Eggers quickly found out how. They had picked the cruciform lock of the only office used by the Germans that faced into the prisoners' courtyard, burrowed through the floor beneath the desk into the storeroom below, and re-emerged, just after the guard changed, as a team of uniformed Polish orderlies under the command of a German

NCO. By good fortune, the German sentry guarding the gate out of the park fell for this disguise and obligingly opened it. Four of the escapers were quickly apprehended, but two, a Dutchman posing as an architecture student and the Australian airman pretending to be a Belgian laborer, evaded the search parties. Eighty-seven hours after leaving Colditz, they crossed into Switzerland at the Singen salient wearing civilian clothes.

The hole in the office floor was sealed up, and yet more security measures were imposed: a machine gun tower on the northwest corner of the terrace with a clear line of fire down the northern and western sides; a catwalk manned by a sentry over the barbed wire gate on the east side; more powerful floodlights in the inner courtyard. The "seam" where the prisoners' quarters adjoined the German quarters, always the weakest point of security, was networked with alarm wires under the plaster. Every escape attempt, successful or otherwise, made the next a little harder.

For Hauptmann Reinhold Eggers, the war had so far proven to be if not exactly enjoyable then perfectly tolerable. He missed his wife back in Halle. He worried for the safety of his two sons, one fighting in North Africa and the other in Nazi-occupied Norway. The prisoners could be extremely irritating, and their insolence continued to vex him. Yet he relished the challenge of pitting his wits against the escapers, in what he called a "permanent game of leapfrog: first we were ahead with our security barriers, then they were, scheming around them." Eggers was making quite a name for himself within the German military prison service. When General Henri Giraud escaped from Königstein Castle, a camp for senior French and Polish officers in Saxony, Eggers was sent to investigate. "Sure enough, my Colditz methods yielded the desired result." He concluded that the French general had escaped by scaling down the outside of the fortress using telephone cable smuggled to him by his wife, hidden inside a large ham. When the prison authorities opened a central escape museum in Vienna, Eggers was flattered to be asked to supply "specimens of our best escape material from our collection of photographs of tunnels, contraband, fake passes, keys, disguises etc." He gave tours of Germany's highest-security

prison to visiting dignitaries, and in October, to his intense grat-
ification, he was invited to a conference on prisoner policy in
Dresden. "Fame at last!" he wrote, without irony. "The Colditz
Escape Academy was now getting some recognition." His "museum" was becoming an obsession. He made six German sentries dress up as Polish orderlies in order to photograph a
re-enactment of the September escape. When a French officer
was caught trying to walk out disguised in overalls as the civilian
camp electrician Willi Pönert, Eggers had him pose for a photograph alongside his doppelgänger, adding another remarkable
image to his growing collection.

Eggers was fifty-two years old, and he had found his calling.
He was fast becoming Germany's foremost expert on escapology, the Sherlock Holmes of the *Sonderlager*. A bright future
beckoned, whenever Germany won the war.

But that victory, once an imminent certainty, was starting to
look more distant by the autumn of 1942. German soldiers were
being fed into the slaughter fields of the Eastern Front at a terrify-
ing rate. The tide of war was turning in North Africa, where
Rommel was now in retreat after the Second Battle of El Alamein.
With the increasing demand for frontline troops, the Colditz garrison was reduced. The coal ration was cut by a third. Despite the
enmity between the guarded and the guards, inside Colditz this
was still a gentlemanly war between soldiers who adhered to similar military codes of honor. But, as Eggers observed, "the war
outside was taking an unpleasant turn," and the ugliness was
seeping into the camp.

The German high command was increasingly enraged by Allied commando raids launched against targets in Nazi-occupied
Europe: the Dieppe raid, the capture of prisoners on the Channel
Island of Sark, the assassination of the brutal SS tyrant Reinhard
Heydrich in Czechoslovakia. The perpetrators of these assaults,
the Nazis claimed, were criminal bandits, tying up prisoners and
executing unarmed captives. In July came the order that captured parachutists should be handed over to the Gestapo.
Downed bomber crews were in increasing danger of being
lynched by enraged groups of vigilantes. "These pilots were safe,
and by that I mean comparatively safe, only when they got into

Wehrmacht hands," wrote Eggers. Escaping was becoming more dangerous: prisoners found outside the walls, in civilian clothes or disguised as German soldiers, were more likely to be accused of espionage and handed over to the Gestapo or the SS, brutal fanatics with no interest in following even the most basic rules of war. As the tide of war began to turn, the Nazi Party tightened its grip. The party leaders in Colditz town were taking a greater interest in what was happening in the castle; visits from the Gestapo to inspect security arrangements became more frequent. Within the German mess itself, the split was widening between those, like Eggers, who felt that the prisoners should be treated in accordance with regulations, and the hawks who favored more ruthless measures to keep the inmates in line.

On October 7, seven new prisoners arrived in Colditz to be photographed, before being swiftly hustled off to the town cells, away from the other inmates. No one knew who they were, or where they had come from.

Dominic Bruce was still in the town solitary cells following his failed packing-case escape, and during an exercise session he managed to exchange a few words with the leader of the group.

"Who are you?" Bruce whispered.

"Who are you?" the man responded.

"I'm an RAF officer."

"Where from?"

"I'm a Tynesider, but I haven't been there for a while," said Bruce. "Where are you from?"

There was a pause before the soldier replied.

"Norway."

"Well, if you want any messages sent home to England, we can send them for you," said Bruce.

"Tell them things went all right in Norway."

The man's name was Captain Graeme Black, a thirty-one-year-old Canadian from Ontario and the leader of "Operation Musketoon," one of the most daring secret sabotage missions of the war.

Two weeks earlier, Black had led a team of nine British and two Norwegian commandos in an attack on the Glomfjord power plant in Nazi-occupied Norway, a large hydroelectric works powering an aluminum factory that supplied important war matériel to the Germans. Transported to the coast of Norway by submarine, the saboteurs paddled ashore in dinghies in the dead of night, armed with rifles, Sten guns, pistols, and fighting knives. The team was also carrying dried meat, wire cutters, halibut oil, tinted spectacles against snow blindness, Horlicks, binoculars, and Benzedrine tablets. Having scaled a sheer cliff to the plant, they ushered the Norwegian night staff to safety, attached delayed-action plastic explosives to the machinery, pipeline, and generators, and headed inland. They were a mile away when it blew up, "with a colossal explosion which made the echoes ring from all the mountains round about." An hour later they were intercepted by a search party: two Germans and one of the commandos were killed in the ensuing firefight. The attackers then split into two parties: one group of four made it safely to neutral Sweden; the remaining seven were captured and taken to Colditz.

Three days after their arrival, Eggers was seen accompanying four Gestapo officers to the town jail. Black and his second-in-command were removed. Three days later, a routine inspection of their vacated cell revealed that the window bars had been sawn through in three places. "The cuts are filled with chewed bread, very neatly and hardly visible," wrote an impressed Schädlich. "This unit has been really well trained." Inside a comb sheath belonging to one of the commandos the Germans found a steel saw blade. One of the men, twenty-one-year-old Private Eric Curtis, scribbled in a diary: "We feel really happy, as if we were on holiday. Red Cross parcels with English food, chocolate, tea, milk, sugar. Tonight we really feel terrific . . . Red Cross marmalade makes bread taste like home." That was the last entry in Curtis's diary. Schädlich found it in his cell. The next day Curtis and his four companions were escorted under heavy guard to a waiting bus, and driven away. Three of them were just twenty years old. The oldest was twenty-eight. Their names and ranks, obtained by the orderly Solly Goldman while serving them breakfast in solitary, were passed on to MI9 in a coded letter that would later feature in evidence at the Nuremberg trials. When the Senior British Officer at Colditz demanded to know what had become of these men, Glaesche equivocated: "They were merely passing through the camp, coming from a place he did not know and going to a destination which he did not know."

On October 18, Hitler issued his *Kommandobefehl*, or "Commando Order," a glaring breach of the Geneva Convention ordering that all captured Allied commandos, in or out of uniform, should be summarily executed without trial, even if they had surrendered. "All men operating against German troops in so-called Commando raids are to be annihilated to the last man . . . no pardon is on any account to be given." The order warned that any German officer who failed to carry out this execution order would be punished. The last vestige of Nazi respect for international law was evaporating.

The survivors of Operation Musketoon were locked into the basement cells of the Reich Security headquarters in Berlin. There they were personally interrogated by Gestapo chief Heinrich Müller, one of Hitler's most brutal functionaries (and one of the few whose post-war fate has never been ascertained). On October 22, the seven commandos were chained together, loaded onto a truck, and taken to Sachsenhausen concentration camp, an hour's drive north of the city. At dawn the next day, the men were led out and then murdered by their SS guards, one by one, with a single pistol shot to the back of the neck.

The German authorities told the Red Cross and the Swiss "protecting power" that the commandos had escaped. Letters addressed to the seven at Colditz were returned unopened, marked *geflohen* (fled). Kommandant Glaesche must have known this was a lie. So, presumably, did Eggers. In his otherwise comprehensive account of life in Colditz, this terrible episode goes unmentioned, the queasy silence of guilt.

Further evidence of Nazi depravity arrived in Colditz a few weeks later. Kit Silverwood-Cope was another of Mrs. M's "boys." For fourteen months he had lived in Warsaw under the protection of Jane Walker's Anglo-Polish Society network, moving between safehouses. The first winter, struck down with typhus, he was nursed back to life by a Jewish doctor. But soon after Michael Sinclair made his abortive dash for the Bulgarian border, the network was infiltrated, and destroyed. Under interrogation two intercepted POWs revealed several key addresses.

A Pole, working for the Germans, worked his way into Mrs. M's confidence by offering to spirit escapers out through Switzerland. The Gestapo pounced. Silverwood-Cope and a dozen other escapers were arrested. The Jewish doctor and his family were sent to Auschwitz. Mrs. M was tipped off just in time, and went into hiding in the Polish countryside, disguised as a peasant. Jane Walker's one-woman resistance campaign was over, but Mrs. M left a remarkable legacy: she had stiffened the sinews of countless fugitive soldiers, helped dozens to get away, and instilled in Michael Sinclair an escape-lust that grew more urgent by the day.

The Gestapo accused Silverwood-Cope of spying and locked him in Pawiak civilian prison. Starved, repeatedly interrogated, confined to a tiny, freezing cell, he lost a quarter of his body weight in three months. The prison was a place of unspeakable cruelty. "By day, the screams of agony from prisoners being flogged was incessant." The Wehrmacht was still upholding the rules where possible; the army interceded and almost certainly saved Silverwood-Cope's life by removing him to Colditz. He arrived an emaciated, traumatized ghost. Eggers at first refused to believe his description of conditions in Pawiak. "The most dreadful things: Jews pushed down under manhole covers into drains full of dirty water and left to drown; dogs set on prisoners . . . prisoners beaten and hung by their wrists." Like many Germans, Eggers had hitherto dismissed tales of Nazi barbarity and mass murder as Allied propaganda. He was profoundly shocked. "It was the first information that I had personally had from firsthand sources, of what to me had till then been only rumors." Eggers was a prig, but he was neither a heartless man nor a stupid one. A small worm of doubt burrowed into his soul: not only could Germany lose the war; she might deserve to.

Pat Reid had planned, aided, approved, or taken part in virtually every escape attempt organized by the British. But of all the plans he vetted during two years of captivity none was quite so foolhardy, so very likely to fail, as the one he was invited to join in November 1942. Four prisoners proposed to climb out of a window in the POWs' kitchen, creep across the flat roof of the German kitchen in full view of the *Kommandantur* windows, sneak behind a sentry when his back was turned, and then crawl to a shallow pit on the south side of the German courtyard. In the corner was a door to a disused staircase that might lead to the empty upper floors of the German quarters, from which they planned to clamber down the outside walls on bedsheets, past rooms filled with sleeping German soldiers, and into the moat. Then they would take a train to the Swiss border, disguised as Flemish workmen. They had no idea what was behind the door, or whether they could open it. "The scheme was lunatic," declared Reid. He accepted the invitation without hesitation. This would be his sixth escape attempt and, he knew, his last. "I resolved I would not come back if I ever escaped again."

On October 14, Reid and three other British officers, dressed in civilian clothes and carrying suitcases as additional disguise, climbed onto the German roof, "a floodlit stage overlooked by several hundred windows." At that moment, Douglas Bader was conducting the Colditz orchestra in a rehearsal of Mozart's Oboe Concerto, and the music was clearly audible in the German courtyard. Stooges were watching, and signaling to the conductor: when the sentry turned his back Bader would lower his baton; as the guard turned around, Bader would resume conducting and the orchestra struck up again. Reid strained to pick up the musical cues; the music kept jolting to a halt, and then raggedly restarting, possibly because most of the orchestra, unaware of what was happening, could not follow Bader's bizarre conducting technique. Reid decided to chance it: one by one, the men dropped onto the cobbles, dived into a flower bed, and then crawled over to the shallow pit. Anyone glancing out of the windows would have seen them. The ancient lever-lock securing the staircase door resisted every effort to pick it, perhaps because it had not been opened for years. After an hour Reid gave up. The orchestra had dispersed, and the courtyard was silent. A few yards away, the sentry paced up and down. It was already 11 p.m. From the pit, Reid could see an archway with stone steps leading down into a cellar. That door was unlocked. The men slipped inside. At the far end of the cellar, a thin ray of light from the exterior floodlight revealed a ventilation shaft or disused chimney flue. Reid peered up it: "I could see that it led to a barred opening on the far side of the building, where lay the moat." Reid stripped off his clothes and wriggled up the narrow brick chute. One of the bars was loose in its socket. He pried it up and bent it back, and then dragged himself, inch by inch, through the wall, finally flopping onto the terrace outside. The next man, Hank Wardle, was stouter. Reid hauled on his outstretched hand. The others pushed from below. "At the end of 20 minutes, with a last wrench, I pulled him clear. He was bruised all over and streaming with perspiration." It was now 3 a.m. The four men dressed quickly, descended the three twelve-foot terraces into the moat, and set off down to the park. In the bushes on the far side of the wall they shook hands, whispered farewell in the darkness, split into pairs, and parted.

Three weeks later, Rupert Barry, the code-maker, received a postcard from Switzerland. It read: "We are having a holiday here and are sorry you are not with us. Give our dear love to your friend Dick." Dick Howe had taken over from Reid as British escape officer. The card was signed "Harriet and Phyllis Murgatroyd." The H and the P were heavily inked. Hank Wardle and Pat Reid were in Switzerland. Their two companions had reached safety a day later: it was the most successful single breakout to date.

Reid remained in Switzerland for the rest of the war, where he worked for MI6, gathering intelligence from other escapers. Once back in Britain, he forged an astonishingly successful career as the principal eyewitness historian of Colditz even though, as some of his fellow inmates sourly pointed out, he had been in it for under half its life as a POW camp.

The British were now top of the unofficial escapers' league for 1942, having achieved seven "home runs" in the space of a year. Michael Sinclair was determined to be next. With approval from the international escape committee, he teamed up with a French officer named Charles Klein, and on November 25, in broad daylight after the midday meal, they climbed out of the lightwell of the theater, through the German kitchens, into the *Kommandantur* courtyard, and then walked out of the gate: an exit so brazen that it worked. Then they split up. Klein was recaptured at

Plauen. With Mrs. M's Polish network broken up, Sinclair instead headed south for Singen. He was caught just a few miles from the Swiss border. Eggers collected him from Weinsberg police station, and found the recaptured officer in a filthy mood, monosyllabic and uncooperative. Sinclair later lodged an official complaint that Eggers had behaved in an "ungentlemanly" fashion by ordering a meal in the station restaurant without inviting the prisoner to join him. "This beats everything," wrote Eggers. "Such arrogance!" (Ever punctilious, Eggers formally noted that he had given Sinclair "a bottle of lemonade and some soup.") Sinclair was not so much arrogant as ferociously frustrated. He was the ideal escaper: young, energetic, imaginative, and brave. He merely lacked the one resource essential to every successful escape: luck. Sinclair longed to rejoin the battle, but with every failure the prospect of playing a useful part in the war seemed to recede a little further.

Colditz prisoners were not supposed to know what was happening in the wider conflict. Incoming letters were rigorously censored, and the German newspapers permitted inside the camp offered a uniformly rosy and misleading version of events. Yet the prisoners clearly had access to other news sources. Occasionally they dropped demoralizing remarks to the guards, pointing out that Germany's war was not progressing in the way Nazi propaganda claimed: the Allies were advancing in North Africa, the German army was bogged down in the Russian winter. The French seemed particularly well informed. "Neither gossip nor incoming prisoners could account for all they now and then admitted to knowing," Eggers noted. The French knew more about the war than he did, and early in December a traitor in the French camp revealed why: they were listening to the BBC. The ingenious lock-picker Frédo Guigues had smuggled in a three-valve radio through the parcels office, concealed inside a food package from his wife. The radio, codenamed "Arthur," was hidden behind a wall on the top floor of the French quarters, in a room occupied by the curate. It was disguised by a large map of Africa drawn on the wall. "The black dots marking towns on the map were in fact sockets for the headphone plugs; the tuning knob was underneath Dakar." News was gathered nightly from the

BBC French Service and passed on to the other nations without revealing the whereabouts of the radio.

Eggers "found" the radio on December 15 ("French make, tuned to London"), after conducting an elaborate investigation of the *Kellerhaus* to make it appear as if the discovery was the result of a routine search. His underlings knew better. Schädlich wrote in his diary: "A radio installation as cleverly hidden and disguised as this one would not have been found without being betrayed." Years later Eggers admitted that he had been tipped off by a French informant, and though he passed on the name of the spy to Guigues after the war, he insisted that this not be revealed until 2000. In that year the spy was identified as Julien Kérignard, an NCO from Marseille and the assistant curate. Kérignard was set free in return for revealing the radio's hiding place. "In order not to arouse suspicions we transferred him with some others to a different camp." Eggers put it about that the Frenchman had subsequently been released "on health grounds." Kérignard abandoned the priesthood after the war and died with his treachery unrevealed.

"There are no more radios in the camp," Eggers reassured Berlin emphatically, and wrongly. As "insurance," Guigues had already built a second radio, from parts shipped in different parcels by the resourceful and obliging Madame Guigues. Arthur II, hidden in the attics under a pile of broken tiles, was up and running on the very evening that Arthur I was confiscated. "There was no break in our radio service," wrote Guigues.

The flurry of successful escapes, and the encouraging war news, lent a prematurely optimistic flavor to that Christmas, a belief that captivity might soon be at an end. The men took bets on when the war would be won. A Christmas Day truce was agreed with the Kommandant, under which "the prisoners promised not to escape, and the Germans left the lights on until 1:00 a.m." Time was beginning to concertina, one year merging into the next. "Tonight's celebration had nothing new in it," remarked Padre Platt. "It was just a repetition of last year and the year before—but with more hope." This Colditz Christmas differed from its predecessors in one other respect: it was spectacularly drunken.

The illicit production of alcohol had come a long way since the crude and fearsome spirit brewed up by the early Polish distillers. Prison moonshine was made by mixing sugar and yeast with ersatz jam, mashed fruit, or vegetables. The resulting mixture was left in a warm cupboard to ferment for six weeks, before being distilled with a rustic Liebig condenser constructed from stolen toilet piping, to produce a clear alcohol of 120 degrees proof. This hooch still had to be made palatable by flavoring it with whatever came to hand: more fruit, brown sugar, or, in one instance, Chanel No. 5 aftershave sent in a care package. "Jam Alc" was grim stuff. It resulted in inebriation, to be sure, but also blurred vision, vomiting, nightmares, black teeth, a swollen tongue, and, as the effects wore off, headaches of cataclysmic violence. One Colditz distiller named his "whisky" "Glenbucket." Left overnight it could eat through the bottom of an enamel cup. Prisoners who overindulged were said to be "jam happy."

The Germans at first tried to prevent alcohol production but eventually tolerated it as a welcome distraction: pickled prisoners were often less trouble than the sober variety. Though one drinker developed cirrhosis and a few went briefly blind, no one died of alcohol poisoning, and as the former medical student Peter Storie-Pugh observed, alcohol in moderation had "an enormously good effect" on morale. The quality of the homemade hooch steadily improved. Michael Farr, a vintner and oenophile whose family owned Hawker's Gin, emerged as chief purveyor of wines and spirits to Colditz, with the encouragement of Eggers, who "not only allowed us to continue brewing but in fact helped us by giving us rough clay wine jars." Over the course of his imprisonment, Farr developed a pure white schnapps and a sloe gin, as well as "remarkably good" rosé and white wines from a variety of dried fruits including apricots, prunes, raisins, and sultanas. Farr's *grand cru* was "Chateau Colditz," a demi-sec sparkling wine made using the *méthode champenoise* pioneered in 1863 by Veuve Clicquot, the *grande dame* of champagne. This wine was fermented in Eggers's jars using raisins, water, and sugar, clarified and filtered through charcoal, bottled, and laid to rest cork-down for a fortnight, until all the sediment had gathered at the neck. Then it was placed upside down on a window ledge in a tray of snow, ice, and salt, until the cork and first inch of wine had frozen solid. Then the cork and iced sediment were removed, leaving a "bright, clear wine with all the yeast removed." Farr added a little more sugar to each bottle before recorking: "An excellent sparkling wine resulted which was served chilled."

Christmas dinner was tomato soup, steak and onions, sardines on toast, and Christmas pudding with custard, washed down with prodigious quantities of this prisoners' prosecco and *digestifs* of various sorts. Instead of dining in their separate messes, the British officers crammed into the Long Room. The orderlies dined separately, and no less lavishly. "Le vin de Chateau Colditz flowed freely in all quarters," wrote Platt. A sweepstake was held on when Tripoli would fall to the Allies. National songs were bellowed in the courtyard. The booze, Farr noted, created "a lot of merriment and high spirits and we forgot where we were for a short time."

Nineteen forty-three dawned with a thumping hangover. The effects of the Jam Alc wore off, bringing back the grim knowledge that the war might not be over by the next Christmas, or the one after that. Unlike ordinary convicts, for prisoners of war the day of freedom is not set by judge or jury, but by events in a distant theater of conflict. Liberty is an unknowable appointment with fate that might come soon, eventually, or never. Alan Campbell, one of several Colditz poets, wrote: "Our cross is the curse of waiting." Frustration was mounting.

Apart from the possible murder in the parcels office, no prisoner had ever attacked a guard in Colditz. But a few days after New Year's, Eggers was standing in the prisoners' courtyard talking to another German officer, when a large lump of snow fizzed past his head and smashed into the door of the canteen with a loud thud. This was no ordinary snowball. "It was thrown with such force," wrote Eggers, "that in the mush left on the door I found a very large piece of bottle glass stuck into the wood." The snowball thrower had intended serious injury. The war, inside and outside Colditz, was growing nastier.

1943

10

The *Prominente* Club

War stories are usually about what happened. The story of Colditz, by contrast, is largely a tale of inactivity, a long procession of duplicate days when little of note occurred, punctuated by moments of intense excitement. The ennui was not confined to the prisoners. "It's boring in the camp," Schädlich wrote in his diary. "The French have caught a mouse and are letting it drift down on a parachute from the 4th floor." The prisoners' existence followed a set pattern: morning roll call, breakfast in their quarters, dishwashing and tidying, then study for some (mutual language teaching continued to thrive), the midday meal when the cookhouse bell rang and the orderlies collected the rations from the German kitchen. Then lying in bed, reading, or playing cards until the afternoon roll call, a game of stoolball or another sport, more cards, escape-plotting or kit-making for some, tea at four o'clock, then trudging around and around the courtyard "in the eternal circle." The hours between meals and roll calls were worn away in a cycle of "smoking, sleeping and self-abuse."

Colditz was a highly literate place, with regular literary discussions, lectures, and a wide variety of books available, including numerous works in German, ranging from Nietzsche's philosophy to translations of Hitler's speeches. Reading matter was supplied via the Red Cross, and Penguin Books set up a system whereby, in return for an annual subscription of three guineas, individual prisoners received a monthly parcel containing a selection of ten books. These books had to pass censors in Britain (to ensure no vital information was transmitted to the enemy), and German ones (in case the pages contained secret intelligence to aid escapes). A handful undertook correspondence courses, to obtain qualifications that might be useful when and if they returned home. Eggers proudly opened a prisoners' library. Padre Platt was the librarian and moral arbiter of the prisoners' reading habits: "A minority read good literature," he decided, "but far too large a section of the camp reads nothing but fiction."

Some passed the hours inventing ever more ingenious forms of goon-baiting. When a large wasps' nest was discovered in an ivy-covered wall, the British came up with a new way to irritate their captors: individual wasps were trapped, and then a cigarette paper bearing the words *Deutschland Kaput!* was carefully attached to one leg by a thread, before the insect was released, in the hope that the angry wasp would sting a German citizen and pass on the message. At one roll call, in a unique act of entomological propaganda, dozens of message-bearing wasps were released simultaneously: "It was like a reversed snowstorm with the wasps flying upwards in furious mood," recalled an eyewitness.

Such diversions were short-lived. There was seldom anything new to talk about, and so the prisoners tended to say the same things, to the same people, again and again. Even the most interesting individuals become crashing bores in prison. Lights-out, at 9:30 p.m., came as "a blessed relief, for it meant the end of another wasted and useless day." It was an existence that many of the inmates had been prepared for by "the harsher side of public school life," wrote one prisoner, the worst privations being "the lack of exercise and sex."

No Colditz prisoner ever had intercourse with a woman. With one possible exception.

The Czech fighter pilot Čeněk Chaloupka, inevitably nicknamed "Checko" by the British, was a debonair figure, with a plausible manner and a rakish mustache. Flight Lieutenant Chaloupka had flown in the Czechoslovakian air force, and then for the French after the German invasion of his homeland, before coming to Britain and joining the RAF. He liked to number his medals from three different air forces as if they had been awarded for amorous conquests: "This is for loving a blonde, this is for loving a brunette, this is for loving a redhead." Assigned to 615

Squadron, he was shot down in his Hawker Hurricane fighter off the Belgian coast on October 6, 1941, and was captured. "Puckish, dynamic, uproarious and explosive," Chaloupka was a most unruly prisoner, and in January 1943 he was dispatched to Colditz.

On the train to Oflag IV-C, Chaloupka and his guards found themselves sharing a compartment with an extremely attractive young woman. Irmgard Wernicke was nineteen years old, four years younger than the Czech airman. Checko spoke fluent German. "It was quite a long trip," Chaloupka later recalled. "And we had time to get to know each other." Irma explained that she worked as assistant to the Colditz town dentist, Dr. Ernst Michael. Her father, Dr. Richard Karl Wernicke, was headmaster of the nearby agricultural school and a senior figure in the local Nazi Party whose home backed onto the castle grounds. Checko, in turn, described his flight from Czechoslovakia, his adventures as a pilot, and his capture. Like Checko, Irma was a romantic and a rebel. By the time the train pulled into Colditz, she was smitten.

As they alighted, Irma whispered that Checko should feign a dental emergency so they could meet again. A few weeks later, Chaloupka deliberately chipped a tooth. The resulting dentist appointment turned out to be more thrilling than most. He left his muffler behind. Irma ran up the hill to return it to him. They kissed on the road to Colditz, with the amused German guard looking on, the unlikely start to a passionate love affair between an imprisoned Czech fighter pilot and a German dental assistant.

In the early days of Colditz, Dr. Michael and his pretty assistant had visited the castle once a week to attend to the prisoners' teeth, but this arrangement came to an end early in 1942 when the dentist's winter coat was stolen from a locked cupboard, along with his scalpels, drills, and even his surgical gown. After that, he insisted that prisoners needing treatment must be brought to his surgery in the middle of the town. According to a fellow prisoner, "Checko managed to get to the dentist five times, by smashing a few teeth so badly on rocks that they needed a series of treatments." Word swiftly went round that the Czech was now "the only inmate of the castle ever to have kissed a girl."

Chaloupka hinted he had done a lot more than kiss Irma on these occasions. If they did have sex, this can only have been done with the connivance of Dr. Michael, and may well have been achieved by bribery, Checko's other principal talent.

Within weeks of his arrival, Chaloupka had emerged as the chief coordinator and controller of the camp's illegal barter system: using cigarettes as enticements, he established friendly terms with several of the guards. Through these "soft goons," Checko seemed to be able to obtain almost anything: railway timetables, eggs, tools, fresh onions, and information. From there it was a short step to blackmail: threatening to report a guard who had taken a bribe was a most effective way to force the man to accept another. Checko was a master dealmaker: if the price of enjoying sexual relations with Irma was a few damaged teeth and a lot of cigarettes for the town dentist, then that, in Checko's view, was a bargain.

A man of "considerable charm and presence, possessed of an irresistible exuberance," Checko was also a fantastic show-off who reveled in his reputation as a black market fixer and lothario. Chaloupka later described his typical day: he liked to rise late, enjoy a leisurely breakfast cooked by his personal chef, wander up to the second floor of the east wing to observe, through a lecherscope, his "favorite popsy in her panties as she was dressing"; then a light lunch, some profitable trading with the guards, a game of cards, back upstairs to watch Irmgard disrobing in her bedroom, an "excellent supper," a conversation about the progress of the war, and so to bed. How much of it was actually true may never be known, but this was exactly the kind of account to excite the envy and admiration of Checko's sex-starved fellow inmates.

Opportunists like Chaloupka thrive on upheaval, and his arrival coincided with another regime change in the camp. In February, the Kommandant was sent to take over the administration of camps in Ukraine. Glaesche never came to grips with the combative culture of Colditz, and in recent months he had seldom emerged from his private quarters. His replacement, Oberstleutnant (Lieutenant Colonel) Gerhard Prawitt, the third and last Kommandant of Colditz, was a "typical Prussian martinet" redeployed from the Eastern Front. At forty-four he was younger and more active than most of the men under his command. One of his first acts was to dismiss the easygoing alcoholic Hauptmann Priem, who took early retirement and soon after drank himself to death. New machine gun posts were erected, and fresh fields of barbed wire rolled out around the castle's slopes. To instill greater discipline, the number of roll calls increased to four a day: the prisoners now had to form up for counting at 7 a.m., 11 a.m., 4 p.m., and 10 p.m. "If this doesn't work, six to eight roll calls a day," Prawitt warned the Senior Officers. From the start, he refused to tolerate the sort of rebelliousness that had taken root under Glaesche: "If a POW does not obey orders," he told the guards, "repeat the order and push your rifle into his back. If he continues disobeying, shoot him on the spot." Eggers favored a more subtle approach, and confided to his diary: "Prawitt is the most ignorant Kommandant I have ever had." He was about to face a challenge to his authority from a most unlikely quarter.

Birendranath Mazumdar still wrestled, in secret, with the most difficult decision of his life. A discreet word with Eggers would see him back in the first-class compartment on the train to Berlin; soon after that, he might be the senior medical officer of an army fighting for Indian freedom under the leadership of the great Subhas Chandra Bose. It was a painfully tempting vision. But to take that step would be to exchange integrity for freedom, and that Mazumdar could not do. "Honor and fidelity are not double-edged," he reflected. "One can be honorable when times are not hard, but when honorable intentions are changed in a crisis, such as captivity, then that person can no longer be called honorable. The same is equally true of fidelity. To honor one's own promise is the bounden duty of every individual who so pledges. Come what may. Anyone who diverts from that sacred path, no matter for what reason, is despised and looked down upon. An honorless person is not a human being: he ought to be classified with the quadrupeds."

The Indian doctor nursed his principles in solitude. When a second doctor, an Irishman named Ion Ferguson, arrived in late 1942, Mazumdar greeted him gloomily: "You'll rue the day you came to this madhouse. Most of us are cracked here and it won't be long before you're the same as the rest."

Life in Colditz had become "unbearable," Mazumdar reflected. He had to get out. "I was fed up. I had to prove that I could escape."

In accordance with the Nazi insistence on racial stratification, the Germans had set up a handful of camps in Germany and occupied France containing only Indian prisoners, mostly soldiers of the British Indian Army captured in North Africa. The security at such places was well below Colditz standards. If Mazumdar could get himself transferred to an all-Indian camp, he calculated, there might be a better chance of escaping; if not, he would at least get away from the rumors of disloyalty that dogged him in Colditz, find someone to talk to in Bengali, and resume his medical work. He asked the new Kommandant for a transfer, insisting he had a right to be imprisoned with his compatriots; he pretended to be vegetarian, claiming that the camp food was a violation of his religion; whenever the Swiss, as the protecting power, came to inspect, he lobbied them to ask the prison authorities to move him. Nothing worked. "I keep trying to force the Germans to let me return to work in a Stalag," he told Dr. Ferguson. "But they take no notice of me." The Germans pointed out that Mazumdar was officially *deutschfeindlich,* and therefore in exactly the right place.

One February morning, in conversation with the Irish doctor, Mazumdar announced: "You know, Ferguson, I have decided not to stay here any longer. There's no good an Indian trying to escape through Germany, so I shall just have to arrange to go out through the main gate. I'm prepared to bet you that I shall not be here in a fortnight."

Ferguson was astonished.

"You think I am joking, don't you, Fergy? Well, I will show you that you are wrong."

The Indian doctor had decided to deploy what he called "the sole weapon open to me": he would go on a hunger strike.

During the 1930s, Mahatma Gandhi, Mazumdar's political idol, had staged a series of highly publicized hunger strikes to demand an end to British rule in India. On February 10, 1943, detained without charges by the British, Gandhi began his fifteenth such protest, insisting he would eat nothing until he was released. Two days later, Mazumdar launched his own hunger strike. He told Ferguson: "The Jerries will not find it very good propaganda in the Far East if the news gets around they have allowed an Indian to starve to death." He then took to his bed, declaring he would consume nothing but water and a little salt until the Kommandant relented and moved him to another camp.

Food was the second most widely discussed topic in Colditz, after escaping. The idea that a prisoner might voluntarily forgo nourishment struck the others as bizarre. The British officers mocked him—"Jumbo is doing a Gandhi"—but the little doctor just smiled and said: "I know what I am doing. We shall see what we shall see."

The Germans were initially surprised by Mazumdar's one-man protest, then mildly amused, and finally deeply alarmed. After a week of starvation, Mazumdar had lost half a stone. Ferguson urged him to call it off. He politely refused. The German doctor examined him and reported back to Kommandant Prawitt that Mazumdar was sinking fast: "He could not keep the anxiety out of his voice." Eggers was becoming seriously concerned. The Senior British Officer appealed to the new Kommandant to "rescue the little Indian doctor from his self-imposed fate." Messages flew between Colditz and Berlin. By the end of the second week, Mazumdar was too frail to leave his bed, but he remained resolute. "I have never seen a man more determined about anything," wrote Dr. Ferguson, who issued bulletins on Mazumdar's health every four hours. Unteroffizier Schädlich noted in his diary: "The English-Indian doctor has not eaten for 14 days, he only drinks tea and smokes." His eyesight was starting to fail, and his heart rate was dropping, yet "he continued to smile and reiterated: 'We shall see what we shall see.'" Delirious from hunger, Mazumdar tried to focus on the Hindu fasting ritual of *Upanayana* he had undergone as a boy, the sacred thread ceremony, and willed his body to fight on. "I was getting weaker and weaker," he recalled. His father's words kept coming back to him: "Never forget what you are, how you were brought up, what good luck you had."

On day sixteen, the German army blinked. A message arrived from army headquarters in Berlin: "Dr. Mazumdar should cease forthwith his hunger strike and prepare to leave the camp as soon as he has regained his strength."

Mazumdar's hunger strike had borne fruit. (Gandhi's protest didn't. The British ignored it, and he resumed eating after twenty-one days.)

The other inmates instantly forgot how poorly they had treated Mazumdar in the past: "The Indian doctor was the hero of the hour." The suspicion and prejudice that had always clung to him evaporated overnight, and as he emerged into the court-yard, weak and gaunt but grinning broadly, he was greeted with loud cheers. People who had shunned him now declared they had always liked him: "We were all sorry to lose such a deter-mined personality from our midst." They plied him with food to build up his strength. "The British officers fed me up sumptu-ously." Harry Elliott, the officer who had accused him of spying and ended up being pummeled on the washroom floor, now apologized. "I am very sorry," he said. "I am extending an invi-tation to stay with me and my family after the war."

Mazumdar had been barred from escaping on account of his skin color, but now, as he prepared to leave, the escape commit-tee presented him with a brand-new arse-creeper filled with Ger-man banknotes—a gesture of racial solidarity that was heartfelt, if somewhat unusual.

On February 28, 1943, just as he had predicted, Mazumdar walked out of the front gates of Colditz.

After a week in a fetid Indian camp on a former polo field at Bayonne in southwest France, he was loaded onto another train with a group of prisoners heading north. "You are mad," a fel-low Indian officer told him, when Mazumdar confided that he intended to jump off the train. Near Angoulême, with the help of two Indian sappers, he levered out the carriage window and jumped through it. The train was still moving "pretty fast." With a broken finger, he set off south on foot, hoping to cross the Pyr-enees into neutral Spain. French peasants provided food, cloth-ing, and directions. But in a small village near Toulouse his luck ran out. "I foolishly inquired from an old Frenchman the whereabouts of a bridge." The man led him to a building, which turned out to be the police station. Mazumdar was arrested and handed over to the Germans. "My first contact with the Gestapo was anything but pleasant," he recalled, with ringing understatement. "I had a rough time with them." He was interrogated and badly beaten up, first in the cells at Agen, then at Gestapo headquarters at Toulouse. After one particularly savage thrashing his nose bled for an hour, but he adamantly "refused to admit the names of the French civilians" who had helped him. The Gestapo seemed to know all about his meeting with Subhas Chandra Bose.

"We'll give you one more chance to join us," they said.

"I'm not doing anything of the sort," he replied. So they beat him up again.

Mazumdar assumed the Gestapo would eventually run out of patience and kill him. At best, they might send him back to Colditz. Instead, on April 17, he was taken to Frontstalag 153 at Chartres in central France, a camp for "colonial prisoners" where 500 captive Indians were guarded by a garrison of French-Algerian troops under German command. As the only officer with a British commission, Mazumdar was the most senior soldier in the place. "I had joined my compatriots," he wrote. "I had reason to be pleased." He began planning his next escape attempt: "I was determined to get away, come what may."

At the same moment, back in Colditz, another solitary prisoner also found companionship. Giles Romilly, Churchill's nephew, spent his nights alone in his cell, and his days under constant surveillance. But in February he was joined by a second VIP prisoner, a captured commando who had avoided execution through a heroic feat of bogus name-dropping. The Germans believed him to be the nephew of General Sir Harold Alexander, the British commander of Allied Forces in the Middle East. Which he was not.

Lieutenant Michael Alexander was a twenty-two-year-old officer in the Special Boat Section (SBS), the marine equivalent of the Special Air Service (SAS) founded by David Stirling in 1941. Where the fledgling SAS had pioneered a new form of warfare in

North Africa by crossing the Libyan desert to attack Axis air-fields along the coast, the SBS performed a similarly destructive and secretive role, but by sea. Alexander had been playing tennis in Alexandria in the summer of 1942 when he received a message summoning him on a mission to sabotage a munitions dump behind enemy lines. He had no time to change into uniform. The team of twenty SBS commandos traveled forty miles up the coast by high-speed torpedo boat, and then, in darkness, paddled ashore in rubber boats, only to find they had landed in the wrong place: a tented encampment of the German 90th Light Infantry Division, a crack unit of the Afrika Korps. The mission was aborted, but while the others returned to Alexandria, Alexander, and one other man, Corporal Peter Gurney, insisted on continuing alone. This proved to be an error.

The two men walked through the German camp in the dark, attaching time bombs to two tank transporters, an armored car, and an ammunition depot, before setting off on foot for the British lines, some twenty-five miles to the east. By daybreak, they were hungry and thirsty, and in the middle of another encampment. They entered a tent, captured six German soldiers at gunpoint, tied them up, stole their Luger pistols, and then ate their breakfast of spaghetti bolognese and coffee. They were both captured soon after. Alexander was not dressed for his role as a commando: he was still wearing his gabardine trousers and silk shirt from the tennis court, now supplemented by a stolen Afrika Korps cap. A young German officer, who "spoke perfect English and said that he had been up at Oxford in 1938," politely informed them that they would now be killed: they had murdered two Germans asleep in the tank transporter and were dressed (at least partially) in German uniform, and thus suspected of espionage. Under Hitler's Commando Order they were liable to summary execution.

Alexander had a timely brainwave. "Intending to play on the caste snobbism that was part of German military tradition," he encouraged Gurney to mention that he was "not just a vulgar saboteur" but a nephew of General Alexander, already a figure of repute among the Germans. The new commander of Allied forces in Cairo was, in fact, his second cousin once removed, but

Alexander reckoned he knew just enough about the family to bluff his way through an interrogation on the subject. Rommel himself ordered a stay of execution. When an aide pointed out that Hitler had ordered the killing of all captured commandos, the Field Marshal replied: "What! Shoot General Alexander's nephew? You damned fool." The other British captive could claim no illustrious relatives. "Corporal Gurney was taken off in another direction," wrote Alexander, who spent the rest of his life wondering what terrible fate had befallen his companion. Gurney was never seen again.

Alexander was moved from one prison to another until, in February 1943, he was taken to Colditz, marched across the courtyard, and ushered into a small room. "By a barred window was a short, square figure, wearing an old brown dressing-gown and trying to swat a fly."

"Herr Romilly," said the guard. "We have company for you."

These two men would form the nucleus of the *Prominente*, the group of important prisoners held "under rather special supervision," as Alexander put it. The two men had much in common, including "uncles" they barely knew whose fame had brought them to Colditz.

In time, these two would be joined by additional "elite" prisoners, selected from POW camps around the country: the sons of British aristocrats, politicians, senior military figures, and members of the royal family. The Germans followed eclectic criteria for who was, and who was not, sufficiently elevated to be admitted to this small group. Colditz inmate John Arundell, the 16th Baron Arundell of Wardour, was a bona fide blue-blooded aristocrat, but lacked the political or royal clout to be deemed truly prominent. Max de Hamel, a tank commander who became the seventh member of the *Prominente* group late in 1944, had no idea why he was accorded this dubious privilege, until he remembered a recent letter from his grandmother that contained the line: "Met some of Mr. Churchill's grandchildren, who are cousins of yours." This was news to de Hamel, and of considerable interest to the German letter-censors, who alerted the authorities. De Hamel reckoned he was probably the prime minister's third cousin. Every individual has an average of around

850 third cousins, but this slender blood tie to Britain's prime minister was enough for the amateur genealogists of the Third Reich. Max de Hamel was shipped off to Colditz on the basis of a snippet of "homely gossip" in a letter from his family.

To twist Groucho Marx's dictum, the *Prominente* formed a club that its members had never wanted to join. Yet membership brought certain privileges: greater privacy, more space, a gramophone, and better food. Since the VIPs were not permitted to exercise in the park, the Kommandant agreed that they could take "parole walks," like Douglas Bader, accompanied by four guards armed with machine pistols. "It is beautiful country," said Eggers. "Rather like your Cotswolds." As they wandered the lanes around Colditz, Michael Alexander would pick thyme from the hedgerows and later traded it with the French for bully beef. The *Prominente* did not exactly look down on the other prisoners, but, as in civilian life, these men enjoyed a different status. One of the group described prison life in Colditz as "the country gentleman set-up" and was surprised to find so many people who "came from my own walk of life." The exception was Max de Hamel, who was not quite of the same class. "He had the air of a chamberlain looking for an emperor," Michael Alexander observed snootily. Giles Romilly was a communist but, crucially, a socially connected, upper-class one. The lowest and uppermost classes of Colditz were both more securely incarcerated than the middle-class prisoners: the orderlies were not expected to escape, and the aristocracy of Colditz society was kept under such close surveillance that getting out was impossible. When Romilly attempted to do so, disguised as a rubbish collector, he was intercepted and sent back to his cell with the mocking admonition that Mr. Churchill's nephew should not be "getting his hands dirty" in this way. But while they enjoyed a peculiar form of privilege, the *Prominente* knew that their exceptional treatment in Colditz was not a measure of deference but a cynical calculation: they were bargaining chips, to be cashed in when Hitler felt the need.

Clubs were, and remain, a bizarre British preoccupation. Whenever three or more Englishmen are gathered together, a minimum of two will attempt to form a club from which the others are excluded. Allegiance to a particular tribe, whether a soccer team or a gentleman's club in Pall Mall, runs through British (male) culture like veins through marble. Often absurd in ritual, rigidly hierarchical, and rigorously exclusive, these defining grouplets can be hugely significant to their members, and no one else. A certain sort of clubbable Englishman is happiest when admitting a like-minded person into his club, or blackballing someone who isn't. In Colditz, the distinct messes evolved into small clubs: the "House of Lords," the "Kindergarten," a poker school of "White's Club types." The "old school tie" mentality not only persisted but was exacerbated under captivity, as the inmates sought to build a replica of the lives they had known before the war. The Old Etonians, Platt noted, tended to be particularly clannish, to the point of coordinating their bodily functions. "They ate together, paced the exercise ground in twos, threes, or fours; attended the same lectures; and went to the *Abort* [lavatory] together."

Colditz even had its own Bullingdon Club, modeled on the all-male Oxford University private dining club that has since become a byword for elitist philistinism. In the twenty-first century alone, Bullingdon alumni have included two Tory prime ministers and a chancellor of the Exchequer. The Colditz Bullingdon was "mostly Old Etonians with the necessary 'old school' and horsey characteristics," one member recalled. "We got on wonderfully well." The Bullingdon is infamous for drunkenly wrecking restaurants and an initiation rite that allegedly includes burning a £50 note in front of a homeless person. In Colditz there were no restaurants, no real money, and no horses, but the mere existence of a Bullingdon Club was further evidence of a determination to translate pre-war social norms into the artificial world of prison. An officers' camp, Colditz was itself the "Bad Boys' Club"; the *Prominente* represented an even more select society within it ("We were rather cliquey up there," said Michael Alexander); and the Colditz Bullingdon was the most exclusive subgroup of all, a club within a club within a club.

After the war, former inmates tended to portray the Colditz prisoner community as a classless, cohesive band of brothers whose shared determination to escape somehow flattened out the distinctions and dissonances that divided the world outside. Exactly the reverse was true. "The class structure in Colditz was like the class structure of the time," said one new arrival. "There was a working class, who were the soldiers, the orderlies who had to work. Then there were the middle class, officers from minor or major public schools, and then there was an upper class, with the *Prominente* and the Lords of the Realm . . ." Alex Ross, Bader's put-upon dogsbody, referred to these special prisoners as "the big nobs" and noted "they didn't talk to the orderlies." The social divide between officers and their servants was strictly upheld. Ross played the clarinet in the band, but otherwise he and the other orderlies lived separate, very different lives from the officers they served, with their own quarters, and no opportunity to escape. "We didn't even know when the escapes were taking place," said Ross. "They'd never involve us." The orderlies played soccer, but were not expected to participate in stoolball, an officers' game. "It was too bloody rough," said Ross, who was permitted to take part in cricket matches, but only when Bader was playing. "I detested the cricket. He'd hit the ball and I'd do the runs."

Beyond class, there were also divisions of military rank, service, nationality, seniority, and the different ways a man might choose to pass the time. One veteran observed that prisoners "roughly divided themselves into five main categories: escapers, creators, administrators, the students, and the sleepers. Many individuals combined two or more of these approaches in their system of dealing with captivity." As at school, new arrivals were teased and demeaned until they had proved themselves.

In early summer, seventy-six British officers were transferred to Colditz after staging a mass tunnel breakout from Eichstätt camp in Bavaria. The resident prisoners referred to them disparagingly as the "Eichstätt mob." The new bugs did not accord the old lags the respect the latter felt they deserved. "We thought they were all mad," said one of the new intake. "They'd been locked up in the same place for far too long and were terrible show-offs." Some of the recent arrivals regarded the Colditz tradition of goon-baiting as childish and counterproductive; others resented the requirement that all escape attempts had to be approved by a committee. Even escaping had an internal hierarchy, with veteran escapers at the top.

Chief among these was Michael Sinclair, the most obsessive of the obsessives. In May he hatched yet another scheme with Gris Davies-Scourfield, one of the officers who had escaped with him from Poznań: during exercise in the park, they would sit in a corner of the enclosure, leaning against the fence, and then gradually cut through the wire, "working away surreptitiously" behind their backs, with a saw made from a serrated razor blade. When a panel was cut out, the other men would cause a diversion, the two men would break through, "crawl up a bramble-covered bank, and then quickly slip over the wall to freedom." Davies-Scourfield knew the plan had little chance of success, "but Mike's enthusiasm carried me along." The Germans soon discovered the severed wires, repaired the fence, and banned prisoners from leaning on it thereafter. This was Sinclair's fifth escape attempt. "His lust to escape, unclouded by a single distracting thought, made him the dominant figure of British escaping in Colditz in 1943," wrote Romilly. But while Sinclair was involved in every plan, he remained a solitary figure. "Mike Sinclair was a silent person. He walked alone." Even the Germans were impressed: "His red hair and bitter courage earned him the respectful German nickname *Rote Fuchs*," the Red Fox. With leaden irony Eggers dubbed him the "Great Escaper," but he admired Sinclair's persistence: "The number of his escapes, the variety and ingenuity, the thoroughness of preparation and exactness of execution, all added up to an unparalleled accomplishment"; and a unique record of failure.

The arrival of the Eichstätt mob marked a transformation in the essential character of Colditz. After two and a half years, the Wehrmacht had reached the belated conclusion that it was a mistake to cram all the most recalcitrant prisoners, of every Allied nation, into one place. Instead of dampening rebellion, the chemistry of international competition and collaboration had made the place even harder to police. Henceforth, Oflag IV-C was to contain only British prisoners, those from Commonwealth countries, and, in time, Americans. The Dutch contingent left in June; the entire prison population turned out to wave them off. The

French and Belgians were taken to Lübeck camp a few weeks later. A puce-faced Giles Romilly was found hiding in a French packing case on the platform at Colditz station, with a packet of biscuits and a saw; the box had been left upside down and he was close to fainting. "He would undoubtedly have suffocated before the train left because a lot of luggage had been piled on top so that the air hole drilled into the crate was restricted," wrote Schädlich. Kommandant Prawitt, whose neck would be on the line if "Emil" escaped, threw a tantrum and dismissed the chief security officer. The last of the Polish company departed for a camp in Silesia in August, leaving behind 228 British officers, a number that would grow steadily over the coming months. The admixture of British, French, Polish, Belgian, and Dutch inmates had lent the place a peculiarly cosmopolitan atmosphere. "I'm rather sorry to go," said Van den Heuvel, the Dutch escape officer, whose contingent of sixty-eight officers had achieved no fewer than thirteen "home runs."

The French bequeathed an invaluable legacy. The radio, Arthur II, was handed over "in its stronghold, lock, stock and barrel." The British had known of the French radio's existence, but not where it was located. Before leaving for Lübeck, Frédo Guigues, lock-picker and radio technician of genius, led the British escape officer, Dick Howe, to the hiding place: a secret compartment between the floor of the *Kellerhaus* attics and the ceiling below, complete with desk, upholstered chairs, blankets against the cold, walls lined with wool, electricity diverted from the mains for light and power, and maps to enable the secret listeners to follow the progress of the war. "The French have a flair for comfort and convenience," said Howe, impressed by this well-appointed secret lair beneath the floorboards. Henceforth, a two-man British radio team consisting of an operator and a "scribe" climbed to the attic every evening to hear the BBC news at 7 p.m., while an elaborate system of stooges kept watch. Back in the prisoners' quarters, the scribe would then transcribe the news from his shorthand notes; the bulletin was distributed to each mess, and read out during the evening meal. The Germans knew a radio was in operation: "They searched until they were blue in the face without success." The Bullingdon Club established their mess in the room below, on the logic that the Germans were marginally less likely to raid a place containing the Colditz elite. Only a handful of officers were privy to the precise whereabouts of the radio. Arthur II continued to function, undiscovered, until the end of the war, providing a steady diet of reliable information, a daily morale-sustaining ritual reminding the prisoners they still had a home, and might one day return to it.

The battle within Colditz was now a two-sided conflict between the British and the Germans. There was no longer a danger that an escape plan secretly mounted by one nation might trip up another. Colditz became a British prison: the hierarchy of rank was more pronounced, as was the control exerted by the escape committee, and the opportunity for one-man ventures was reduced. The Dutch Hawaiian band, the French cuisine, and the Polish choir were gone. The informal cultural osmosis between nationalities was over, as was the fruitful Anglo-Dutch partnership and the daily babble of diverse languages in the inner courtyard. Padre Platt noticed that as an all-Anglo prison, the place seemed more cliquey, with "small friendship groups, complete in themselves and almost exclusive." From now on, the plays performed in the theater were strictly British: *The Importance of Being Earnest, Gas Light,* and *Pygmalion.*

A man of cosmopolitan tastes, Reinhold Eggers lamented "the end of Colditz as an international camp," but predicted that the camp would "quieten down" as a result. This, he later admitted, turned out to be "wishful thinking." Eggers longed for the war to end, though he never said so openly. He and the other senior officers were under orders to "keep up appearances no matter what the morale of our men and no matter what the news." But that was getting harder. Secretly, he was also listening to the BBC. In May 1943, his twenty-three-year-old son, a Luftwaffe pilot, was shot down and killed. Eggers told no one. As both a schoolteacher and prison guard, his watchword was "show no emotion." On the outside, he maintained an air of poker-faced assurance, and an upper lip as stiff as any of his British captives.

11

Shabash

Knotted sheets, secret tunnels, and elaborate disguises were not the only way to get out of Colditz. As the war progressed, both sides showed an increased willingness to send their prisoners home via a neutral country. Following the capture of large numbers of German soldiers in North Africa, negotiations over prisoner exchanges started in earnest and by 1943 some British soldiers, including medical orderlies, were being selected for repatriation.

In August, Alex Ross, Douglas Bader's put-upon batman, was approached by one of the friendlier German officers.

"Good news, Ross," he said. "You're going home."

The Scottish orderly was overjoyed. "I was very excited at the prospect. It also meant I could get as far away as possible from Bader." He ran to find the famous flying ace in the courtyard, and breathlessly relayed the news that he would soon be going back to Britain.

"No you're bloody not," said Bader. "Look here, Ross, you came here as my lackey and you will stay with me as my lackey until we are both liberated. That's that." Then he "stomped off," leaving Ross speechless.

"I couldn't believe that he was stopping me going home. He only ever thought of himself and I was nothing to him. Just someone to serve him."

The other orderlies urged Ross to appeal to the SBO, but so ingrained was the habit of obedience, he simply accepted the injustice. "Looking back, I should have complained. But I didn't. In those days, you just didn't go against what an officer said."

Ross would spend another two years lugging the legless RAF officer up and down stairs for his bath.

A few weeks later, Frank "Errol" Flinn attempted suicide, having lost his mind. That, at least, was the impression he gave, both to the Germans and to fellow prisoners. Later, Flinn insisted that he had merely been pretending to have gone mad in the hope of being transferred to another prison from which escape might be easier. But where Flinn's feigned madness ended and real insanity began was never quite clear, even to Flinn himself. By imitating psychosis, he may have sent himself in exactly that direction. In Colditz (as in society as a whole) mental illness was seen as weakness. It is possible that after 170 days in solitary Flinn felt his grip on sanity slipping and tried to pretend he was playacting. His behavior had grown steadily more eccentric since his attempt to pick the lock of the parcels office in broad daylight. He spent long hours meditating, chanting in Sanskrit, and standing on his head: "At that time people didn't look upon yoga as being anything other than a bit round the bend." (Stoolball, in which players beat one another to a pulp, was considered a much saner form of exercise.) Sometimes Flinn was voluble, expounding the new religion he had invented, but mostly he was withdrawn and silent. "If you are sitting at a table with people year in year out, you can only say so many things of interest," he observed. "They all get said. All you do is sit there. You know exactly what the man is going to say the next minute, exactly what he's going to do. It's very easy to get into a state where you don't care about very much." At times Flinn exploded in violence.

"Lieutenant Flinn has been locked up as he is again having mental fits and endangering the life of his comrades," wrote Unteroffizier Schädlich, who witnessed one particularly curious scene. "He was sitting at a table with some others when he suddenly gets up, says 'Excuse me,' goes to the next table, where chess is being played, says 'Excuse me' again, grabs the chess board and smashes it on the head of one of the players so his head sticks through the frame. Without batting an eyelid, he then returns to his table and sits down, having again said a very polite 'Excuse me.'"

One evening, Flinn was found hanging from a noose in the lavatory. "I had this rope around my neck and I put it over the cistern, put one foot on the floor and one on the lavatory seat, so if I wanted to ease the pressure on my throat I could. I made sure I had a good red mark on my throat." Flinn was discovered, and the alarm was raised. "The goons charged up the stairs and saw the red mark and thought I'd tried to kill myself." He subsequently claimed that this episode had also been an act; his fellow inmates believed he had genuinely tried to kill himself, and so did Kommandant Prawitt. A week later, Flinn described being transferred, not to another prison, but to a concentration camp. From his cell, he witnessed scenes of appalling cruelty: "I saw barbed wire and starved-looking people walking about in striped uniforms, emaciated, reaching out, wanting help. They had a glare in their eyes like animals trapped and ready to be killed. Some of them were dying. I was thinking, what is this place? Who are these people?" After a few weeks, he was back in Colditz. Over the coming months, Flinn's madness, real or contrived (or a combination of both), would grow ever more extreme.

In the all-Indian Frontstalag 153 at Chartes, Biren Mazumdar was doing his best to drive the German authorities to distraction by constantly complaining about conditions in the camp and, whenever an opportunity arose, trying to get out of it. "Almost every day I had rows with the German camp commander." He sawed through the bars on a window and scaled the twenty-foot outer wall topped with broken glass, before he was picked up by a floodlight beam and forced to give himself up. Emerged from six weeks in solitary, Mazumdar was awarded the peculiar distinction of a personal guard during daylight hours. "He made my life unbearable and followed me everywhere I went, even to the WC." At night he was locked up, with a handful of other troublemakers, in one half of a three-story block guarded by five Algerian guards with machine guns. Here Mazumdar made his first real friend since his capture: Sowar (Trooper) Dariao Singh of the 2nd Royal Lancers. A Jat Sikh from the Punjab, Singh was a giant of a soldier, well over six feet tall, with a flowing beard and hands the size of soup plates. The two men struck up an immediate bond.

On June 3, 1943, the two Indians broke out of Frontstalag 153. First, Singh gouged an opening through a two-foot-thick wall into the empty part of the building. "The way he made a hole with only makeshift tools was really amazing," wrote Mazumdar. Then they forced their way out of a window that had been nailed shut and sealed with two thick sheets of tin. The camp gate was 500 yards away, across a stretch of ground punctuated by barbed wire fences and illuminated by searchlights. "It was bright as day." They crawled to the first fence, seven strands of thick barbed wire, "with loose wires between them." Singh noiselessly snipped the two bottom wires with a pair of cutters fashioned out of pieces of metal bedpost, and they wriggled underneath. Ten yards farther on was another wire fence. And then another. Whenever the searchlights swept over, they flattened themselves into the earth, which turned to mud as the drizzle grew steadily heavier. Mazumdar felt a surge of hope. The rain would obscure the view of the sentries manning the machine gun posts at either end of the compound. On the other side of a track leading to the German garrison lay another four lines of wire. Singh cut the fences, methodically and silently, one after the other. Finally they reached the iron gate, eighteen feet high and surmounted by more rolls of barbed wire. When the searchlight had passed, Singh climbed to the top, snipped the wire, and hauled Mazumdar up after him. "*Shabash*, Doctor Sahib," he whispered, the Indian word for "bravo." They landed heavily on the other side and slid into the shadows. It had taken three hours to crawl from one side of the camp compound to the other. In the moonlight Mazumdar caught the flash of his companion's wide grin: "*Shabash*," said Singh again, taking the doctor's hand and setting off at a jog. They ran for an hour without stopping, a stout Bengali doctor and an enormous Sikh cavalryman, pounding through the rainy night. "He was absolutely splendid," said Mazumdar. "No words of mine can adequately express his daring, courage and perseverance." Singh hurled his homemade tools into a pond. As dawn broke, they hid in a clump of bushes, waited for nightfall, and agreed on a plan: they would make for the Swiss border, avoid speaking to anyone for as long as possible, and walk only during the hours of darkness. "We were clothed in battledress and had only a few cigarettes and shoes. We possessed neither map nor compass."

They headed south, skirting cities and towns, sleeping during the day in woods and under hedgerows. At last, famished, they steeled themselves to approach a secluded farmstead, where they were taken in, given food and clothing, and then sent on their way, with directions to another place of safety. Mazumdar was astonished and moved by the willingness of the local people to risk their lives by helping them. "We were fed as we had never been during our captivity, and wherever we stayed we received enough to eat. We always sought out isolated farmhouses away from the main road, and we even avoided the secondary roads." Mazumdar spoke passable French, and learned that "eighty percent of the population hate the Germans and the Pétain regime. There is great discontent in the country. The average Frenchman is anxiously awaiting the invasion of France by the Allies. We were given every possible assistance by the French civilians." The peasants welcomed them, offered encouragement and sustenance, and tuned their radios to the BBC so the fugitives could listen to news from a world free of Nazi occupation. Not all of the French were so hospitable. "We were told to avoid rich people, and so it proved to be true." When two dark-skinned foreigners appeared at her château asking for help, the Comtesse d'Impley "threatened to inform the gendarmerie" and slammed the door.

The trek across France by Biren Mazumdar and Dariao Singh is one of the great untold stories of the Second World War: two unmistakably Indian soldiers trudged 900 kilometers in six weeks through Nazi-held territory. Mazumdar later listed the French regions they had crossed, as if reciting one of his poems: "Loiret, Nièvre, Cher, Saône-et-Loire, Jura, Ain." They crossed three rivers, narrowly avoided capture by some civilians guarding a bridge over the Saône, and finally reached the foothills of the Jura, the mountain range between France and Switzerland. Their last host had warned that the border region was heavily policed by German guards. "This was the most difficult part," wrote Mazumdar, who was close to collapse. Even Singh's granite constitution was beginning to crumble. In pouring rain they slogged on, covering the last 100 kilometers in three days. Near the frontier at Dôle, they knocked on the door of a farmhouse. It was opened by an elderly woman, who ushered the famished men inside and sat them down to a meal of bread, cheese, and wine. "We had not eaten for three days and were feeling the strain. We must have appeared to her extremely worn and exhausted, and she begged us to stay for at least a day." The woman explained that the Swiss frontier was a few kilometers to the east and offered to find a trustworthy guide to take them to an unguarded border post in the mountains. Mazumdar hesitated, "knowing the penalty for helping a prisoner of war." But she insisted. The next evening, at sundown, a young boy from the village appeared and this "very charming old lady" waved them off into the deepening dusk. Mazumdar never discovered her name.

At 9 p.m. on July 13, 1943, the pair crossed the border near the village of Malcombe. Three hours later, at around midnight, they reached the Swiss village of La Rippe, and staggered into the police station.

After three years of captivity, the Indian doctor was finally free, his deliverance a tribute to tenacity, luck, and the kindness of strangers. Mazumdar's escape odyssey was over, but his trials were not.

On September 3, 1943, Michael Sinclair, wearing a false handlebar mustache and the fake uniform of a Wehrmacht sergeant major, hurled abuse in fluent German at a nervous sentry while brandishing a bogus internal security pass that was the wrong color. In the rooms above, the clustered British officers could hear Sinclair's voice rising, as he impersonated Stabsfeldwebel Gustav Rothenberger working himself into a rage.

The Franz Josef scheme was the most elaborate escape plan since the French Métro tunnel. More than fifty officers had taken part in the preparations, producing escape equipment for a small army: three perfect uniforms and replica guns for the main participants, as well as thirty-five sets of false papers and civilian clothing for the escapers who would climb down the walls and break out when Sinclair opened the gate. The window bars on the sixth floor of the former British quarters on the east side, now deserted, had been carefully severed over several months, the cuts in the metal concealed with black boot polish. For months, Sinclair had studied the mannerisms, bearing, and thick Saxon accent of Stabsfeldwebel Rothenberger, rehearsing his part under the direction of Teddy Barton, one of Colditz's theatrical producers. It took fifteen attempts to replicate Rothenberger's ginger mustache before the result was sufficiently convincing to be approved by the escape committee. Checko Chaloupka bribed one of his "soft goons" into surrendering his numbered pass for an hour, which was swiftly copied and returned.

The escape had been timed to take place when a "particularly dumb-looking" sentry was known to be on duty at the gate. After the evening roll call, the stooges reported that Rothenberger was safely in the guardhouse. The locks to the old British quarters were picked, and the troop of escapers crept up to the sixth floor. A few minutes before midnight, Sinclair and his two "guards" climbed out of the sickbay window, and onto the terrace. The escapers listened intently, as their boots crunched on the gravel and Sinclair barked commands. At the final gate, the first guard handed over the keys and marched off toward the guardhouse, but the second hesitated, unwilling to leave his post as instructed. The "ivory-headed goon" was not so thick as he seemed, or perhaps so stupid that he could not work out why Stabsfeldwebel Rothenberger was now angrily demanding that he should do something he had previously ordered him not to do. "He won't go," someone whispered in the darkness of the sixth floor. "Why the hell won't he go?" The sentry stared at the pass, and back at the red-faced, mustachioed figure berating him; then he lifted his rifle, pressed the alarm bell, and told the three men to raise their hands. What happened next is disputed.

Sinclair was still loudly remonstrating when the duty officer, Gefreiter "Big Bum" Pilz, rounded the corner of the terrace at a sprint, summoned by the alarm from the guardhouse, with two more guards behind him. Everyone was shouting. "Pilz drew his pistol" in what was later described by the Senior British Officer as a "reckless and gleeful manner." In fact, amid the noise and confusion, he panicked. The British claimed afterward that Sinclair had already raised his hands in surrender. The Germans insisted Sinclair was reaching for his own (fake) pistol.

Pilz aimed his gun and fired, and from a distance of three feet a single 9mm revolver bullet thudded into the chest of Michael Sinclair. He sank to his knees, and then toppled sideways. "Good God," gasped one of the German guards, who was having trouble keeping up with events. "You've shot our sergeant major." It was at this moment that the real Rothenberger, panting heavily, came round the corner and entered a surreal scene, bathed in the artificial glare of the searchlights: six German guards, two with their hands up, a corporal with a smoking gun, and what appeared to be himself, lying dead on the terrace. From the upper floor came howls of fury: "German murderers! You bloody murderers!"

The fallout from the Franz Josef affair reverberated around Colditz for months. Prawitt was "almost beside himself," according to Eggers. The SBO demanded that Pilz be court-martialed for shooting an unarmed man. Prawitt refused, claiming his guard had acted in self-defense; but an internal inquiry was launched and "Big Bum" Pilz was dispatched to the Eastern Front. Eggers was quietly pleased that "for once, one of our sentries did what he had been told to." With typical schoolmasterly wisdom after the event, he claimed that the phony Franz Josef's "mustache was the weak spot." He installed Sinclair's German uniform, bloodstained and bullet-holed, in his museum.

Michael Sinclair survived. No one was more surprised by this than Sinclair himself. The bullet had glanced off a rib, passed through his lung, and exited below his left shoulder blade, missing his heart by three inches. After just a week of convalescence in the hospital at Bad Lausick, the Red Fox was back in Colditz, his arm in a sling, planning his next escape.

The war beyond the castle walls was getting closer. The prisoners could hear it: on the radio, and in the night sky, as Allied bombers pounded the major German cities in the escalating strategic bombing campaign. "Operation Gomorrah" in July saw 9,000 tons of bombs hurled at Hamburg, killing 37,000 people in the most ferocious aerial bombardment the world had ever seen. In October it was the turn of Halle, just fifty miles away, the hometown of Reinhold Eggers. The electricity supply to Colditz was cut off for twenty-four hours. "It was the closest evidence of bombing that we had ever had," wrote Eggers. On a single night in early December, British bombers killed 1,800 residents of Leipzig, just thirty miles to the north, and razed much of the ancient city. Padre Platt observed the "steadily mounting glow" in the distance. As the horizon blazed, the prisoners listened to the carnage with a mixture of elation, awe, and fear. The evening radio roundup brought news of the invasion of Sicily, the Allied landings in mainland Italy, and finally the capitulation of Italy itself and the flight of Mussolini. The prisoners began taking bets on where the "second front" against Germany would be launched from.

The progress of the conflict could be measured in other, less obvious ways. In late August some 2,000 Red Cross parcels arrived, the largest consignment yet, including forty-five parcels of tobacco, coffee from Venezuela, and sugar from Argentina. The prisoners estimated they now had enough food to last for five months, but it was hard to avoid the conclusion that the Red Cross was encouraging prisoners to stock up on essentials, in anticipation of a time when supplies might no longer get through. As the official protecting power, Switzerland sent regular delegations to inspect the camp and ensure that the Geneva Convention was being observed. These noted that while the prisoners were not starving, living conditions were steadily deteriorating, with inadequate electric light and hot water, no fresh vegetables, and shortages of toilet paper. "The walls are so thick that in winter the rooms cannot be sufficiently warmed," noted a Swiss report in October 1943. Yet morale among the prisoners remained high. "These are stubborn characters, embittered due to long imprisonment and humiliations, however with unbroken spirit. They received the Delegate with cordial hospitality, it is a pleasure to meet such men." The same Swiss official noted, however, that "Flight Lieutenant Flinn is in a very bad mental state" and recommended he be moved to another camp "as a matter of urgency." His recommendation was ignored.

The mood in the German garrison, by contrast, was growing darker. Some of the German soldiers had lost their homes or relatives in the bombing raids. Red Cross parcels began disappearing before they were delivered. Hungry guards were increasingly willing to risk trading with prisoners. Eggers noticed "a lot of friction" in the German officers' mess. Those urging tougher measures to keep the prisoners in line took their lead from the Kommandant. Whenever Prawitt was informed of fresh acts of disobedience, his response was draconian: "Why don't you use your gun?" The chief of the German High Command, General Keitel himself, sent a personal letter of commendation to Prawitt, along with official "confirmation of his right to enforce discipline by any and every means." Prawitt's deputy, a strutting little man known as "The Turkeycock," was also "a man of violence," in Eggers's view, itching to show the prisoners "who's boss here." The Germans still had the power of life and death over their captives, and as the possibility of defeat loomed closer, some were keen to exercise it.

Hitherto Colditz had been exclusively the preserve of the Wehrmacht, but the Nazi security services and the SS were becoming more involved in the camp and its occupants. An eighteen-strong squad of SS under the command of the Dresden criminal commissioner appeared one morning and carried out a "mass search" of the castle, but uncovered little. A new "rapid response" unit was installed at nearby Bad Lausick, amid fears that the British might deploy a snatch squad of commandos to try to seize the "special prisoners" from Colditz, including Giles Romilly and Douglas Bader. The British had no such plans, but this sinister deployment was evidence of growing Nazi paranoia: the *Prominente* would not be surrendered without a fight.

By October 1943, the prison population numbered 205 British officers, 14 Australians, 15 Canadians, 33 "Fighting French"— (formally a British auxiliary force)—and 2 ghosts. When RAF pilot Jack Best and navy lieutenant Mike Harvey vanished back in April, the Germans thought they had escaped. In fact, they were hiding in a secret compartment under the chapel pulpit that had once been part of the great French tunnel. At night, they would emerge and be replaced by two other prisoners, while Harvey and Best slept in the vacated beds: the Germans sometimes conducted head counts of sleeping prisoners. They both took the names of other officers, in case they happened to be intercepted by the guards, and circulated like normal prisoners, until the next roll call: Harvey was "D. E. Bartlett" and Best became "Bob Barnes." After an escape, a ghost would take the place of an escaper, to buy time, before disappearing back into the hole. This troglodyte existence took a toll. Best was a chain-smoking ex-farmer from colonial Kenya; a photograph from the time shows a man with the staring eyes of one who has spent too long underground, reading by the dim light of a candle made from cooking fat. In recognition of their sacrifice, the ghosts were bumped to the top of the escaping list.

As autumn turned to winter, into the drab confines of Colditz fluttered a creature of dazzling color and flamboyance: Micky Burn was a journalist, novelist, and poet, a former Nazi sympathizer who had since embraced Marxism, a spoiled, louche, funny, good-looking, feckless man who had displayed astonishing bravery during one of the most daring commando raids of the war. He was also bisexual, openly and actively. The rest of Colditz never quite knew what to make of Micky Burn.

Burn's rich father was the royal family's solicitor. His mother's family had developed the French gambling resort of Le Touquet. Burn grew up, in a grace and favor house provided by the royal family opposite Buckingham Palace, in a world of parties, smart weekends, fast cars, and unmerited admiration. "I only had to lift a finger and it was all laid on." He went to Oxford, where he did no work whatever and was sent down after a year, before breezing into a job at *The Times*, the establishment newspaper. He began a passionate affair with Guy Burgess, the Foreign Office official and communist later exposed as a KGB spy. When Burn confided to his father that he was sexually attracted to men, he was sent to George V's doctor, who gave him Benzedrine injections: these made him hyperactive, but not heterosexual. A love of Wagner's music drew him to Germany in 1933, where he fell under the Nazi spell. "My mix of ignorance, blindness and semi-criminal benevolence, let loose in a world of intensely organized falsehood, turned me into a dupe," he later wrote. The fervent British fascist Unity Mitford introduced him to Hitler, who signed a copy of *Mein Kampf* for the smitten young Englishman. Burn was thrilled by this gift, and immediately lost it. He attended a Nuremberg rally, and breathlessly described the "great lights in the sky, moving music, the rhetoric, the presentation, timing, performance, soundtrack, exultation, and climax. It was almost aimed at the sexual parts of one's consciousness." He found himself sitting next to a Dutch aristocrat, Baroness Ella van Heemstra, with whom he started an affair. After the Nuremberg show, Burn was given a tour of Dachau concentration camp with Mitford and her sister Diana, soon to be married to the British fascist leader Oswald Mosley. Burn entirely (perhaps deliberately) failed to recognize the horror he was witnessing. "I kept trying to convince myself it wasn't as bad as it seemed." But on returning to Britain he spent a week as the paying guest of a Barnsley miner, and for the first time witnessed poverty at close quarters. The scales fell from his eyes with a resounding thump: "What Hitler was offering me as soul-saving was shit." Burn abandoned his right-wing views overnight, and set off on a headlong charge to the left, embracing socialism and then communism as fervently as he had once supported Hitler's National Socialism.

When war came he joined the Special Service Brigade, a volunteer unit formed for commando operations, determined to compensate for his flirtation with fascism by joining the riskiest missions, armed only with "a Jane Austen and a little ammunition." He trained in Scotland until he was "unbearably fit," and then took a leading part in "Operation Chariot," an amphibious attack on the dry dock at St. Nazaire on the Atlantic coast of France, where large German ships put in for repairs. On March 28, 1942, Captain Burn led his unit of twenty-eight commandos on a mission to destroy the port's machinery and gun emplacements while the destroyer HMS *Campbeltown,* disguised as a German ship and laden with delayed-action high explosives, rammed into the dock gates. Half of Burn's troop were killed when their motor launch took a direct hit from a German shell. Burn fought his way ashore, reached the objective alone, and was finally captured with bullet wounds in his arm and thigh, and a shard of shrapnel in his back. "I had led no one, destroyed nothing, protected no one," he wrote, underplaying an episode for which he would be awarded the Military Cross. The Germans published a propaganda image of Burn being led away under guard with his hands raised: the photographer had failed to notice that Burn's left hand was surreptitiously raised in the V for Victory sign, an act of bravery and foolishness that was entirely characteristic. Aware of his earlier sympathy for their cause, the Nazis tried to recruit him as a stool pigeon; when that failed, he was bundled off to Colditz.

"I am now living in a castle, as most of the best people do at this time of year," Burn wrote to his parents.

A few Colditz inmates suspected Burn of being a German spy. Others mistrusted his loudly expressed left-wing views. But as a former pupil at Winchester boarding school he was soon knitted into the strange social fabric of the place. "When I arrived at Colditz I was asked to join this very smart mess nicknamed the Bullingdon, made up of close relations of the royal family, and a few Lords and lairds. None of them knew that I had been blackballed from the real Bullingdon when I was at Oxford." Back in 1930, he had been considered "not the type" for the exclusive club because he was bisexual.

Micky Burn emerged as the radical philosopher-poet of the castle, "a born optimist, and one of the few men in Colditz who never got depressed." He wrote the only good novel to come out of the camp, entitled *Yes, Farewell*, a study of the psychology of prison life that captures the dreary decrepitude of the place, the "smell of musty decay," and the pervasive atmosphere of "tense inactivity." The novel's title bids adieu to the liberal certainties of the pre-war world. Burn wrote poetry, and sent it to his mother, who passed it on to various literary luminaries: J. B. Priestley thought Burn's verses "very promising," but T. S. Eliot considered his poetry "immature, and often awkward." His father was even blunter: "I hate poetry unless it rhymes." As for sex, Burn later asserted that "anything of that sort" was a challenge, since it was "very difficult to find sufficient privacy to make it enjoyable . . . the crowded conditions and a general censure made satisfaction almost hopeless." Almost, but not entirely. Burn would emerge from Colditz convinced (wrongly, as matters turned out) that he was exclusively homosexual. At the age of thirty, Burn feared he was losing his looks. "I now weigh no more than 10 stone. My cheeks have fallen in . . . my hair around the ears has gone the grey of a distinguished stockbroker, and has deserted the temples entirely."

With his reporter's shorthand and journalistic experience, Burn was the natural "scribe" for the nightly news service: every evening, while the jazz musician Jimmy Yule operated the radio, Burn scribbled down the BBC highlights, edited them into readable form, and distributed the result around the various messes. Making up for earlier academic failure, he studied for an Oxford diploma in social sciences; he read the economist John Maynard Keynes, the Beveridge Report of 1942, which would form the cornerstone of Britain's welfare state, and works on employment theory. Burn was determined to try to understand what the postwar world might be like. His views moved further leftward, and he reached a conclusion: the ruling class, of which he was so fortunate a product, was damned and doomed. He learned Russian, and by the end of 1943 declared himself "well on the way to Marxism."

There were unhappy rumblings in the Bullingdon Club over the Red revolutionary in their midst. But one of the *Prominente* found, in Burn, an ideological soulmate. Giles Romilly had hitherto kept his communism if not hidden, then certainly veiled. The two men now made common cause, and began giving joint lectures on Marxist theory. These were well attended, particularly by the orderlies. Some of the more conservative inmates were deeply alarmed by what they saw as communist propaganda. One warned Burn, with mock joviality, that "nice fellow though he was," he would end up "hanging from a lamppost." Another demanded that he be "tried for treason." Douglas Bader called Burn "a dangerous menace," banned his fellow RAF officers from attending Romilly's lectures, and gave his own rival talks on such themes as "Stalin's War Aim—the total military occupation of Germany" and "Opening a Second Front to ensure that Russia does not win the war alone." But the so-called Colditz commies continued to spread the gospel of Marx, exploring this unlikely "foothold of free speech" inside a Nazi prison. The ideological schism reflected and prefigured events in the wider world: a battle between the forces of communism and capitalist democracy, between defenders of the British empire and those who saw it as a crime, between the class warriors and the traditional governing class. As winter fell on Colditz, a shiver of the looming Cold War could be felt inside it.

Micky Burn had no desire to escape, and in this, too, he represented a different way of thinking. "I wasn't interested," he wrote. "I did what I could to help, but I felt someone should consider why we were there at all; why the war had started; why there should be any wars. It gave me a sort of escape within myself without having to get out." Unlike the earliest soldier-prisoners in Colditz, enraged and emasculated to have been captured without much of a fight, many of the newer arrivals had been bloodied before their captivity and felt they had already "done their bit." "I'd seen quite a lot of action," said Michael Alexander, the commando who had sabotaged a German ammunition dump wearing his tennis kit. "I didn't want to escape. They could get on without me quite well." Others quailed at the scale of the challenge. "It would have been too difficult for me to escape from Colditz," said John Watton, an accomplished artist. "I did not consider myself competent to achieve the level of effort and skill required." Most would seize the opportunity to abscond if one arose, and almost all prisoners were willing to contribute to escape efforts, but a growing number were happy to leave the difficult and dangerous business of escaping to a hardened few. And so emerged a new and subtle distinction within the prisoner community, between those determined to escape and others for whom that prospect had receded to the point of near indifference. "Young men have grown old from weariness and hope deferred," Padre Platt wrote in his diary. "Conversation has almost stagnated except for topics of war news, letters, and sex perversion." Every letter from home was avidly devoured. Micky Burn's former lover Ella van Heemstra spotted him in the newsreel of his capture, and sent a photo of herself "to remind you of the good old days!" She was now living under German occupation in Holland, her dalliance with Nazism, like his, a thing of the past. Her teenage daughter, Audrey, was training as a dancer, she told him: "We'll send you tickets for a box on her first night in London," she promised.

The fourth Colditz Christmas came and went, and Reinhold Eggers totted up the escape scores, as he had every year since 1940. Just twenty-six escape attempts had been made in 1943, fewer than half the total of the previous year; only one Frenchman had made it home, and he had done so after being transferred to a hospital outside the camp. Not a single prisoner had managed to escape from inside the castle. A "Christmas Truce" was agreed between prisoners and jailers: there would be no escape attempts between Christmas and New Year's, in return for a German promise to launch no midnight roll calls or searches. The intensity of the struggle between the jailers and the jailed was dissipating; Colditz would never be "escape-proof," as originally intended, but it was far more secure than it had been at the outset; as in the wider war, exhaustion was setting in, along with the faint hope of an ending.

Before Christmas, Allied aircraft launched another massive bombardment of nearby Leipzig. The festive lights that year came in the form of high explosive that engulfed the city in fire, and lit up the night sky: gone were the theaters, most of the university, more than 1,000 commercial buildings, 472 factories, 56 schools, 9 churches, and the Café Zimmermann frequented by J. S. Bach, the backdrop for the first performance of his Coffee Cantata.

While Nazi hardliners still insisted victory was just around the corner, Eggers knew "the end was only a matter of time." Among most of his fellow officers, he detected "a complete lack of confidence in our military and political leaders." Eggers was no defeatist. Like many patriotic Germans he would battle to the end, whatever his private feelings about the Nazi leadership. Yet he had sensed what others were not prepared to put into words: a gradual, almost imperceptible shift in the balance of power within the camp.

"How was it all going to end?" Eggers wrote. "A catastrophe for Germany was inevitable."

1944

12

The Dentist Spies

The escape hiatus came to a dramatic end on January 19, when two burly officers hoisted up one end of a long, highly polished table, and the man lying on it, wearing a balaclava helmet and with a ninety-foot rope tied around his waist, slid down the makeshift launchpad at high speed and shot out of the second-floor window feetfirst into the darkness. Michael Sinclair was attempting another escape, his seventh.

Fully recovered from the bullet wound to his chest, Sinclair had spent months studying the western side of the castle where the British were now quartered, pipe clamped between his teeth, suffused in smoke and deep in thought: finally, he spotted a gap in the German security cordon. Beneath the windows ran the upper terrace with a balustrade; thirty feet below that was a lower walkway, the garden terrace; this was protected by a wire perimeter fence, beyond which the ground fell away steeply for a hundred feet into the back gardens of the town. At night, the side of the castle was lit up by powerful floodlights. Shortly before these were switched on at dusk, the guards transferred from their day to night positions: this meant that for roughly one minute, the upper terrace and the face of the building were unobserved, and in semi-darkness.

Sinclair's companion in this escape attempt would be an RAF lieutenant, Jack Best, one of the "ghosts" promoted up the escaping list by dint of having hidden undetected for nine months.

At 5 p.m., on a "dull, dark evening with a little rain," the men took up their positions. The stooges gave the "all-clear," and Sinclair slid down the table and out of the window, dressed entirely in black, with socks over his shoes and a pair of wire cutters strapped to his left leg. The rope, laboriously stitched out of bedsheets, uncoiled with a fizz; just before Sinclair hit the ground, two strong officers braced at the other end and he landed almost silently. In a couple of paces he was over the balustrade, and being lowered down to the second terrace. Best slid down after him. Sinclair cut the three strands of the wire fence; they wriggled through and scrambled down the bank. "It was a forty-five degree slope of shale with eighteen inches of barbed wire all over it which ripped our clothes to shreds," Best recalled. At the bottom, they climbed over the roof of a garden shed and dropped into a cottage back garden, while a woman stared at them in astonishment from a rear window. Then they walked off down the main street of Colditz. The floodlights came on just in time for the guard to see a ninety-foot rope being hauled back up the building into a second-floor window. The episode immediately became known as the "sixty-second escape." It was, declared an admiring Eggers, "a quite fantastic affair."

In the Colditz woods, the pair patched the worst holes in their civilian clothes and set off for Grossbothen station: there they boarded a train for Dessau, another to Minden, and then a third toward Osnabrück. At Rheine, near the Dutch border, they were stopped by a policeman. Best's pallid complexion, after so long underground, gave them away: "He told us that my face and hat had aroused his suspicions as they did not look Teutonic." The Gestapo accused them of being spies. "We were kept overnight in a cell with the walls caked with blood," but finally they were released to the army authorities.

Yet again, Michael Sinclair trudged back through the gates of Colditz, and into the solitary cells. For "Bob Barnes," however, this was a first recapture. That was the false identity Best had been living under since his disappearance into the bowels of Colditz, and he now reassumed it, while the real Barnes went into the hole beneath the chapel. Two months later, Eggers finally cracked the ghost mystery. In March, two officers were found hiding inside an air raid shelter in the mistaken belief that it had a secret underground exit. One was "Bush" Parker, the Australian lock-picker; the other gave his name as Bartlett, but by means of an early photograph Eggers worked out that the man in front of him was really Mike Harvey, who was supposed to have escaped a year before. And if Harvey was still inside the camp, where was Best, the man who had disappeared with him? Eggers issued a photograph of Best to his guards and told them to memorize the face. "Get this officer," he said. "Go in when they're all having their tea. That's when you'll find him." Sure enough, Best alias Barnes was found leaning against a wall, sipping a cup of tea. The two ghosts had managed to evade detection for a year, successfully missing 1,326 roll calls. Eggers was impressed. "It was a hell of a story." The army command in Berlin refused to believe it. Rather than admit they had been duped, the authorities arrived at the hilarious conclusion that the two men *had* escaped back in April 1943, but found it impossible to get out of Germany and had then secretly broken back *into* the castle. Kommandant Prawitt exploded: "Is this place a damned hotel where people come and go as they wish? It's nearly as difficult to get in here as it is to get out!"

After more than three years inside, some prisoners were starting to decay mentally—and dentally.

Julius Green was a Jewish dentist from Glasgow who injected irony into every aspect of his life, as an anesthetic against the miseries of Colditz. A captain in the Army Dental Corps, he measured out his war in impacted wisdom teeth and carious molars, extractions, fillings, mended dentures, and improvised crowns. His surgical equipment consisted of a foot drill, a few probes, mouth mirrors, and filling instruments, a pair of forceps, and a syringe salvaged from a medical truck during the retreat to Dunkirk. Mostly, he used pliers. "The average visit for extraction lasted only a minute or so," wrote Green, whose technique for removing rotten teeth was "a very quick and purposeful movement" before the victim knew what was happening. His patients left "sometimes swearing gratitude and sometimes just swearing." Green turned whatever he could scavenge to dental use. He made cement fillings from building plaster, and false teeth from acrylic resin that he bartered from the guards in exchange for Red Cross supplies. In lieu of gas, he believed that the best way of preparing prisoners for dental work was to make them laugh. When he wasn't mending, making, or pulling teeth, Julius Green thought about food, of which he was extremely fond. At night he lay recalling meals he had eaten in the past and imagining those he might consume in the future. By the middle of 1943, after three years "in the bag" in various camps, Green's legs were swollen from edema and he had lost two and a half stone from amebic dysentery, but he sustained himself by drawing up make-believe menus for the meals he might be eating were he a free man. The other prisoners adored him. They called him "Toothy" or "Toothwright," or, after a particularly painful session, "Fucking Toothwright."

Green insisted he was "a devout and practicing coward, a short-sighted, flat-footed dentist with a tendency to overweight." This was camouflage: the Jewish Scotsman with the infectious giggle was not only a fine dentist and an exceptionally brave man, but a secret agent for British intelligence.

At the outbreak of war, two years after graduating from the Dental School at Edinburgh's Royal College of Surgeons, Green left his home in Fife, reported to the 152 (Highland) Field Ambulance unit of the 51st Highland Division in Dundee, and then marched off to France in his kilt. The twenty-seven-year-old dentist assumed this conflict would be much like the last: "A nice easy positional war with forward trenches and weekends in Paris." As the German forces swiftly advanced and the French and British were thrown back, Green found plenty to do, and plenty to eat. One day in June 1940, he was sitting down to a banquet laid on by a local mayor consisting of "*potage aux légumes, filet de veau normand* and *fraises des bois au Champagne*"; the next he found himself trying to patch up soldiers with appalling facial injuries, "removing any pieces of shrapnel, completely dislodged teeth and other debris, and temporarily wiring and bandaging to support their mandibles." Many men owed their faces to Green and his rustic battlefield surgery. Two days later, with the British army in pell-mell retreat, the dentist was wandering the streets of Saint-Valery-sur-Somme looking for casualties, when he turned a corner and walked into a German tank. A Panzer officer emerged from it and pointed a pistol at Green's then ample stomach.

"You are a prisoner," he said.

"I did not see any point in arguing," he wrote.

On his way to captivity, Green recalled, "one of Hitler's supermen belted me in the base of the spine with his rifle butt." The dentist would suffer back pain for the rest of his life. "It was beginning to dawn on me that this was going to be a pretty grim war."

For the next three years, Captain Green traveled between POW camps, performing dental work on both prisoners and guards, as well as other surgical procedures, including gangrene amputations. "I don't mind the sight of blood so long as it isn't mine," he observed. His services were in high demand. People tend to confide in dentists, partly to delay the moment when they have to "open wide." In 1941, Green was approached by a subaltern who told him "there was a way of communicating with home" and asked whether he would be prepared to collect "useful information" from his patients, including the German ones, that might be of interest to London. Green was inducted into the secret of the "5-6-O code" (see Appendix), and swiftly became one of the most prolific coded letter-writers of the war: these were dispatched to family members in Dunfermline, then forwarded to the War Office and sent on to MI9. Airey Neave had never met Green and yet, through the magic of code, they were now secret pen pals.

Green gathered information on German troop movements, railway and shipping timetables, the latest news about U-boats and the Luftwaffe, clues to Germany's industrial production, civilian morale, and much more. While sitting in the dentist's chair, recaptured escapers passed on whatever they had gleaned from the outside. Back in London, British intelligence compiled shopping lists for the peripatetic dentist, which were sent on by his family in coded letters drafted by MI9. "I was getting replies to my signals and requests for specific items." Green's letters home made little sense, but the War Office reassured the family: "You will see that your son refers to certain matters which will have no meaning for you. These remarks are intended for us, so please do not worry about them, nor refer to them in any way when replying to your son. We are very glad to tell you that your son is continuing to do most valuable work." Using homemade secret ink, he drew a map on a standard War Office letter form, indicating the precise location of bombing targets, including railway sidings, army barracks, and factories. MI9 was delighted with his productivity: "Congratulations on really excellent work keep it up." He knew the risk he was running: if the Germans discovered what he was doing, "the enemy would be quite cross and the best you could hope for would be a relatively quick demise." During the day, the dentist-spy extracted teeth and information, and at night he dreamed of bread-and-butter pudding with custard.

In January 1944, Julius Green was abruptly moved to Colditz. Reinhold Eggers greeted him in the courtyard, as he did all newly arriving officers.

"What is this place?" asked Green.

"Oflag IV-C, Colditz," said Eggers. "This is a *Sonderlager*, a special camp."

Green had heard of Colditz, the camp for unruly prisoners, and the name set running a series of conflicting emotions: "It was a photo finish between panic and pride, with curiosity a short head behind."

The dentist never knew quite why he had been sent there. Perhaps his secret activities had been discovered. Alternatively, he suspected the censors might have intercepted a letter in Hebrew he had received from a Jewish prisoner in another camp, and drawn the obvious conclusion. Green described himself as a "more or less practicing Jew," but the Wehrmacht prison authorities had hitherto seemed oblivious to the fact. The real reason for his transfer was probably nothing to do with either his Judaism or his espionage. A few weeks earlier, Green told a German security officer that the British secret service had discovered a revolutionary new way to pass secret messages, "by crossing carrier pigeons with parrots and giving them verbal messages, so if they are shot down they can't talk." The German duly reported this breakthrough in avian wartime communications to his Kommandant, and entirely failed to see the funny side when it was pointed out that this was a typical British joke. Green's "unfortunate sense of humor" had been "sufficient to get in to Colditz."

"Toothy" Green set up his dental surgery in the sickbay and swiftly became a popular figure in Colditz even though, as he wrote, "the lack of equipment and anaesthetics made my ministrations less than pleasant." Despite being unmarried and probably a virgin, he combined dental work with the role of relationships counselor, advising his patients on their romantic and marital anxieties: "I suppose an onlooker gets a better picture of the game, even if he doesn't play, than a participant." He baked cakes from ground millet and discovered that adding an indigestion tablet to water in which dried peas were boiled made them softer and more palatable. "This was my greatest contribution towards gracious living in Colditz," he wrote.

Green's arrival meant that Checko Chaloupka could no longer wangle a visit to the town dentist and a carnal encounter with his "favorite popsy" by bashing his own teeth with a rock. That relationship, however, continued to blossom, based on a heady combination of sexual attraction, epistolary romance, and espionage: in one of those odd coincidences that history occasionally produces, Julius Green was not the only dentist-spy in Colditz.

Irmgard Wernicke was much more than just an infatuated dentist's assistant. The Nazi Party still held a firm grip on Colditz town and the surrounding country. Irma's father was a senior party official, and most of her neighbors were keen party members. Every November, on the anniversary of the National Socialists' ascent to power, the town held a celebration, with a parading brass band and much cheering. "Several of us were detailed to attend the Party Show down in the town," Eggers noted sourly. As the war news worsened "in many towns these celebrations were called off. Not so, however, in Colditz." But some of the townsfolk were not Nazis. Particularly among the younger generation, there was growing resistance to the regime, a secret alliance of people profoundly opposed to Hitler, longing for his downfall and secretly preparing for it. One of them was Irmgard Wernicke.

Irma had access to lots of useful information. She had lived in Colditz all her life and knew everyone in the town. Richard Wernicke's Nazi friends and colleagues frequently gathered at the family home, where their host's attractive daughter served beer and schnapps, and listened. The dentist's waiting room was a hotbed of local gossip. Irma began to collect useful nuggets of intelligence and passed them on to her imprisoned lover in the castle above the town: the layout of the town, train times, hiding places in the countryside. The guard who had condoned their first kiss was willing to act as a go-between, carrying what appeared to be love letters back and forth. (The town baker also proved amenable to bribery. "During the winter of '43 this girl supplied up to 20 loaves of bread daily, which were brought into the camp by the German soldier," Chaloupka wrote.) In June 1944, Colonel Tod, the new Senior British Officer, instructed Checko to use his "reliable anti-Nazi contact in the village," as well as the softer goons, to "find out everything that was going on in the camp." Like many spies, Irma's romantic feelings entwined with her ideological inclinations. "I obtained a great deal of information from Fräulein Wernicke," Chaloupka later wrote, "and passed it on to the escape committee." Irma was taking a far greater risk than Checko himself. He was protected by the Geneva Convention. She was not. Her neighbors, and probably her family, would have turned her in to the Gestapo without hesitation had they discovered what the demure dentist's assistant was really up to. Having a relationship with a prisoner was hazardous enough, but working as a secret agent for the British was a task so dangerous that only someone besotted, fearless, or fanatically anti-Nazi would have undertaken it: and Irma was all three.

Julius Green combed through the intelligence collected by Checko and extracted whatever might be of interest to MI9: in coded letters, the information passed under the eyes of the German censors and then onward to a little village in Fife. The prisoners now had their own fully functioning espionage network, with its roots in dentistry.

But Checko's "repeated dental appointments" did not escape the notice of Reinhold Eggers. The "excessive contact" between the dentist's "attractive assistant" and the "tall, dark, and handsome" Czech officer had seemed harmless enough at first, an impossible long-distance flirtation, but as time passed Eggers "suspected that the girl's soft heart must have provided something more than love letters for her amorous airman." He resolved to keep an eye on young Irmgard Wernicke.

In February 1944, Eggers was promoted to the rank of Senior Security Officer, reporting directly to the Kommandant. In reality, he already fulfilled the role of chief jailer. "I was the only person who could do the job properly," he wrote. "I had been in Colditz over three years, knew practically all the inhabitants by sight, and was familiar with the details of nearly every escape that had ever taken place." He could not resist a glow of pride, for Eggers was now the longest-serving Colditz officer, the last of the old guard: Stabsfeldwebel "Mussolini" Gephard had been sent to the Eastern Front, and never returned; Unteroffizier "Dixon Hawke" Schädlich was deployed to Italy, where he, too, perished. The additional responsibility meant more work, but Eggers was eager to make an impact in his new position as security chief. "It was a relief to be busy on this small battle-front," he wrote. "It momentarily enabled me to ignore the mounting catastrophe outside."

New prisoners continued to arrive throughout the spring, sometimes in groups, more often in ones and twos. On March 8, 1944, Eggers escorted through the gates a young naval officer with a broad, handsome, rather empty face and a distracted air. His name was Walter Purdy, a twenty-two-year-old sub-lieutenant from Barking in Essex, who had worked as an engineer aboard merchant ships before being transferred to a Royal Navy armed cruiser, the *Van Dyck*. He was captured in June 1940, when the ship was sunk off Narvik during the disastrous Norway campaign. Julius "Toothy" Green recognized Purdy from Marlag camp, where both had been imprisoned in 1941, and offered to show him around Colditz. Chatty as ever, Green inquired why Purdy had been sent to a place for "escapees and people not generally liked by the Germans." Purdy replied that he had indeed escaped, and then lived "with a bird" in Berlin before being recaptured. He asked Green the same question. "I think they suspect me of being a Jew," the Scottish dentist replied, "and they may have rumbled that I was concerned in the code-letter business." Purdy was now listening intently. Green proceeded to describe how secret messages were hidden in ordinary letters, or passed on to a friendly German guard who posted them to an address in Switzerland. "As he was a British officer whom I had previously known, I did not think any harm could be done in talking to him," said Green. The two men were passing through the British quarters on the first floor of the *Kellerhaus* when an officer, covered in dust, suddenly emerged from beneath a window seat. This was the mouth of a tunnel known as "Crown Deep": it started below the window and dropped twenty feet inside the wall to the bottom of the circular staircase. "We had been working for several months and had made fair progress," recalled the tunneler, Ian Maclean. "Purdy saw me coming out of the trap after completing my shift . . . he appeared very interested in the activities and mentioned that it was a very good trap." Green continued the guided tour. On the top floor of the British quarters, concealed beneath a built-in bedside cupboard, was the "Colditz Bank," the best hiding place in the castle, which held 2,250 Reichsmarks, 4,500 French francs, forged passes, two sacks of clothing, tools, and a miniature radio constructed by Clayton Hutton of MI9 and recently smuggled in via the parcels office. Eggers got wind of the escapers' "treasury" and had spent the last three years searching for the hoard. One of the occupants later recalled that "someone was getting something out of it just as Purdy went through the room."

That evening Green and Purdy sat side by side as Micky Burn read out the evening BBC news bulletin. The new arrival was deeply impressed that the prisoners had successfully rigged up a secret radio.

Green was beginning to get a queasy feeling about Purdy. He seemed "strange and jittery," and his escape story "sounded a bit thin." The harder Green pressed him for details, the jumpier Purdy became. The dentist passed on his misgivings to his seniors, and the next morning Purdy was interrogated, first by the camp's internal security committee, and then by the stern-eyed

Senior British Officer, Willie Tod. Purdy tried to bluff it out, elaborating on the account he had told Green: he claimed that after escaping he had found refuge with a friend of his sister's, a milliner in Berlin, until her home had been bombed and he had been pulled from the debris, only to be arrested by the Gestapo. With each embellishment, the story sounded less credible. Green gently took Purdy aside and advised him to "make a clean breast of it."

A few moments later, he confessed: "I've behaved like a rat and a traitor."

Purdy's journey to treason started in 1937 at a meeting of the British Union of Fascists in Ilford. The merchant seaman precisely fitted the profile of people being recruited by Oswald Mosley's fascist party, being young, racist, angry, and very gullible. Purdy was intoxicated by the anti-Semitic oratory of the speaker that day, an American-born brawler and bigot named William Joyce, Mosley's Director of Propaganda. Purdy's fascist leanings survived capture, and early in 1941 the German security officer at Marlag camp spotted the young naval officer reading *Twilight over England,* a book written by Joyce extolling the virtues of Nazi Germany and predicting Britain's defeat. By this time Joyce had moved to Berlin, adopted German citizenship, and become infamous as the radio voice of "Lord Haw-Haw," broadcasting virulent propaganda blaming the war on international Jewry and urging Britain to surrender: the role the Germans had tried, and failed, to persuade Mazumdar to undertake. The German security officer offered to have Purdy's book signed by its author. In May 1943, Purdy was taken to Berlin to meet Joyce himself, who offered a deal to his fellow British fascist: if Purdy made ten broadcasts, within a period of five weeks, "he would be allowed to escape to a neutral country." Purdy readily agreed. Joyce's wife, Margaret, was unimpressed by her husband's new recruit, considering him "dotty, without much brains, and what he had was in a whirl." But the Nazis needed every British fascist they could get, and Purdy became "a willing and enthusiastic" employee of the Büro Concordia, the German radio station broadcasting black propaganda to Britain. Using the adopted name "Robert Wallace," Purdy read out whatever was put in front of him. It was grim stuff: "This is British Radio National, the only entirely uncensored radio station run by Englishmen . . . These Jewish armament kings are sending the youth of the world to their death. They are prolonging the war so they may profit. We have no quarrel with the Germans . . . Jews are the power behind the government, the real culprits and instigators of this futile war without end." People in Britain were officially discouraged from listening, yet some six million tuned in to hear, and mock, the vicious rantings of "Lord Haw-Haw" and "Robert Wallace": "Germany calling. Germany calling. Germany calling . . ."

For almost a year, Purdy lived a most enjoyable life in Berlin. He was paid 400 marks a week. He started a relationship with a pastry cook named Margaret Weitemeier, known as Gretel, and moved into her flat. "An exceptionally good Christmas with Gretel," Purdy wrote in his diary. "Plenty to drink." He had the SS emblem tattooed on one arm. Gretel taught him German. He made her pregnant. The German authorities flattered Purdy, calling him "the man with the golden voice," and, as it so often happens, a tiny amount of celebrity went straight to his head. "He was a most conceited and loud-mouthed individual," said another POW briefly employed at the Büro Concordia. "He told me he was a first-class broadcaster, much sought after by other German radio stations."

In March 1944, Purdy was told he was going to Colditz. It is not clear whether the Wehrmacht ordered him to work as a stool pigeon or if he volunteered for the task, but, either way, Eggers was delighted, observing: "I had a chance, this time a real chance, of an agent of my own, to pass back to me such information on escape and security matters as he could collect in the camp." With a spy among the British prisoners, Eggers could ensure that no one ever escaped again.

The security officer traveled to Berlin to brief Purdy before his arrival. Their conversation was an odd one.

"Who's going to win this war?" asked Eggers.

"England, of course," Purdy replied.

"What's going to happen to you then?"

"Oh, I'll go back home and spread National Socialism in England."

Purdy appeared to have no conception of the gravity of what

he had already done, and the further treachery he was about to commit. It is unclear whether the young officer was motivated by greed, lust, fear, or fascist ideology. But on one aspect of his character there is no debate: Walter Purdy was incredibly stupid.

The stool pigeon had been in place less than twenty-four hours before being exposed and making a full confession. He now made another spectacular blunder.

"If you are allowed to remain in the camp, will you give an understanding that you will do nothing prejudicial to British interests?" asked Colonel Tod.

Purdy considered this question for a moment before replying: "I cannot do that . . . if the Germans ask me to give them information in return for my liberty, I could not resist that. I want to get back to my woman in Berlin."

Not only had Purdy admitted to spying on his fellow officers, he was too thick to conceal that he intended to continue doing so. Which gave Tod little choice over what happened next. He ordered Captain David Walker to put on his uniform, place Purdy under close arrest, and bring him for court-martial. Walker described Purdy as "a haunted, spent creature, anyone's tool, yet dangerous." Everyone understood what the outcome of a trial would be—except, perhaps, Purdy himself.

A rougher sort of justice was meanwhile being prepared. Feelings were running high in the British quarters, and an ugly atmosphere was spreading. Dick Howe, the escape officer, approached Gris Davies-Scourfield.

"What do you think of this fellow Purdy?"

"Not much," came the reply.

"Some of us think he is a traitor and should be hanged. I've got some volunteers assembling in one of the rooms in the attic and we're going to string him up."

Davies-Scourfield described a macabre scene. "Upstairs in this little room there were people sitting round and a rope was swung over a beam in position. The wretched Purdy was being held between two stalwart officers."

Howe addressed the assembled group. "We are all here because we agree that it is our very painful duty to carry out the hanging of the traitor Purdy. He came here as a stool pigeon, and unless we put him away for good and all he'll be taken away by the Germans and sent to another camp, and discover more secrets. So it is quite clearly our duty to do it, is it not?"

This speech was greeted with a mumble of agreement. Howe was not alone in advocating summary justice. Davies-Scourfield felt the same. So did Michael Sinclair.

"Right," said Howe. "All we need is a couple of volunteers to do the deed."

This suggestion was met with silence. There might be a general accord that Purdy deserved to hang, but no one was actually willing to perform the execution, including Howe himself. It was, said Davies-Scourfield, a "very British situation": an agreement in principle that nobody wanted to put into practice.

The lynch mob mood dissipated. Purdy was escorted back to his room.

Colonel Tod, meanwhile, demanded an urgent meeting with the Kommandant.

"Purdy must be removed from the presence of British officers. He is a stool pigeon," said Tod.

"I will not have him moved," replied Prawitt.

Here the Kommandant's adjutant broke in: "But Purdy will be safe, will he not?"

Tod said he could guarantee no such thing. "Having worked for the Germans, he is no longer a British officer. You have been warned of what may happen, and it's your affair now."

Within the hour, Purdy was whisked to the safety of a solitary cell in the *Kommandantur*, where he demanded Red Cross chocolate, and lots of cigarettes.

He was still there when Eggers uncovered the stash beneath the cupboard. "We found their main hoard," crowed Eggers. "I had always hoped I would find that money." He also unearthed a still for brewing moonshine, parts for constructing a typewriter, and the miniature radio, "the first ever discovered in any POW camp." (Eggers remained unaware of Arthur II, the inherited French radio in the attic.) A few hours later a squad of German soldiers with sledgehammers broke into the wall at the foot of the staircase, exposing the Crown Deep tunnel and the shaft to the window seat above. Eggers later claimed he had been "acting on a hunch," and that the only useful information provided by Purdy concerned the unidentified guard willing to post letters outside the camp. But the prisoners had no doubt Purdy had passed on everything he had seen and learned since his arrival. As Eggers was walking through the courtyard, Douglas Bader bellowed from an upper window: "Pay the fellow who gave the hole away with your own food parcels and not with ours!" If the stool pigeon had still been in the hands of the prisoners, he would have been lynched. Alerting the Kommandant that Purdy had been unmasked probably saved his life.

After a few weeks, Purdy was removed from his cell and escorted back to Berlin, to resume his comfortable existence of collaboration, broadcasting to Britain and living with Gretel the pregnant pastry cook.

Some felt that Purdy had deserved to die hanging from the rafters in the attics. "We had failed in our duties," wrote Davies-Scourfield. But others were relieved the traitor had been removed "to keep anyone from doing him up good and proper," as Green put it. The gentle dentist was not ready to forgive Purdy, particularly given the secrets he had unwittingly revealed to him, but he did try to understand the man. Purdy was "a poor, unbalanced fool, a weak character who, for the sake of food, comfort and the use of a woman, had helped the enemy propaganda and betrayed his comrades." David Walker, the officer who arrested him, was also glad to see Purdy leave Colditz alive: "I never did like the idea of executing people for their beliefs, however misguided." The British courts would take a less lenient view.

"Toothy" Green had an additional reason to worry about which secrets Purdy had told the Germans. During his incautious conversation with the spy, Green had mentioned he was Jewish, and Judaism was potentially a death sentence. Green had seen gangs of Jewish slave laborers on his dental rounds between camps, and at one railway station he heard "the moaning of Jews locked in cattle tracks at a siding," bound for Auschwitz. He had already destroyed the identity disc identifying him as Jewish, reflecting: "The less the Germans concerned themselves about me, the better Mrs. Green's boy liked it." Eggers was either unaware that Green was Jewish, or more likely he did not care. But a letter had recently arrived from an aunt in Scotland relaying gossip from the synagogue. Green was hauled in front of the German doctor and ordered to take his trousers down for "an examination." Green could hardly disguise the fact that he had been circumcised, but he claimed the operation had taken place "in later life" for medical reasons. He vowed he was a Presbyterian Scot and pretended to be offended at the suggestion he was Jewish. The German doctor was openly skeptical. "It is not easy to date a circumcision," wrote Green, "and apparently faced with this problem the German medical officer let it go." As ever, Green made light of it, but this had been an unpleasant encounter, and it did not bode well.

Hitherto, POW camps run by the German army had been comparatively safe places to be a Jew, and hitherto anti-Semitism in Colditz had gone no further than a willingness to confine French-Jewish officers to the attic "Ghetto." But this apparent indifference was unlikely to continue. The Holocaust was plumbing new depths of savagery, and at some point the attention of the anti-Semitic butchers could turn to the prisoner population. Toothy Green did not wish to be around when that moment came. So in March 1944 he decided to go mad.

13

Madness

Prisoners who were certifiably maimed, incapacitated, or seriously unwell were now eligible for repatriation. The Medical Commission of the Swiss Red Cross assessed which POWs were sufficiently sick, injured, or disturbed to return home, and made recommendations to the prison authorities. Sorting out the genuine cases from the malingerers was a tricky task, for prisoners were willing to go to extremes to appear seriously ill: swallowing soap or tin foil to mimic tuberculosis, or eating cigarettes to color the skin yellow suggesting liver failure. In one camp a man injected his penis with condensed milk, using a fountain pen, to simulate gonorrhea. MI9 connived with the medical subterfuge, dispatching a game of checkers to Colditz with a piece that unscrewed to reveal a pill "which generated symptoms of jaundice." Evidence of serious mental illness was also considered grounds for being sent home.

Here was Green's opportunity. "I boned up on the symptoms of paranoia and started a campaign which I had cleared with the senior medical officer." He claimed to be dying of indigestion, and exhibited extreme neurosis whenever the Germans were watching. He read *Vanity Fair* a dozen times until he could recite large chunks from memory, and did, *ad nauseam*. It became easier to insert secret messages into his letters, since these increasingly made no sense at all. He wandered around the courtyard insisting that all the other prisoners in Colditz were potty, and only he was sane. He appeared before the prison doctor "wearing only my boots, socks and glasses," and loudly declared that he was being held against his will among a group of lunatics with "barbed wire fever." The doctor "made soothing noises, and after examining my chest and making sure I was not homosexual, I was dismissed."

Two weeks later, Green was told that he and Frank Flinn were going to Leipzig to be examined by Professor Wagner, a celebrated psychiatrist at the university. A peculiar quartet boarded the train at Colditz: a dentist pretending to be mad, an RAF officer on the very cusp of real insanity, and two "extremely apprehensive" armed guards, who had been told they would be held responsible if these two madmen tried to kill themselves, or each other.

No sooner had the train pulled out than Green shouted: "I am the only normal man in Colditz."

"Be quiet," said Flinn. "You're sick."

"Who's sick, you crazy bastard?" shouted Green, lurching to his feet.

Flinn leaped up and the two prisoners set upon each other, fists flailing. "The guards threw themselves on us and pushed us back on to our seats." Green and Flinn were moved as far apart as the small compartment would allow, with the sentries forming a human barrier between them. "The rest of the journey we spent glowering at one another."

Allied bombs had reduced Leipzig to a wasteland of ruins and rubble. "Look what your communist Jewish Churchill has done to our city!" shouted an old man as the British prisoners were marched through the desolation at gunpoint. Trudging past the wreckage of the Deutsche Credit-Anstalt, headquarters of one of Germany's oldest banks, Flinn let out a shout of triumph. "Bloody good bombing! The bastards have asked for it!" The civilians picking through the debris stared angrily.

"Shut up, Flinn," hissed Green. "Do you want to get us lynched?"

Green was no longer in doubt: Flinn was completely unhinged.

Professor Wagner ushered Green into his consulting room with a courtly bow. The psychiatrist was "a tall, slim, distinguished-looking man" with an air of detached amusement.

"Do you cry? Are you depressed?" he asked, as soon as Green was seated.

"I don't cry," Green replied. "But who wouldn't be depressed being locked up with a crowd of loonies who dislike me because I am sane?"

The professor took copious notes as Green ran through his repertoire of fake insanities.

Finally the German doctor rose, and solemnly announced: "I will recommend you go before the commission."

Their eyes met, the psychiatrist and the dentist, and then Wagner did something that very nearly sent Green into a fit of giggles: "I will swear he winked."

On May 6, 1944, the Red Cross Medical Commission arrived in Colditz, consisting of four medical officers, two Swiss and two German, accompanied by Rudolf E. Denzler, the Swiss government official responsible for overseeing relations between POWs and the camp authorities.

Denzler was by now a familiar visitor in Colditz, a "funny, tall, untidy sort of fellow," balding and stooped, who frequently left "spots of blood on his collar where he cut himself shaving" and wore a pair of pince-nez on the end of his nose. Belying his scruffy appearance, the Swiss diplomat was a man of painstaking precision when it came to rules and regulations. Under international legal custom, when countries are at war, defending the interests of those countries inside the territory of the enemy usually falls to a third nation, or "protecting power." By 1944, neutral Switzerland was acting inside the Reich for thirty-five nations, including Britain and the United States. The protecting-power section of the Swiss legation was based in what had been the U.S. embassy in Berlin. Denzler was responsible for British and American POWs and civilian internees, and he insisted on doing everything by the book; the book, in this case, being the Geneva Convention of 1929, which Denzler had memorized and held in almost biblical reverence. He saw his role as that of an arbitrator, informing the Germans when they were violating the Convention and ensuring the prisoners' rights were known to them, and respected. "In many cases differences of opinion could be successfully sorted out on the spot, either due to concessions by the Wehrmacht or suitable explanations of the POWs' rights and obligations." Whenever a serious dispute arose, Denzler was summoned to mediate: "Thanks to the patience and hardly sur-passed tolerance of Captain Eggers, these confrontations often ended in refreshing humor," he wrote.

Over the course of the war, Denzler visited forty-two different POW and work camps, and wrote up 350 separate reports. He spoke fluent officialese in three languages. He was punctilious and ferociously precise. In most people, bureaucratic pedantry is annoying; but Rudolf Denzler's nitpicking was nothing short of heroic.

A total of twenty-nine officers were selected to appear before the medical commission: some were genuinely incapacitated or seriously ill; others were faking it to "work their ticket" home; and a few, like Frank Flinn, dwelled somewhere in the psycho-logical no-man's-land in between. Douglas Bader, whose tin legs made him the most famously disabled soldier of the war, was on this list, along with Kit Silverwood-Cope, whose brutal treat-ment in Pawiak prison had left him with thrombosis. The day before the commission arrived, the German army authorities, without explanation, struck six names off the list. This provoked a ferocious row, and something close to outright mutiny at the next roll call. Rudolf Denzler demanded to know why the names had been removed. Kommandant Prawitt called Berlin. The Wehrmacht backed down, and the names were reinstated in what Eggers considered a "100 percent capitulation."

The outcome of Frank Flinn's interview was a foregone con-clusion. Everyone in Colditz, British and German alike, believed he had lost his mind. For months, Denzler and the other Swiss inspectors had been urging his removal on medical grounds. His behavior, merely eccentric at the start, had become ever more er-ratic and violent. "Errol" Flinn was no longer acting, if he ever had been. During four years of imprisonment, he had spent six months in solitary. He knew that this would be his last escape attempt. Flinn had decided that if he was turned down for repa-triation, he would make "a dive at the wire" during the exercise hour and try to climb over it in full view of the sentries. He knew exactly how that would end: "I would've been shot." The com-mission took five minutes to issue a recommendation for his im-mediate repatriation.

Green's appearance before the commission was also perfunctory. The panel asked exactly the same questions as Wagner, and the dentist gave identical answers. "You have passed the examination," the Swiss colonel presiding told him. "You can go home to England." Green was about to utter a celebratory whoop, but caught himself just in time and retained his dour expression: "That's no use. I live in Scotland."

"Well, you can go home," the colonel said kindly.

But Green did not go home to Dunfermline. Although all twenty-nine officers were recommended for repatriation (including at least four who were falsifying or exaggerating their conditions), several remained prisoners. Douglas Bader, the Germans argued, had lost his legs back in 1931, and should not therefore be classified as a casualty of war. Moreover, he was simply too valuable a prisoner to be relinquished. Silverwood-Cope had "sustained considerable ill-treatment after recapture by the Gestapo," according to Denzler, and the Germans were unwilling to let him return to Britain as living proof of Nazi brutality. Just as he never knew the real reason for his imprisonment in Colditz, Julius Green never discovered quite why the Germans refused to let him go. Prawitt later told Denzler that the dentist had been detained as a "non-Aryan." Green believed his role in unmasking Walter Purdy lay behind the decision: "I had spoiled their plan to get a traitor into the camp." As the months passed, and it became clear he was not going to be released, Green stopped acting insane, and instead pretended he did not mind staying in Colditz. He put a brave face on it; that was the only sort of face he had.

Flinn's day of liberation passed in a dreamlike blur. "I remember being taken down to the doors of the castle and I was left standing outside. And I thought, this is it, I'm going. It was an overwhelming feeling to see further than the walls." He had passed three years inside Colditz, and longer in solitary confinement than any other prisoner. Only Mike Sinclair had tried to escape more often. Flinn had been discovered tunneling through a wall, trying to break into the parcels office, and hanging from a noose in the washrooms. He had smashed a chessboard over the head of a fellow prisoner and picked a fight in a railway carriage with the placid dentist. He preached his own religion, and spent much of his time in prison standing on his head. Flinn later claimed it had all been playacting, but no one believed him, and in his more lucid moments he knew that was not true. He never fully recovered. On that last day, standing outside Colditz, he broke down. "I could feel water trickling down from my eyes, both eyes, not crying—just water pouring down my face. That is a memory I have of freedom, that's what freedom can mean." The tears did not seem quite real to him. He did not know if he was really weeping or not. Henceforth, and forever, reality would always be just out of reach. He had won liberty at last, but in the process he lost something he never got back. That is what freedom meant to Frank Flinn.

News of the D-Day landings first became apparent in the faces of the guards. Padre Platt noticed "a certain agitation among the German soldiers and officers." This was followed by the rumor, put out by German propaganda, that the invasion had been repulsed. But that night, June 6, 1944, crouched over the radio in the attic, Micky Burn took down the words of John Snagge, the BBC radio announcer, as he declared: "D-Day has come. Early this morning the Allies began the assault on the north-western face of Hitler's European fortress . . ." Behind the walls of their own fortress, the prisoners let out a mighty cheer as the news was relayed. "It was wildly exciting," Burn wrote. Checko Chaloupka made a bet: if the war was not over by Christmas he would run naked around the inner courtyard, three times. "Parties are likely to be in full swing tonight," noted the padre. As Gris Davies-Scourfield noted in his diary: "We are in a kind of daze, mixed up of joy, excitement and anxiety." The homemade hooch flowed in torrents. Only one British soldier stood back from the revelry, "morose and introspective." Every time someone predicted the war would soon be over, Mike Sinclair flinched. "He dreaded that this would happen while he was still a prisoner of war; a failure after all the efforts he had made." In the German officers' mess, Eggers heard the revelry, and recognized the sound of looming defeat. The Allies would insist on unconditional surrender. "Only a military capitulation would be acceptable," he wrote, leaving "no alternative but to go on until the bitter end."

Allied victory seemed increasingly likely, but there was no certainty the prisoners of Colditz would still be alive to see it.

Just two days after the landings, news of a far grimmer sort filtered into the camp. Dozens of prisoners had escaped from the air force camp Stalag Luft III, near Sagan in what is now Poland, but almost all had been recaptured and handed over to the Gestapo. These had been "shot out of hand," Padre Platt reported. "The Great Escape" is celebrated in film and literature as an episode of epic valor; it was also an appalling human tragedy. A year earlier, the prisoners at Stalag Luft III had embarked on an astonishing feat of engineering: a set of tunnels over 100 meters long and 10 meters deep, constructed out of 4,000 bedboards. On March 25, seventy-six men crawled down the tunnel and emerged beyond the barbed wire. Of these, seventy-three were caught. An enraged Führer initially insisted that every single one of the recaptured officers should be shot, but in the end Hitler settled for a butcher's bill of "more than half." The SS selected fifty of the escapers at random and then murdered them, singly or in pairs. Perhaps the most remarkable aspect of the Great Escape was not the ingenuity of the mass breakout, but the utter barbarity with which it was punished. Word of the slaughter spread swiftly to Colditz. Colonel Willie Tod, the SBO, sent a message to the Kommandant demanding to know if the rumors were true. Prawitt replied, with studied vagueness, that the number "shot while escaping" was as yet unknown. But Reinhold Eggers, who was subsequently dispatched to Stalag Luft III to inspect its security arrangements, knew the truth: the carnage reflected a dramatic power shift within the Third Reich. "Himmler had ordered that any recaptured POWs were not to be sent back to their camps but were to be handed over to the SD," the Nazi Party security organization. The German army was losing the war, and with it the struggle for power inside the regime: Himmler and his SS thugs were gaining the upper hand, ensuring that the end of the Nazi story would be written in a welter of blood and fury.

A few weeks later, Eggers was playing cards in the mess and

listening to the radio, when regular broadcasting was interrupted for an emergency message: there had been an assassination attempt on Hitler's life, a bomb detonated in the Wolf's Lair, his field headquarters. At first Eggers assumed the report must be a hoax, elaborate Allied propaganda, but he was still listening intently at 1 a.m. when the Führer himself, hoarse but very much alive, came on the airwaves to demonstrate that the attempted coup had failed. The July Plot, led by Claus von Stauffenberg, had been hatched in the upper ranks of the German army, the military old guard long seen as suspect by Nazi hardliners. The reprisals, led by the Gestapo, were breathtaking in their savagery: 5,000 suspects were executed, "hanged like cattle" on Hitler's specific orders; under the new *Sippenhaft* (blood guilt) laws, relatives of the plotters were also arrested and condemned. Himmler, already chief of the SS, the Gestapo, and the SD, now took over control of the Reserve Army, that section of the Wehrmacht responsible for backup troops, guard duties, and military prisons. The POW camps, hitherto run by soldiers who largely respected the regulations on treatment of prisoners, were now under the control of Nazi fanatics, and to oversee the prisoner bureaucracy Himmler appointed one of the worst: Obergruppenführer (General) Gottlob Berger of the SS High Command, a figure of outstanding unpleasantness even by Nazi standards. An obedient Hitler crony and ardent anti-Semite, from 1940 Berger ran the SS main office in Berlin: he had played a central role in building up the Waffen-SS (the military wing of the SS), created a unit of convicted criminals known as the "Black Hunters" that committed a wide range of war crimes, and personally initiated a plan to kidnap 50,000 Polish children as slave laborers. Described by one historian as "unscrupulous, blunt, and inelegant in manner and expression, yet also full of genial loquacity and racy humour," Berger was nicknamed *der Allmächtige Gottlob*, the Almighty Gottlob, a play on his name, *Gott* being German for God.

This, then, was the man who now held the future of Colditz, and its inmates, in his hands.

The tightening Nazi grip was felt inside Colditz in ways small and large, some merely symbolic and others highly significant.

From then on, the stiff-armed *Heil Hitler* salute became obligatory, not just among the Germans, but between prisoners and guards. The bloodletting after the July Plot introduced a fresh layer of paranoia into the German mess. The more committed Nazis looked on some of their comrades with distrust. "No one would catch another's eye," wrote Eggers. Down in the town, the Nazi Party bosses staged a parade "to express thanks for the safety of our leader at the hand of providence." The castle garrison were instructed to attend, and all did, with an enthusiasm born of pure fear.

"People did not wish to seem lukewarm in their loyalty," recalled Eggers, who vigorously concealed his own tepid allegiance to the Nazi regime. An SS squad would appear from time to time, unannounced, and carry out a search of the castle. "A small army" of self-important officials from the SD arrived from Dresden to conduct their own investigations. "These people were more trouble than they were worth," sniffed Eggers. The organs of Nazi enforcement were taking a sinister interest in the running of the camp. His professional pride was affronted by the intrusion, but Eggers was far too astute to show it.

The life expectancy of an Allied soldier captured inside Germany shrank dramatically. In the early part of the war, captives were routinely delivered into the custody of the Wehrmacht. Now they were more likely to be handed over to the Gestapo, the SS, or the SD. As the Swiss official Rudolf Denzler noted darkly, "It became extremely difficult to protect POWs who were held by the paramilitary organizations." In the past, downed airmen like Douglas Bader had been taken into captivity with formal military correctness, even respect. Henceforth bomber crews forced to bail out could expect to be "left to the fury of the population." Hitler had already ordered the death of every commando captured in German-held territory; as the Stalag Luft III carnage showed, that execution order now extended to escaped prisoners. Back in January, a Canadian officer named Bill Miller escaped from the outer courtyard of Colditz by clinging on to the underside of a truck. "Dopey" Miller spoke excellent German. A discarded jacket was found in the nearby woods, but Eggers frankly admitted: "We never discovered how he had got away." Miller's disappearance was initially a cause for celebration, then mystery, and finally deep gloom. Months passed without a word. Miller was never heard from again. His precise fate has never been ascertained, but the most likely theory is that he was captured wearing civilian clothes near Lamsdorf, handed over to the Gestapo, taken to Mauthausen concentration camp east of Vienna, and murdered there on July 15, 1944.

The SS was now actively hunting down and exterminating its enemies. "As things got worse," wrote Eggers, "Himmler began taking it out on the most helpless of all, the prisoners and concentration camp inmates." On August 14, without warning, Čeněk Chaloupka and another Czech air force officer were pulled out of the lines during roll call, put on a train to Prague, and locked up in a jail cell. Under German military law, any German citizen taking up arms against Germany was guilty of high treason and liable to execution. Since the Nazi occupation of Czechoslovakia, in German eyes Checko Chaloupka was no longer Czech, but a German wearing an RAF uniform, and therefore a traitor liable to court-martial. Colonel Tod launched a furious objection, pointing out that any such prosecution was a violation of international law. From the Swiss legation in Berlin, Rudolf Denzler fired off "numerous representations on their behalf." Checko, meanwhile, was undergoing Gestapo interrogation, and already resigned to his fate: "I thought I would never come back from Prague." But then, without explanation, after two weeks in prison, the two men were loaded back onto the train and returned to Colditz. Irma Wernicke was waiting on the platform. "I've met every train from Prague hoping you would come back," she told Checko. "Thank God you have."

The prisoners were now safer within the castle walls than outside them, but only for as long as the German army remained in charge. With the SS in the ascendant, the future of Colditz was highly unpredictable. Its prisoners were defined by their antipathy to the Reich. The *Prominente* were prize hostages, captive status symbols. If defeat seemed inevitable, the SS might be tempted simply to murder them all in a final symbolic act of barbarity. The Great Escape massacre had demonstrated the Nazi willingness to wreak collective revenge on prisoners. "If the enemy, desperate in defeat, should seek a target among the prison camps, Colditz was the obvious bulls-eye," wrote David Walker. "We thought of that but did not speak of it."

Escaping had always had its dangers: a trigger-happy guard, a local lynch mob, a collapsed tunnel, an ill-tied sheet rope. By the summer of 1944, in contrast, the most likely outcome of a failed escape was a bullet in the back of the neck and an unmarked grave. Unsurprisingly, this had an impact on escape activity: most prisoners now knew the best chance of getting home was to stay put, and hope that the Allies turned up before the SS did. This was not cowardice, but sensible actuarial calculation. David Walker, a man of unquestionable bravery, spoke for many when he totted up the new arithmetic of escaping: "If the odds might be ninety-nine to one *against* getting out of Germany, and if the odds might be, as the enemy became more desperate, ninety-nine to one *on* being shot when recaptured, the odds were somewhat loaded. So, perhaps ignobly, we stopped trying." When Pat Reid was escape officer, escaping had been a game, albeit a serious one: now it was strictly a matter of life and death, with a heavy emphasis on the latter.

Yet for a hard core escaping remained a central preoccupation; the increased danger, the threat from the SS, and the ever tighter security measures merely compounded the challenge. For men like Mike Sinclair, the humiliation of capture so early in the war could only be expunged by getting away, whatever the odds. Three officers were found hiding in a drain under the castle archway after a guard heard sounds of digging. Another managed to slip away during the Park Walk—just as the first escaper, Alain Le Ray, had done in 1941. He hid in a pile of rubbish under a blanket camouflaged with twigs and strips of cardboard, but was captured within two miles of the castle. "The escaping spirit was dying hard," wrote Eggers. "In some cases it would not fade at all." On August 8, a white wooden sign with black lettering was nailed to the door of the *Kellerhaus*: "Camp Order No. 21: POWs escaping will be shot at." One prisoner already knew what that felt like. As Padre Platt noted in his diary, "Several officers have taken pleasure in informing Mike Sinclair, who was shot at a year ago, of the new order." Sinclair's reaction to this gentle gibe is not recorded. It certainly did nothing to dent his determination, but his close friends had noticed a marked change in his demeanor. Sinclair had never been much of a smiler, but now "he wore an almost perpetual frown, and looked well beyond his years."

The war might end before he got out. The Americans had already landed at Normandy, and they would soon arrive in Colditz; not as liberators, but as inmates.

14

The Sparrows

Rudolf Denzler was making a routine inspection of Kaiserstein-bruch POW camp outside Vienna in the summer of 1944, when he learned that a group of inmates in American uniforms had been spotted in the punishment cells. The Swiss official demanded to see the Americans, and found that "for all these men had suffered hardship, bad food, and continuous humiliations" they were "possessed of unshakable morale." There was nothing Denzler relished more than tying up the Nazis in red tape. "I immediately informed our embassy in Berlin," he wrote, before firing off a message to General Westhoff, head of the POW Division at German High Command, with whom he had a "friendly and agreeable" relationship. Westhoff ordered that the men be handed over to the Wehrmacht at once.

A few weeks later the three Americans, along with a squad of seven British commandos captured after an abortive parachute landing in Albania, were loaded onto a train for Colditz. "To my great pleasure I could greet them," wrote Denzler. "Only when these people entered the castle yard, exhausted and neglected, did they become Wehrmacht POWs and thus protected by the Geneva Convention."

The new arrivals were led by a mustachioed figure who strode through the castle gates as if arriving as guest of honor at a Manhattan soirée, a "tall, slim, good-looking man with greying hair who looked exactly like a distinguished Englishman," in the words of Douglas Bader.

Florimond Joseph Du Sossoit Duke was the first American prisoner in Colditz, the second-oldest paratrooper in the American air force, and one of the least successful secret agents of the Second World War.

As the flourish of his name suggests, Duke was a scion of the American upper class, an East Coast WASP from a privileged world that had thrived and prospered as the Jazz Age boomed, and then sidestepped the worst of the Wall Street crash. One branch of the family had founded Pan American Airways. Another owned some of the most valuable real estate in Connecticut. Duke graduated from Dartmouth College, played pro football for a season for the New York Brickley Giants, and caught the end of the First World War in France as an ambulance driver before taking peacetime employment as the advertising director for *Time* magazine in New York, a job that involved plenty of socializing and very little effort. Florimond Duke was wealthy, happy, good-looking, and crushingly bored.

On September 2, 1939, he sat sipping a cocktail in the garden of his country home, listening to the radio and looking out over the well-tended lawns. It was, he recalled, a "golden, late summer afternoon in Greens Farms, Connecticut." Germany had just invaded Poland. But life was good for Florimond Duke, with "an enviable job, a stylish house and a handsome family." He was forty-seven years old and had already played his part in one world conflict. "I could have sat this one out," he reflected, but "things were too quiet for my taste." Florimond Duke put down his martini and headed to war.

Duke was too old for the front line, but having "pulled every string to get back into the army," he was assigned to the Office of Strategic Services, the fledgling wartime intelligence organization formed to coordinate espionage, sabotage, and subversion behind the lines in Nazi-dominated Europe. The OSS would eventually evolve into the CIA. Lieutenant Colonel Duke was placed in charge of the Balkans Desk, an area of the world he had never seen and knew nothing about.

The landlocked state of Hungary, hemmed in by borders with Germany, Czechoslovakia, Romania, and Yugoslavia, was having a most uncomfortable war. Hungary had been the fourth country to join the Axis Powers in June 1941, alongside Germany, Italy, and Japan, and Hungarian troops had taken part in the invasion of the Soviet Union. Hungary's oil was vital to the German war effort. But by 1944 the Hungarian government under its prime minister Miklós Kállay had begun reaching out to Britain and the United States. A series of top-secret meetings took place in Switzerland, accompanied by a flurry of coded messages exploring how the country might extract itself from the steel embrace of the Nazis without falling under the control of the Soviet Union. Hitler knew exactly what was going on. German counterintelligence agents had bugged the telephones in Berne and broken the American codes: unknown to either the Hungarians or the Western Allies, the Führer was actively planning to prevent the defection of his disloyal ally by invading and occupying Hungary.

In February 1944 the OSS, with no inkling of these invasion plans, worked up a scheme to drop a squad of agents into Hungary to contact the anti-Nazi plotters, discover their bona fides, and generally gather useful intelligence.

Florimond Duke immediately volunteered to lead the three-man mission, codenamed "Sparrow."

"But this is a parachute mission," Duke's boss pointed out. "And you've never jumped."

"I can learn," he replied.

Duke would be accompanied by a radio operator, Major Alfred Suarez, a tough Hispanic New Yorker who had fought in the Spanish Civil War, and Captain Guy Nunn, a Californian adventure novelist who spoke perfect German and was "big enough and handsome enough to play the part of the hero in one of his own yarns." Their orders were somewhat vague: the three agents would drop unseen into Hungary, and then "help shorten and win the war" by liaising with "the highest authorities and carrying out negotiations as to how Hungary could leave the German camp." Duke was told that he should on no account agree to a deal. The OSS informed MI6: "Party is not repeat not authorized to make or accept peace feelers." The Hungarians seeking to break away from Hitler were hoping for a full-scale Allied military intervention to protect their country against the

Nazis—what they got was a middle-aged advertising executive armed with thousands of American cigarettes, nylon stockings, and gold, for the purposes of bribery.

Duke's parachute training lasted an hour and involved jumping out of the side door of a stationary plane parked on a runway in Algiers. In the early hours of March 16, the three American officers were dropped from a British Halifax somewhere near the border with Yugoslavia. Duke nearly castrated himself when his parachute opened with a violent jolt and he discovered the "harness straps had slipped too high on his crotch." Amazingly, the men landed without further injury, buried their parachutes, and set off to find some Hungarians who could put them in touch with the government. A message arrived at OSS headquarters in London: "Sparrow dropped successfully."

That message was also read in Berlin, where preparations for "Operation Margarethe," the invasion of Hungary, were well advanced. Hitler threw a tantrum when told the Americans had landed. "I always told you that the Hungarians ultimately will try to stab us in the back," he shouted. "And this is what's happening right now." According to Wilhelm Höttl, SS Chief of Intelligence and Counter-Espionage in Central and Southeast Europe, "Duke's arrival set the machinery in motion."

The three Americans were picked up by Hungarian soldiers and escorted to Budapest by a cheerful air force officer named Kiraly, a former bush pilot in western Canada who spoke perfect North American English. "We've been expecting you for some time," he drawled. They were lodged in a basement room of the foreign ministry, fed a sumptuous meal from a nearby restaurant, and politely asked to surrender their Colt 45s. The next morning, Kiraly reappeared, looking crestfallen: "At this moment Hitler is invading Hungary. The Germans will be in Budapest within the hour." He was most apologetic: "You must think we are a bunch of dopes. I swear we didn't dream Hitler would go off the deep end. We must turn you over to the Germans as prisoners of war." Kiraly advised them to get rid of any incriminating evidence, including their code books. Survival would depend on convincing the Germans they were not spies but innocent soldiers who had accidentally parachuted into Hungary while en route to join the Yugoslavian partisans. Finally, they handed over their money belts, containing $6,000 in *Louis d'or* gold coins, confident they would never see the money, or Kiraly, again. Mission Sparrow had achieved exactly none of its aims; far from shortening the war, it had helped kick-start the Nazi invasion of Hungary. Kiraly tried to cheer them up: "The rumor is that Hitler had to stop you before you got started . . . Sixteen German divisions to stop three American officers. Not a bad ratio."

For five terrible months, the Sparrows, as they called themselves, were shunted from one prison to another, in Belgrade, Berlin, Budapest, and Vienna. They were repeatedly interrogated by the Gestapo's "accomplished bullies." "We are soldiers," Duke insisted. "Not criminals. Not political prisoners. I demand that you get us out of here right now and send us to a POW officers' camp." On at least three occasions, Duke was told they would all be executed the following day. They tried to keep up their spirits by holding fly-swatting competitions and comparing their nightly tally of bedbug bites. Duke spent his fiftieth birthday in the basement cells of Gestapo headquarters in Berlin. He lost thirty-five pounds, and grew an elaborate air force–style mustache, which he twisted into points. They slept in their flying jackets. Back in Washington they were listed as Missing in Action, "presumed dead"; which is almost certainly what they would have been, had Rudolf Denzler not found them languishing in Kaisersteinbruch POW camp.

Florimond Duke might have been a hopeless spy, but he was a natural leader, and the arrival of the first Americans sent hope fluttering around the castle. "They added a freshness and a new outlook to our lives." Prisoners locked up since the start of the war had never seen an American soldier in uniform before. With his patrician self-confidence Duke personified America's manifest destiny, an assurance that the Allies would triumph eventually. The British called him "Dookie." He was "intelligent, older and wiser than we younger men," observed Bader. "A consoling personality." Duke "took in good spirit a fair amount of ribbing about his improbable first name," and the Americans were soon woven into the fabric of Colditz society. Checko Chaloupka began teaching Al Suarez to speak Czech. Florimond Duke joined the Bridge Club. After the horrific experiences of the last five months, he wrote, Colditz Castle "seemed, for a while, like freedom."

And yet, for prisoners who awoke every morning in the same dank, stone cage, the prospect of freedom itself remained a distant, cruel dream. A febrile atmosphere pervaded the camp, with "morale soaring or plummeting on the slightest pretext." One wit suggested that the place should be renamed "Hot-and-Colditz." Formations of Allied bombers flew overhead to pummel the German cities, and "gleamed in the sun like great beautiful things." The communist Micky Burn, only half-joking, declared that if the Soviet army reached the camp before the Americans, he would join its ranks as a commissar. But then, often without obvious reason as Padre Platt observed, "an air of sadness spread over the camp; the eternal optimists had little enthusiasm left for the victory that was always 'next month' and 'just around the corner.' They were nearly played out."

Wearied by their own thoughts, the prisoners pried into those of their fellow captives: "People are now at such a loose end that they occupy their time minding other people's business . . . if one goes and stands looking out of a window for a few minutes, up comes somebody and asks what one is doing." A series of plays in the castle theater helped to take the prisoners' thoughts off the uncertain future. Drama in Colditz had come a long way since the days when men dressed up in paper tutus and stomped around the stage belting out music hall songs to an ill-tuned piano. "The superior productions of 1944 were a far cry from the early days," wrote Platt, though he disapproved of the homosexual undertones in a production of Noël Coward's *Blithe Spirit*, declaring it "completely amoral." Ever vigilant for sins of the flesh, the padre detected a "decrease in moral resistance and an increase in perverted interest." The padre feared that "homosexualism" was on the rise, and while the majority were making "efforts to resist its development," others, unobtrusively, were not. At the same time, religious enthusiasm seemed to be waning. "It is at a low ebb," he wrote, unlike the early days of captivity when "church service was one of the biggest things in camp life."

As the days grew shorter, the prisoners "gritted their teeth once more to stand another winter behind the bars"; in one case literally. Mike Sinclair's friends noticed that "the stems of his pipes were always quickly bitten through."

A similar tension gripped the German garrison. Some of the Wehrmacht officers privately resigned themselves to defeat, while others clung to the hope that Hitler's secret weapons would finally win the war for Germany. "I'll shoot myself and my family," said one diehard Nazi. "But, before that, I'll go into the yard and finish off a few of the prisoners." Eggers had no intention of doing away with himself, or anyone else. But even that arch-realist tried to force himself to believe the Nazi propaganda, imagining an outcome in which Germany emerged intact, with honor. "We lived in two worlds—of fact and of illusion," he wrote. Eggers had no doubt that when the end came, there would be an accounting. The bloodstained fake uniform worn by Sinclair during the Franz Josef escape attempt had once been a historical souvenir. Now it looked more like a piece of incriminating evidence that could be presented in a post-war trial. Eggers quietly removed the grisly artifact from the Colditz Museum and burned it.

The internal power dynamic of the camp was changing fast in the autumn of 1944, bringing with it a strange new gentleness between some of the guards and the guarded. Eggers borrowed a box of films made by the German Educational Film Society from the town schoolmaster and arranged a Saturday night cinema club in the theater. *The Life of the Cabbage Butterfly* was hardly gripping cinema, but it was marginally better than nothing. Prisoners who gave their parole, a promise not to escape, were permitted to go down to the town under guard to play rugby on the village green and bathe in the river. In early September, when an officer was found hiding in a pile of leaves during the Park Walk, the guards merely hauled him out and walked him back up the path. "There was none of the accustomed abuse or threatening to shoot." The vicious goon-baiting of the early years abated, and then all but disappeared. Only Douglas Bader kept up the torrent of insults and impertinence. The mockery had once been an expression of defiant resistance; now, as the bombs cascaded onto Germany and the Soviet and Allied armies grew closer, it seemed like bullying. Reinhold Eggers, so long the target of cruel derision, found that the prisoners had begun to treat him and the other German officers with something that felt almost like kindness: "Typically British, they began to feel sympathy for the underdog." On his visits to the castle, Rudolf Denzler noticed that the mutual aggression was dissipating: "As the war worsened for the Wehrmacht, fewer incidents took place and a spirit of comradely consideration developed." The prisoners and their jailers were growing closer.

In the wider war, the men who had escaped from Colditz waited, wondered, or fought on, as the last chapter opened, the ending unknown.

Airey Neave and MI9 had successfully smuggled more than 5,000 British and American soldiers and airmen through the escape lines in occupied Europe and back to Britain. In the immediate aftermath of D-Day, Neave was deployed to France to organize "Operation Marathon," a mission to gather hundreds of downed airmen into forest camps where they could be rescued by the advancing Allied armies. Alain Le Ray, the first escaper, had taken over command of French Resistance forces in the Vercors, launching sabotage raids against the Nazi occupiers, and by 1944 he was chief of de Gaulle's French Forces of the Interior. Fellow Frenchman Pierre Mairesse-Lebrun, the exquisite equestrian who had vaulted over the wire in 1941, joined the Allied landings in Provence in August, and was now part of the Liberation Army fighting northward to the Rhine. Hans Larive, whose discovery of the route into Switzerland had made possible his own escape and so many others', was commanding the Dutch Motor Torpedo Boats helping to liberate the Netherlands. Jane Walker, a redoubtable Scotswoman disguised as a peasant and speaking perfect Polish, hunkered down in a small village on the east bank of the Vistula: the Red Army was approaching, and

Mrs. M was not at all sure she wanted to be liberated by communists. Frank "Errol" Flinn was repatriated via neutral Sweden. Back in Britain, he suffered a mental breakdown and was sent to a hospital near Blackpool. "I was unfit for fighting. Life seemed meaningless for a long time. Four years was a long time in prison, the best years of your life. Recovery was slow."

Two notable Colditz escapers who had reached Switzerland were trapped there after the escape route through southern France was closed following the Nazi occupation of Vichy France in November 1942. Their experiences were very different.

Pat Reid was serving as Assistant Military Attaché in Berne, secretly working for MI6 and enjoying life as a free man. There he met a young American woman and swiftly married her, news that electrified Colditz when it reached the castle: "Pat Reid married an American heiress in Switzerland!" Padre Platt reported. The myth of the irrepressible Colditz escaper was already taking shape.

Meanwhile, Birendranath Mazumdar was billeted in a hotel in Montreux on Lake Geneva. To begin with, Switzerland felt like paradise. "It was a good life. Good food. Good wine." He went back to work tending to the ailments of the various Allied servicemen who had reached Switzerland, including a number of Indian soldiers. The British had set up a social club, where he played billiards and bridge with a naval petty officer named Hammond. He enrolled for another medical degree at the specialist tuberculosis clinic in Locarno. He even started a love affair with a young Swiss woman named Elianne whose wealthy parents lived in Basel.

Yet an air of suspicion still surrounded the Indian doctor. Soon after arriving in Montreux, he was summoned by Lieutenant Colonel Henry Foote, a tank commander who had won the Victoria Cross in North Africa before being captured and imprisoned in Italy, and then escaping to Switzerland. "I cannot say that I took a liking to Mazumdar," Foote reported to London after interviewing the Indian officer, whom he described as "needlessly verbose and somewhat cantankerous." The British authorities were deeply distrustful of the doctor's contact with the Indian nationalist leader, Subhas Chandra Bose. In 1943, Hitler had provided Bose with a submarine to take him to southeast Asia, and the figurehead of Indian independence was now in Japanese-occupied Singapore, recruiting more Indian soldiers for his army of liberation and establishing, with Japanese support, the Provisional Government of Free India. MI5 set up a special unit, Section Z, to investigate Indian subversion, and a file was opened on Dr. Mazumdar. During what felt like an interrogation, Mazumdar described his visit to Berlin, pointed out that he had turned down every invitation to collaborate, and then tried to change the subject. Foote duly reported that Mazumdar "did not want to talk" about Bose and "certainly displayed no keenness to do so." This was hardly surprising in the circumstances, but it was enough to mark him out as a potential traitor.

Officers who had served in British India, like Foote, regarded Mazumdar with particular mistrust. Some referred to him as a "Bengali Baboo," a pejorative term for an Indian perceived as overeducated and "uppity." At the Montreux club, it was pointed out that his guest was only a petty officer, and the snooker table was strictly reserved for commissioned officers. The message was clear: they did not want Mazumdar in the club.

One afternoon he was accosted by a British colonel.

"Speak to your countrymen," the officer instructed. "Tell them not to socialize with Swiss girls."

Once again, Mazumdar knew that the order was aimed directly at him, and his relationship with a white woman.

"Colonel, I shall not do it," he replied. "As long as British officers socialize with Swiss girls, then I will."

"It is an order."

"I refuse to obey that order. You're wasting your time. I'm supposed to be free, so don't chain me. You can't chain me."

Lieutenant Colonel Sidney Lavender of the 16th Punjab Regiment was the Senior British Officer in Switzerland. He had won a Distinguished Service Order (DSO) in North Africa and escaped from an Italian prisoner of war camp. Having spent most of his adult life in British India, Lavender was convinced he understood "the Indian mind," and he did not like what he thought

he saw in Mazumdar's. Late in 1944, he spotted an opportunity
to bring the Indian doctor down a peg.

Many of the escaped prisoners were suffering from eye conditions, and to establish a better diagnosis Mazumdar decided he
needed an ophthalmoscope, an expensive handheld magnifying
tool with a light to see inside the eye. He ordered one from Geneva, obtained a chit from the senior medical officer, and bought
it with petty cash.

A day later, he was summoned to see Colonel Lavender.

"You're a bloody liar, Mazumdar," the colonel bellowed.

"I beg your pardon," said Mazumdar. "I'm not used to that
kind of language, Colonel."

With a torrent of expletives, the senior officer accused Mazumdar of theft, claiming he had embezzled the money intended
for the purchase of the ophthalmoscope. (Mazumdar later discovered that the girl who sold him the instrument had been
"wined and dined" and persuaded to sign a statement that she
had not sold him the ophthalmoscope.)

"You didn't buy it."

Mazumdar pointed out that he could produce the brand-new
instrument as proof, but Colonel Lavender had by now launched
into a furious diatribe about Indian corruption and the reasons
why that country would never be ready for independence.

"I disagreed with everything he said," Mazumdar recalled.

Both men were now on their feet, shouting. Lavender went
from pink to purple.

Finally Mazumdar exploded: "The difference between you
and me, Colonel, is this: You have lived in my country for twenty-
five years and you can't speak one of its languages. I have lived
in your country for fifteen and speak five languages, including
yours."

Mazumdar was placed under house arrest in a Locarno hotel
to await court-martial on a charge of stealing. "I had nobody to
help me," he wrote. A prisoner of war for four years, the Indian
doctor had escaped only to find himself a prisoner once more,
but now in British custody.

If and when Mazumdar finally made it back to Britain, MI5
would be waiting for him.

. . .

By the autumn, celebrity prisoners were arriving in Colditz in numbers that seamed increasingly ominous. October saw the appearance, under heavy guard, of a small, self-effacing New Zealand sheep farmer named Charles Upham. He was so shy, and the atmosphere in the camp so jittery, that some immediately assumed he must be another spy. In reality he was the only combat soldier to have won the Victoria Cross twice for outstanding bravery, in Crete and then in Egypt. Riddled with bullets, he was captured during the First Battle of El Alamein, and refused to have his arm amputated despite the urging of Italian military doctors. After numerous escape attempts, he was taken to Colditz, where he flatly refused to discuss his heroics. He preferred talking about sheep.

Another new arrival, equally brave but a lot more talkative, was David Stirling, the founder of the SAS. Under his quixotic command, the fledgling special forces unit had caused mayhem during the North African campaign by slipping onto the Axis airfields at night, planting bombs on the parked German and Italian aircraft, and then disappearing back into the Libyan desert as they exploded. Nicknamed the "Phantom Major" by an admiring Field Marshal Rommel, Stirling was finally captured in January 1943. He tried to escape five times, from camps in Italy, Austria, and Czechoslovakia, before being shipped to Colditz, where his reputation for extreme waywardness preceded him. "David is regarded with the gravest suspicion by the prison staff," a fellow prisoner wrote. "They daren't leave him alone for a minute."

The distinguished ranks of the *Prominente* were also swelled by the arrival of a stream of blue-blooded prisoners plucked from other camps. The first to join Giles Romilly and Michael Alexander in elite semi-isolation was the Earl of Hopetoun, son of the Marquess of Linlithgow, Viceroy of India between 1936 and 1943. Captain Charlie Hopetoun of the 51st Highland Division had been captured at Dunkirk, and now found himself in Colditz for no other reason than because "he was his father's son." They were joined by two nephews of King George VI: Lieutenant Viscount George Lascelles, sixth in line to the throne at the time of his birth, who would become 7th Earl of Hare-wood, and Captain John Elphinstone, later 17th Lord Elphin-stone. The Nazis had always been obsessed by the British royal family, and these royal captives were blandly informed they were being "protected." Of equal propaganda value was Captain George Alexander Eugene Douglas Haig, 2nd Earl Haig, the son of the late Field Marshal Haig, Britain's most celebrated First World War soldier. "Dawyck" Haig was a pallid, depressive artist who "wore silence like a dark cloak" and suffered from amebic dysentery. According to Michael Alexander, "captivity had affected him more severely than the other *Prominente*" and he seldom spoke, finding painting "more expressive than speech." Haig had been president of the Bullingdon at Oxford, and Hopetoun had been a member. The new arrivals were immediately inducted into the camp's most exclusive club. The addition of Max de Hamel, Churchill's distant cousin, brought the contingent of *Prominente* to seven. They dined together, shared rooms, and were securely locked up by 7:30 p.m. They were no longer allowed to take walks in the countryside.

Evidence that the Germans were corralling valued prisoners into Colditz reached London, and this disquieting development was immediately relayed to Downing Street and Buckingham Palace. "The King thought it rather sinister that the Germans should have collected in one Oflag all these young men who are near relatives of prominent people in this country," Sir Alan "Tommy" Lascelles, the King's private secretary and a cousin of the new Colditz inmate, wrote to Churchill. "These sudden transfers have an unpleasant significance." The prime minister briefly considered trying to exchange the *Prominente* for senior German prisoners in British hands, or launching a commando raid to seize them, but it was decided that "special action on behalf of individual prisoners would only serve to emphasize to the Germans our particular interest in them." Instead, a formal request was sent to the Swiss Protecting Power to monitor the welfare of the "special prisoners." At the same time, a pamphlet was drawn up by the Political Intelligence Department of the Foreign Office, to be dropped on POW camps, containing a "Solemn Warning" that the Gestapo, Kommandants, prison officers and guards "would be held *individually* responsible for the safety and welfare of Allied prisoners of war in their charge." That might make the ordinary camp administrators pause before resorting to murder, but it was unlikely to have much effect on Himmler and his SS killers. Rudolf Denzler knew that his power to intervene on behalf of the *Prominente* was limited: "POWs are hostages in the hands of a warring nation, and Colditz contained especially valuable ones," he wrote. Sir James Grigg, the secretary of state for war, warned Churchill: "The high-ups in Germany are keeping the 'prominenti' [*sic*] with the intention of trading them against their own skins later on. Our people are in no danger until we get some of the main war criminals into our hands. But it would mean a terrible dilemma for us later on."

The *Prominente* were now unwilling guests in what David Stirling called "the Third Reich's most closely guarded hostelry," with no idea whether they had been herded together to be kept safe, swapped, or slaughtered. The Romanovs had also been gathered together in 1917, before they were massacred. When Hopetoun asked why he had been moved to Colditz, the response was chilling: "We do not wish to happen to you what happened to the Russian royal family."

The castle lit by floodlights and the full moon.

A guard on duty at night in winter, watching for escapes—and being watched in turn by the "stooges."

Christmas, 1943. A seasonal truce was agreed upon: no escape attempts in return for no roll calls. Birendranath Mazumdar middle row, fourth from left; Peter Allan bottom left.

A stockpile of Red Cross provisions found in the canteen tunnel and confiscated.

A German soldier re-enacts an escape attempt in 1941 from an upper window using a rope made from bedsheets.

The Colditz Museum: a collection of fake uniforms, ropes, insignia, and other escape aids amassed and displayed by Reinhold Eggers.

The exit of the canteen tunnel, where Pat Reid and eleven other escapers were captured in May 1941.

Christopher Clayton Hutton, "Clutty" of MI9, the unsung genius of wartime escapology.

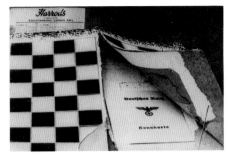

A chessboard with hidden identity card.

A compass concealed inside a walnut.

A Nazi eagle stamp carved out of linoleum.

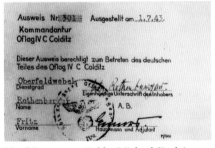

The fake pass carried by Michael Sinclair as Sergeant "Franz Josef" Rothenberger.

German cash concealed inside gramophone records.

The French radio smuggled into the castle in food packages, codenamed "Arthur."

Badminton racquets with concealed maps and money.

Fake cardboard weapons confiscated and displayed in the Colditz Museum.

Rubble and a ladder found in the clock tower after the foiled French Métro escape.

Photo labeled by Eggers "Three foxes leave their hole": another failed escape re-enacted for the camera. Dutch escape officer Machiel van den Heuvel, center.

Peter Allan at the exit to the "toilet tunnel," discovered in July 1941.

A rope ladder into a tunnel in the Dutch quarters, discovered in February 1942.

Émile Boulé, a bald forty-five-year-old French officer who attempted to escape dressed as a German woman, in a wig and a skirt.

Doppelgängers: French officer André Perodeau, left, disguised as Willi Pönert, the camp electrician, right.

Michael Sinclair, the Red Fox, the most dedicated escaper in Colditz, and the most unlucky.

Gustav Rothenberger, nicknamed "Franz Josef" by the prisoners for his elaborate mustaches.

New Year's Eve, 1942: two hundred inebriated prisoners formed a long conga and paraded through the snow.

Commando Micky Burn flashes a V for Victory sign with his left hand as he is led away after the St. Nazaire raid in March 1942.

Walter Purdy, the British fascist and pro-Nazi broadcaster recruited to spy on the other prisoners.

Frank "Errol" Flinn, top row, right, a psychologically fragile figure who spent more time in solitary confinement than any other prisoner.

Čeněk "Checko" Chaloupka, the louche and debonair Czech flying officer who ran the black market in Colditz.

Irma Wernicke, assistant to the Colditz town dentist, who became Chaloupka's lover, and then his spy.

Julius Green, a dentist, gourmand, coding expert, and secret agent.

The dentist at work in Colditz with foot drill and pliers, illustrated by John Watton.

Polish general Tadeusz Bór-Komorowski, commander-in-chief of the secret Polish Home Army, imprisoned in Colditz in autumn 1944.

The last Polish prisoners are marched out of Colditz.

The Polish quarters, where inmates brewed a ferocious homemade spirit and treated their German guards with withering disdain.

David Stirling, founder of the SAS, who arrived in August 1944 and set about establishing the Colditz Intelligence Unit.

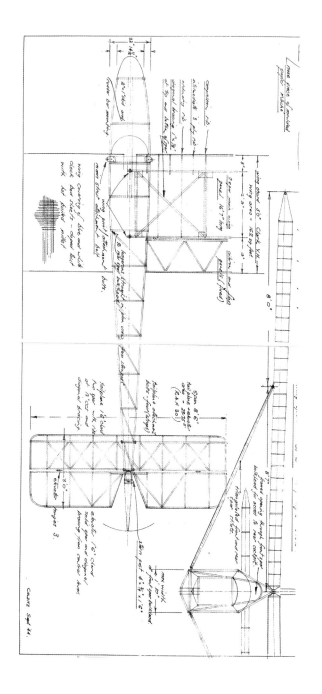

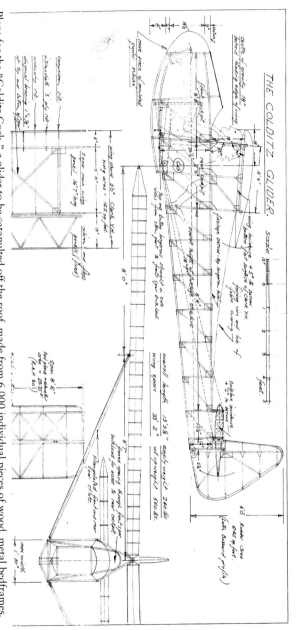

Plans for the "Colditz Cock," a glider to be catapulted off the roof, made from 6,000 individual pieces of wood, metal bedframes, stolen telephone cabling, and mattress covers.

The only known picture of the glider, a photograph taken by the journalist Lee Carson in April 1945.

American troops cross Colditz bridge, with visible damage from the failed German attempt to destroy it.

Lee Carson, American war correspondent for the International News Service: resourceful, brave, and "the best-liked news chick who ever beat a male reporter to a story."

Florimond Duke was the first American prisoner in Colditz, the second-oldest paratrooper in the U.S. Air Force, and one of the least successful spies of the Second World War.

Obergruppenführer Gottlob Berger of the SS High Command, a Hitler crony and ardent anti-Semite appointed to oversee the POW camps.

SS Oberst Friedrich Meurer, Berger's aide-de-camp, who escorted the *Prominente* hostages on their final journey.

The *Prominente* reach the American lines. From left to right: Max de Hamel, George Lascelles, John Elphinstone, Swiss diplomat Werner Buchmüller, and Michael Alexander.

Lists of Jewish prisoners transferred from Buchenwald concentration camp to the labor camp at Colditz.

Häftlingsschreibstube
K. L. Buchenwald

Februar 1945.
22.

196a

Transport Colditz

1	114336	62	Zylberger,A.	51	114652	62	Diament,A.
2	328		Baruch,A.	52	635		Fissel,A.
3	353		Dymant,A.	53	639		Czajkowski,.
4	355		Gelbart,B.	54	642		Arbusman,H.
5	363		Feiweles,J.	55	644		Gros,B.
6	367		Wolman,J.	56	650		Rand,M.
7	398		Davidowicz,C.	57	650		Kossmacher,K.
8	399		Profesorski,J.	58	661		Winogradski,.
9	409		Satajnbuch,M.	59	664		Koja,M.
10	412		Wajngarten,J.	60	666		Gelberg,J.
11	413		Rosenfurt,P.	61	667		Gelbuch,A.
12	414		Rosenfrucht,J.	62	671		Kopels,A.
13	405		Silberman,G.	63	672		Kopec,J.
14	435		Lerner,S.	64	677		Grynschpan,Sz.
15	400		Kalka,J.	65	678		Faust,H.
16	442		Königsberg,C.	66	687		Jakubowicz,J.
17	444		Fraeworski,K.	67	689		Lesman,J.
18	445		Goldstajn,K.	68	690		Glikman,A.
19	449		Tenenberg,M.	69	691		Sztajnberg,M.
20	460		Apolot,A.	70	692		Sztajnberg,B.
21	463		Fukman,A.	71	693		Diament,A.
22	466		Rozengarten,J.	72	695		Zajdler,Sz.
23	473		Bendel,J.	73	696		Zajdler,Ch.
24	474		Morgenstern,A.	74	698		Nordman,L.
25	477		Wielinski,J.	75	705		Sidman,S.
26	492		Filkenstein,M.	76	706		Misner,H.
27	501		Rubin,B.	77	708		Rubin,.
28	504		Loos,L.	78	709		Blausztein,Ch.
29	515		Grünbaum,F.	79	712		Brendes,B.
30	526		Wolowski,H.	80	713		Reisman,B.
31	527		Josefowicz,P.	81	714		Grynman,G.
32	534		Nordkovski,M.	82	716		Rajmann,C.
33	539		Erlich,A.	83	719		Blech,M.
34	540		Gnessanower,H.	84	725		Szerman,B.
35	541		Czessanower,J.	85	729		Blankowski,J.
36	548		Rosenstajn,Ch.	86	732		Najman,C.
37	559		Wajnryb,J.	87	744		Rocak,U.
38	563		Rosenzweig,B.	88	745		Seewan,L.
39	567		Rusbaum,J.	89	752		Gutmanowicz,D.
40	569		Apfelbaum,N.	90	757		Fajgenblatt,F.
41	572		Stajnfeld,Sz.	91	761		Klajnic,S.
42	575		Nachman,D.	92	764		San,J.
43	581		Deren,Sz.	93	765		Altusli,M.
44	585		Lubliner,J.	94	766		Lestny,B.
45	586		Grünblatt,B.	95	778		Fropanstor,J.
46	592		Danziger,.	96	780		Kaufman,N.
47	593		Daneyger,J.	97	782		Krupc,.
48	594		Rosenzweig,W.	98	787		Grube,B.
49	616		Rosenberg,B.	99	789		Fajtel,S.
50	625		Ajzenburg,J.	100	792		Szpiro,J.

U 14415

Steingutfabrik labor camp, the secret armaments factory near Colditz Castle where hundreds of slave laborers were worked to death.

Starving and emaciated Hungarian-Jewish slave laborers freed by the advancing American troops.

The pipe-smoking GIs who liberated Colditz. From left to right: Walter Burrows, Alan Murphey, Frank Giegnas Jr., and Robert Miller.

Colditz unchained: the freed prisoners celebrate, April 16, 1945.

15

The Red Fox

Lieutenant Colonel Willie Tod would never again lead his men in battle, but he would do whatever was necessary to lead them home.

Tod was the embodiment of Colditz itself: tall, graying, battle-battered, and as tough as granite. The Senior British Officer was a Scotsman, with a long, equine face and an extravagantly broken nose. "Peace-loving, courteous and gentle," he was quite different in character from earlier SBOs. Tod disapproved of goon-baiting, which he considered bad sportsmanship. "The Germans were taking a licking," wrote Padre Platt. "He did not believe in kicking a man when he was down." Tod did not actively inhibit escaping, but as the risks mounted and the end of the war inched closer, he did not encourage it either. The escape committee continued to function, but "he would only approve future attempts if they provided a real chance of success." For most prisoners, that half prohibition came as a relief. Adored and revered by the younger men, "Auld Wullie" wore his own sadness on the inside. In January 1944, a few months after Tod arrived in Colditz, his son and only child was killed fighting in Italy. He did not tell a soul, and when word leaked out and his fellow prisoners offered condolences, Willie Tod simply gazed into the distance and said: "It happens, to soldiers." But he was utterly determined to make sure it did not happen to the soldiers under his care. In this resolve, he was joined by Florimond Duke. The American persuaded the Germans to recognize him formally as the Senior American Officer (SAO) in the camp. As such, he would be party to any confrontation with the Kommandant. "We'll be two against one," Duke told Tod.

These, then, were the two men tasked with steering Colditz through the menacing endgame: their role, as they saw it, was to protect the prisoners under their command, ensuring that as many as possible survived the war.

One afternoon in late August, the men trooped down to the park for an exercise session. For the first time in several months Michael Sinclair was among them, wearing a large khaki cloak he had bought from a French officer. The guards knew to keep a close watch on the redheaded Sinclair, and sure enough a routine inspection revealed that beneath his uniform he was wearing homemade civilian clothing. This was plainly preparation for some sort of escape attempt, and Sinclair was duly sentenced to fourteen days in solitary.

"I was a little hurt that he had told me nothing of any escape plan," wrote Gris Davies-Scourfield. The two men had been the closest friends since the early days of their captivity. They had escaped together from Poznań, hidden out in Poland under the protection of Mrs. M, and plotted each escape together. But in recent months Sinclair had seemed increasingly unreachable. The death of Sinclair's younger brother at Anzio had deepened his detachment. "Even I, his old friend and comrade, just could not get through to him at all and, to be frank, after a number of rebuffs I ceased to try very hard." When Davies-Scourfield asked what he was up to, Sinclair simply shrugged and said: "You never know when an opportunity might arise." For someone so meticulous in his planning this, too, seemed out of character.

Sinclair emerged from solitary on September 18. Five days later, a new notice was posted on the courtyard wall in stark red and black lettering, with many exclamation marks, italics, and underlinings.

> To all prisoners of war!
> The escape from prison camps is no longer a sport!

The poster accused Britain of deploying "gangster commandos, terror bandits and sabotage troops," and declared: "Germany is determined to safeguard her homeland." This was followed by a threat, disguised as a warning. "It has become necessary to create strictly forbidden zones, called death zones, in which all unauthorized trespassers will be immediately shot on sight. Escaping prisoners of war, entering such death zones, will certainly lose their lives. *Urgent warning is given against making future escapes!* In plain English: Stay in the camp where you will be safe. Breaking out of it is now a damned dangerous act."

But most prisoners were no longer thinking about escaping. They were thinking about food.

Autumn brought with it the first pangs of a great hunger that affected every inhabitant of the castle, both prisoners and guards, gnawing at body and soul alike. The flow of Red Cross parcels had steadily diminished throughout the summer, and stockpiles built up over the previous year were dwindling. In the chaos engulfing the Third Reich and with rail networks severely disrupted by bombing, supplies were no longer getting through; those that entered the country from Switzerland were heavily pilfered or vanished long before they reached the camps. Germany was starting to starve. Personal packages from Britain reduced to a trickle, and then ceased altogether. Letters from home stopped arriving.

Supplementary foodstuffs in Red Cross parcels had made the German rations more palatable and nutritious. Henceforth the prisoners were increasingly (and soon wholly) reliant on what little the German prison system provided: moldy potatoes, black bread, and millet, all strictly rationed; a thin and indefinable soup. The few vegetables coming into the castle consisted of turnips and kohlrabi, and those rarely. Tod gave orders to pool the remaining Red Cross packages as an emergency supply. Food had always been a staple topic of castle conversation. It now became all-consuming.

On September 25, two days after the notice appeared prohibiting escape attempts, Reinhold Eggers stood on the eastern ramparts looking out over the park as the prisoners shuffled into formation for the walk down to the exercise enclosure. It was a beautiful early-autumn afternoon. The foliage of the woods was turning, and the first leaves were already falling, dancing across the park on a warm breeze. This was "the finest view in Colditz," Eggers reflected, "with hornbeams, beeches and sycamores flaming away up through the *Tiergarten*." The war seemed far away.

Gris Davies-Scourfield spotted Mike Sinclair heading down to the park.

"I see you're going on the walk. Would you like me to come with you?" he asked.

"No. I'd rather be alone. Thank you," said Sinclair and turned away. His voice seemed "peculiarly deadpan."

Nettled, Davies-Scourfield thought: "To hell with you . . . Go for a walk alone if that's what you want." He wandered back up to his room to write a letter home. Davies-Scourfield did not spot that beneath the French cloak, his old friend was wearing another set of civilian clothes. The day before, without telling anyone, Sinclair had removed some cash from what was left of the escapers' kitty.

Down in the park, the guards took up their positions around the wire fence, eight feet high and topped with barbed wire. A game of soccer started. Some of the men relaxed in the autumn sun or chatted in groups, while others strolled around the path worn into the earth just inside the perimeter.

Sinclair walked alone for half an hour, up and down the wire, and then stopped to watch the game. One of the players looked up and saw that his face was "ashen pale." No one noticed when he took a pair of thick black gloves out of his pocket, and put them on.

It was almost 3 p.m. when Sinclair suddenly whipped off his cloak, jumped over the first tripwire, and began climbing the perimeter fence. For a moment he seemed to be "spreadeagled in mid-air" before he seized the uppermost strand of barbed wire and hauled himself up. He had reached the top, "balancing astride the swaying wires," before the German guards understood what was happening.

"*Halt!*" they shouted, unslinging their rifles almost in unison. "*Halt oder ich schiesse!*" ("Stop or I'll shoot!")

The German NCO on duty that day was one who knew Sinclair, and "greatly admired" him. He unlocked the gate and ran around to the exterior, while unholstering his pistol. The game had stopped, and the players were now staring in rapt excitement.

Sinclair landed hard on the other side, just as the German NCO arrived, panting.

"It's no use, Herr Sinclair," he said, not unkindly.

Sinclair knocked the man's pistol aside and sprinted up the slope, jinking as he ran, "an extraordinarily fixed expression" on his face.

He was already halfway to the outer wall when the first shot echoed around the park. Then two more, followed by a ragged volley from a dozen guards at different positions on the perimeter. Up in the castle, the prisoners heard the gunfire and shouting, and crowded to the windows. "My God, it's Mike," thought Gris Davies-Scourfield. "It must be him." Sinclair was now crouching low and racing toward the tree line. "*Nicht schiessen*," shouted the soccer players. "*Nicht schiessen!*" The machine gun opened up from the emplacement beside the path up to the castle, with a clear line of fire across the little valley.

Sinclair was still ten feet from the outer wall when he staggered, and dropped to his knees. The men behind the wire gasped. "Then, slowly, he crumpled forward among the autumn leaves." A single bullet had ricocheted off his right elbow, directly into his heart.

Within the hour, the stunned prisoners were assembled for an emergency roll call in the inner courtyard. The count was held in shocked silence. The German officer of the guard saluted, and then solemnly marched his men out through the main gate, leaving the prisoners briefly alone. "Attention!" commanded Willie Tod, a prematurely aged man grown suddenly older. "Gentlemen, I am sorry to tell you that Mr. Sinclair is dead."

Just ten prisoners were permitted to attend the funeral at the town cemetery the next day. Kommandant Prawitt provided a Union Jack to drape over the coffin, and what everyone agreed was a "really lovely wreath."

Among Sinclair's possessions, Gris Davies-Scourfield found a note tucked inside a folded shirt: "I take full responsibility. Safe home to you, all you good chaps."

The service in the castle chapel had all the familiar cadences of ritual military mourning: "Abide with Me," "The Lord's My Shepherd," and the national anthem. A bugler played the "Last Post" from the gallery. Sinclair's achievements were listed: no prisoner had escaped more often or more ardently, or spent so long at liberty inside Germany and Nazi-occupied territory; he had hidden out for months in Poland, protected by a redoubtable Scotswoman; he had reached the borders of Switzerland, Holland, and Bulgaria, without ever getting across them; he had been shot through the chest once already while trying to escape; he never gave up. "You know better than any congregation in the world what that means," Padre Platt told the prisoners. "It isn't just a wasteful tragedy," he added, perhaps inadvertently voicing what many were privately wondering.

The other prisoners sought to find nobility, significance, and comfort in Sinclair's death. "To await freedom at the hands of others would seal his own failure, scar his heart and sear his soul," said one. Another declared that he was "killed through his courage and determination to still try, even after others had given up hope." Gris Davies-Scourfield wondered if the German threat to shoot anyone escaping had acted on Sinclair as "an additional spur."

Though Tod and Duke issued a formal complaint, alleging that Sinclair had been "effectively penned in," there were few recriminations against the Germans. The guards had fired reluctantly, after due warning, and certainly without intent to kill. Which left the grim but unspoken possibility that Sinclair had meant to get himself killed. Some ascribed his actions to a "spontaneous breakdown in reason." But Sinclair was perfectly sane when he died; he knew the most likely outcome of a "dive at the wire."

Michael Sinclair was twenty-four when he was captured, and twenty-eight when he died. He had been born into a military family of rigid conformity for whom dying in battle, as his brother had already done, was the ultimate mark of manhood. Captivity had taken away the certainties he had grown up with. Every failed escape compounded the distance from what he had thought of as his destiny. Perhaps, for Sinclair, death from a German bullet on a hillside in Saxony had brought it back.

An enemy's tribute means more than all the encomia of comrades. Reinhold Eggers had spent years trying to stop the Red Fox from getting away. He was profoundly moved by Sinclair's death, and reached back into Nordic mythology, and his own scholarship, for an adequate way to express his feelings: "If there is indeed a Valhalla for the heroes of whatever nation, if the men who go there are men of courage and daring, if their determination springs from one true motive alone and that motive is love of their country—then in our own German tradition, Valhalla is the resting place of Lieutenant Mike Sinclair."

"Nerves are on a knife edge," wrote Padre Platt. The daily BBC bulletins brought the promise of victory, but the future of Colditz, and its prisoners, seemed anything but assured. They might soon be going home. Equally it seemed quite possible they might be starved to death, taken hostage by the retreating Nazis, or murdered en masse by the SS. In war, preparation is all, but it is hard to organize for the unknown. Colonels Tod and Duke needed information on what might be heading their way, when and in what form. They needed people on the outside to warn them of the probable fate of those on the inside. If the tables turned, and the prisoners seized control of the castle, they needed to know whom they could trust, and whom to fear. They needed some reliable intelligence. They needed spies.

For months, Irmgard Wernicke had been supplying the escape committee with a variety of useful information, and in the autumn of 1944 Colonel Tod decided to expand intelligence-gathering operations in the town. The officer tasked with forming what was now grandly dubbed the "Colditz British Intelligence Unit" was David Stirling, founder of the SAS and an expert in the use of both cloak and dagger. With the help of Čeněk Chaloupka, Stirling drew up a shopping list of secrets to be included in the "love letters" sent to the dentist's assistant: "After the necessary fond preludes, the letters turned into questionnaires." The questions dealt with subjects of national interest: morale, attitudes toward the Allies and toward the Nazi Party, but more especially with the situation in Colditz and its surroundings. The location of the police station, the mayor's office, the telephone exchange, the waterworks, barracks of Russian prisoners of war, and main farm buildings. Who were the leading Nazis? Were there any anti-Nazis? By the end of October, Stirling and Checko were sending Irma two questionnaires a week: "Her answers came back carefully thought out and intelligently written." Irma's father knew everyone in the local Nazi Party, and she "had access to information, both gossip and fact, which could be of great use. She was ready to tell us everything she could." Stirling began to assemble files on the various village notables: "Very soon we had a dossier on all the important local Nazis, not only civilians in the Party, but Gestapo and castle administrative personnel." Stirling drew up a map, showing where key individuals lived and worked, petrol stores, ammunition dumps, food caches, grain barns, and medicine stocks.

The network expanded. The young soldier passing messages back and forth between Irma and Checko was named Heinz Schmidt. "Alert and intelligent," he had been a student at the School of Mines at Freiberg before being conscripted. His father was a local industrialist, and one of the richest men in Colditz. But both father and son were secret anti-Nazis. From the start, Heinz knew he was passing on something other than love letters. Irma recruited Heinz, who recruited his father, who then began feeding back information not only about the local Nazi bigwigs, but the names of others who, like him, were ready to work against the regime. The elder Schmidt's willingness to collaborate was partly motivated by revenge: his wife, Heinz's mother, was the mistress of Irma's Nazi father. Infidelity is not unknown in small villages; rarely, however, does it extend into international espionage. Schmidt "confided in other local anti-Nazi elements," recalled Jack Pringle, Stirling's main assistant. Before long the Colditz British Intelligence Unit had an ideological chart of the locality, and a plan to take over the village by force. Pringle wrote: "From information coming from the three of them, we started to select an alternative local government to replace the Party and the Gestapo when the end came."

If the Third Reich collapsed and the Germans surrendered Colditz to its prisoners, they would know who could be trusted, the name of every important Nazi in a thirty-mile radius, and where to find the weapons.

When food is short, some hoard, some benefit, and some share; only a person who has never experienced real hunger believes that he or she would never hide a few secret calories for themselves, or eye a neighbor's crust with avarice. When Red Cross parcels had been plentiful, the prisoners had been content to pool and share resources with their mess-mates, and trade any surplus. But with growing hunger the internal economy of Colditz altered. The guards, even more famished than the prisoners, were increasingly desperate for the few luxuries remaining in the diminishing stock of Red Cross parcels. The black market boomed, overheated, and then effectively collapsed, gripped by a kind of hyperinflation as tradable goods dwindled. In early December, one prisoner agreed to swap five pounds of chocolate and £10 for the promise of a 1938 Renault Coupé, garaged in England. The guards brought in a few fresh eggs, cheese, and milk to trade for increasingly scarce items such as coffee, sugar, and cigarettes. The nicotine addicts suffered acutely as tobacco supplies steadily decreased. Trading with the guards became so open that Eggers sensibly suggested a barter shop be set up in the courtyard. Prawitt was livid: "What do you suggest next? A brothel?" Padre Platt complained bitterly about the boiled kohlrabi, which he described as the "bastard" offspring of a turnip and cabbage, and "the worst of both." A horse's head, the sort of fare that would once have been disdained, was eagerly boiled and consumed. Enterprising hunters baited hooks on window ledges in the hope of catching an incautious pigeon. In early December, the ration was further reduced to three potatoes a day. Platt gloomily described the daily menu: "Breakfast consists of two very thin slices of rye bread with a cup of ersatz coffee. Lunch is one small potato and two or three spoonsful of boiled vegetable, followed by two-seventh of a slice of bread and one-seventh of a tin of cheese ... the evening meal could be put without difficulty into a four-ounce tobacco tin." Before Christmas, every prisoner was weighed. All had lost weight, some dramatically so. Gris Davies-Scourfield weighed eleven and a half stone before the war. He was now down to eight and three-quarters. A diet of just 1,200 calories a day, Julius Green calculated, "would ensure loss of weight even if one were just lying in bed all the time." The prisoners began to covet one another's shrinking stocks. Douglas Bader noticed that Green had been saving a small lump of fatty bacon, and spotted an opportunity to play the kosher card.

"What are you going to do with that bacon, Julius?"

"Eat it," the Jewish dentist replied emphatically.

"But you're not supposed to."

"Just you watch me."

"Where's your principles?"

"Bugger the principles, I'm assuming I have a dispensation from the Chief Rabbi for the duration of the war."

Malnourishment brought with it a new lethargy, as well as aching joints, skin rashes, edema, and searingly bad breath. Enthusiasm for sport tailed off. Games of stoolball all but ceased; on an empty stomach few were prepared to endure the physical assault inherent in that peculiarly violent game. When bread slices were doled out in fractions, there were opportunities for racketeering: stockpiling desirable foodstuffs and then selling them on at inflated prices. A group of officers broke into the German potato store and began secretly extracting supplies for themselves, prompting outrage and envy. To try to regulate the bartering, Colonel Tod ordered that henceforth only David Stirling and Čeněk Chaloupka could trade with the Germans, and gave them exclusive access to the emergency stock of Red Cross goods: anything they managed to obtain would be fairly shared among all the prisoners, including the orderlies. This restriction immediately strengthened the hand of the British Intelligence Unit, for Checko and Stirling could use barter to extract additional intelligence from the hungry guards. According to Jack Pringle, "they knew just how much information to ask for, how much to offer in exchange to coax out more, when to shut off supplies, when to be amiable, when to be tough." But this approach also exacerbated a political divide. Those on the left, like Micky Burn, regarded the centralizing of food stocks and communal distribution as evidence of egalitarian socialism in action. Others saw it as a suppression of the free market and entrepreneurial enterprise: if a man invested his time and resources in obtaining six fresh eggs, should he not be free to enjoy the fruits of his investment? "You can't divide six eggs between 200 people," pointed out Michael Alexander, who, as a member of the Bullingdon Club and one of the *Prominente,* had access to many more eggs than the orderlies who polished his shoes.

The communist armies were approaching from the east; the forces of capitalist democracy were converging on Germany from the west. As in so much else, life inside Colditz echoed the wider world, a looming ideological confrontation reflected in a fierce debate over the allocation of moldy potatoes and diluted soup.

It was bitterly cold. The coal supply was now insufficient to keep the boilers going, and the castle was frequently freezing. Men slept in multiple layers of clothing. The provision of hot water, never reliable, grew even more erratic. Just before Christmas 1944, the last Red Cross parcel arrived. There would be no more. Food supplies, wrote Eggers, "reached the lowest level ever."

The strain told in different ways. Some prisoners got blind drunk on the remaining stocks of homemade spirit. "The stuff they are drinking is poison," wrote Padre Platt, who nonetheless drank it himself. In spite of the prospect of liberation—or perhaps because of it—some inmates were psychologically overwhelmed by the pressure of waiting. It was not despair that drove a small handful over the edge, but hope. "More prisoners than ever are in mental distress," wrote Platt. The kitchen officer was found wandering around the courtyard with a poker in one hand and a wooden spoon in the other, expatiating "unintelligibly on Egyptology, military technique, religion, or going north." He was quietly removed by the Germans and sent to an asylum. A few prisoners took to their beds, getting up only to eat. Others buried themselves in books.

"It is no longer an adventure to get out of this camp," Colonel Tod told the prisoners, a warning that hardly needed to be made in the wake of Sinclair's death. Hungry, cold, and anxious, most of the 254 inmates had already resigned themselves to staying put.

Most, but not all. For, as the war wound down, a small group of men were hard at work on an escape plan that, for ingenuity and audacity, matched anything that had been attempted before. Climbing or tunneling out of Colditz was now virtually impossible; instead, they would try to fly away.

Flight Lieutenant Bill Goldfinch was watching the snowflakes floating up and over the roof of the castle, when he had an aerodynamic brainwave: the same air currents causing the flakes to fall upward might be sufficient to keep a manned glider aloft as far as the opposite side of the Mulde River, 200 yards away, where a wide patch of meadow would make a potential landing strip.

The glider would have to be built in secrecy in one of the attics. When the time was right the escapers would break through a wall, assemble the aircraft on the roof, and then lay a sixty-foot launch strip along the ridge line of the roof immediately below, out of view of the sentries. A sheet rope would be attached to the nose of the glider, running over a pulley wheel at the end of the platform, secured at the other end to a bath filled with concrete and weighing roughly one ton. In theory, when this weight was dropped from the third floor of the chapel block to the ground sixty feet below, it would pull the glider and its two occupants along the runway and then fling the aircraft into the sky with sufficient momentum to become airborne.

There were, however, a number of obstacles to this plan: the glider would require a wingspan of thirty-three feet; the western side of the castle was heavily guarded; once launched, the glider would be visible to both sentries on the ramparts and inhabitants of the village, and an easy target. The physics were not reliable either. To achieve the required lift, the westerly wind would need to be blowing in exactly the right direction, at the correct speed. The glider would have to take off during an air raid when the blackout was in force, cross over the river, and land in darkness. If the rope did not detach at the critical moment, the heavy bath would drag the glider over the edge and send it plummeting to earth at lethal velocity. If it rained, the glue holding it together would dissolve, and the aircraft would disintegrate. The glider was nicknamed the "Colditz Cock": a cockerel cannot fly, but launched from a height it can glide a short distance.

The Colditz glider was a tour de force of inventiveness, a remarkable combination of lateral thinking, technical creativity, and collective endeavor. It was also extremely unlikely to work. Colonel Tod was fully aware of this when he approved the plan. But he also knew this wildly ambitious project would give the men something to do and think about, forge a fresh spirit of cohesion, and take their minds off the hunger. It would require more than 6,000 individual pieces of wood, metal bolts extracted from bedframes, stolen telephone cabling for the controls, a covering stitched out of blue and white mattress covers, and several pints of glue. It would take a long time to make, and involve scores of prisoners as designers, builders, and stooges. The war would probably have ended by the time it was ready for takeoff; and that, perhaps, was the point. Whether the Colditz glider would ever be launched was, in the end, secondary: this might be the greatest escape never attempted.

The other members of the glider team were the former "ghost" Jack Best and Tony Rolt, an engineer and champion racing driver who had won the British Empire Trophy in 1939. It was agreed that not until just before takeoff would they draw lots to decide which pair would board the glider for its one and only flight.

The prison library included a copy of *Aircraft Design* by Cecil Latimer Needham, the British gliding pioneer and aircraft engineer who also invented the hovercraft skirt. With the help of this seminal text, Goldfinch and Best drew up plans for a lightweight, two-seater, high-wing monoplane glider, twenty feet long, with rudder and elevators. Its thirty ribs would be carved from wooden bed slats. The four wing spars would be fashioned from floorboards. The pores in the cloth covering would be sealed with a "dope" made from boiled millet to form a semi-rigid outer skin. The design drawings and stress calculations were checked and approved by Lorne Welch, an engineer at the Royal Aircraft Establishment who had flown gliders before the war. At the western end of the topmost attic above the chapel, the team constructed a false wall from wood and canvas caked with dust, to create a secret workshop accessible from below through a concealed trapdoor. The guards inspected the attic irregularly; they failed to spot that the room had become seven feet shorter. The builders installed a workbench, electric light, and a set of homemade tools including planes, a gauge made from a cupboard bolt, and a tiny saw fashioned out of a gramophone spring for detailed cutting. Checko Chaloupka obtained glue on the black market.

Construction had started in the summer of 1944. Takeoff was planned for the following spring. Throughout that winter, twelve engineers, calling themselves "the apostles," worked on the glider, steaming and bending the wood, pinning, gluing, silently hammering, drilling, cutting, and stitching the outer fabric and daubing it with the millet-dope to draw the material tight around the frame. Some forty lookouts worked in shifts to warn if guards approached. At least a quarter of all the prisoners in Colditz would be involved in the building of the secret glider, the most elaborate collective construction project since the great French tunnel of 1942. By mid-December, the builders had assembled the fuselage, wings, rudder, ropes, pulleys, and most of the saddle-boards that would be secured along the apex of the roof to form a runway. Colonel Tod made an inspection of the secret workshop and was profoundly moved by the industry and determination of the builders: the glider might never fly, but something magical was taking flight beneath the eaves of Colditz.

Christmas that year was the strangest, the sparsest, and the most sober. Checko Chaloupka honored the wager he had made after D-Day and ran naked around the snowy courtyard three times, cheered on by "a boisterous gallery of muffled up spectators." The spectacle would have been funnier had it not been proof that predictions of an early end to the war were hopelessly optimistic. A "Christmas Draw" was held for the few remaining Red Cross food items: the most coveted being a two-pound tin of pork and beans. Platt's mess of eight men drew three small tins of sardines, a tin of golden syrup, and some oatmeal. "There was only one small drinking party," the padre noted approvingly.

"And I don't believe they had enough alcohol to get tight." A Christmas pantomime, *Hey Diddle Snow White*, was staged in the icy theater, produced by Captain the Earl of Hopetoun, who also played the fairy queen.

Christmas in the German quarters was even more frugal, yet Eggers detected a "momentary happiness" within the guard company, now made up of middle-aged men and boys barely out of their teens. "It must all soon be over," he reflected. "Hitler's New Year speech was simply a call to fight on."

Despite the grinding hunger and intense cold, Platt also noticed a peculiarly festive air among the prisoners. "It is amazing to hear everyone describing this—the Christmas they most hated the thought of spending in Germany—as the best they have spent here."

One reason for that was the flying machine taking magnificent shape in the attic. For the glider was more than just an elaborate escape tool. It was a dream, a flight of near-fantasy that could take the prisoners' imaginations soaring over and beyond the castle walls. The glider was an object of faith, a beautiful blue-and-white gingham-clad symbol of hope, built from stolen bed boards and coated in old porridge.

1945

16

The Rhine Maiden

The American war correspondent Lee Carson was extremely beautiful. For many men that was the first, and sometimes the only, thing they noticed about her. Even her fellow newspaper reporters went into impassioned raptures over her looks. "Lee Carson has wavy red hair that hangs down to her shoulders and cool green eyes that light up when she talks, and full red lips and a throaty laugh . . . and she has dimples," wrote one salivating journalist. "When Lee crosses her legs, it's an event. She's something to look at." Because Lee Carson was so attractive, some of her male colleagues liked to imply that she had only succeeded in journalism by batting her eyelashes.

This was, of course, tosh. In spite of her good looks, Carson was one of the finest war reporters of the twentieth century: resourceful, resilient, witty, and astonishingly brave. She had left school at sixteen to join the *Chicago Sun-Times*. After working in the Washington bureau, and stints at *Good Housekeeping* and *Ladies' Home Journal*, at the age of twenty-two she was sent to Britain to cover the D-Day landings as a war correspondent for the International News Service. Women were officially barred from the front lines. But, in June 1944, Carson persuaded a U.S. pilot to smuggle her aboard a spotter plane and she witnessed the bombing of Cherbourg, the only woman reporter to come close to the Normandy invasion. When she landed back in Britain, an army press officer berated her: "Don't you know an article of war states women are not allowed with combat troops?"

"Sure," she replied. "I knew it, but it was my job to get the news. That came ahead of any articles of war or maidenly modesty."

Mixing with the invasion troops, she was confusingly addressed as "Ma'am Sir." Wherever she went Carson was met with cheering and catcalls from the American GIs. "I always reminded them of their wives, or sisters, or sweethearts. Here I was, filthy dirty, in ragged, muddy jacket and trousers, and just the fact that I was an American girl was enough . . . they thought 'Well if she's here, hell, it can't be that bad.'" In August, Carson was confined to a hotel in Rennes with a dozen other women correspondents as Allied troops converged on Paris; she broke out, attached herself to a unit of the Fourth Army, and rode into the French capital in a Jeep with the Reuters correspondent Bob Reuben. She insisted on sitting in the front seat, which made her the first journalist into liberated Paris. The writer Ernest Hemingway was later celebrated for liberating the bar of the Paris Ritz, running up a tab for fifty-one dry martinis. But he reached Paris after Lee Carson, who preferred highballs.

No woman was ever officially accredited to a fighting unit, yet Carson attached herself to the American First Army press camp, along with the British-born *Boston Globe* correspondent Iris Carpenter. They designed their own "uniforms": a khaki denim boiler suit, belted at the waist. A few weeks later, as the Allied troops fought their way eastward in pursuit of the retreating Germans, Carson was driving on a rutted road when her Jeep swerved and overturned at sixty miles per hour; she survived, but "tore open an old appendectomy wound." The army medics patched her up, and did so again when she broke her hand diving into a foxhole under fire. For the next six weeks, Carson typed one-handed, on a German portable typewriter she had found in an abandoned dugout. At Eschweiler on the Siegfried Line, the defensive line running along Germany's western border, she came under sustained mortar bombardment in a ruined house. "For two hours we lay there, with the walls coming down around our ears. Then we decided to get out." During the Battle of the Bulge she described the German planes "zooming down from the pink-streaked winter skies to shower our front-line positions with streams of hot lead, and tearing the world apart with their heavy artillery barrages." Some of her frontline companions remained perplexed by her gender: "Lee Carson is a regular 'guy' to travel with in the field," one wrote. "She does a man's job, and the way she does it wins the admiration of her competitive colleagues. She is constantly the subjects of whistles, shouts, and wisecracks, but she just takes it in her stride." Lee Carson went wherever she wanted, and no one dared stop her, for in addition to her beauty and journalistic skills, she had a formidable temper.

In December 1944, Carson reported the "Malmedy Massacre," where the Waffen-SS slaughtered eighty-four disarmed American POWs. She spent Christmas Day in a shell hole. As the First Army pushed deeper into Germany, Carson went with them. She described "the battle-stained, First Army doughboys, with rifles slung over their shoulders and beard-stubbled chins," and watched American army engineers laboring to lay pontoon bridges across the Rhine—"machine gun fire poured across the river . . . they fought the current, they fought the enemy, they fought cold, wet and fatigue, and they fought time." The soldiers called her "The Rhine Maiden." At Berrendorf, she watched seventy members of Hitler's Home Guard (the *Volkssturm*) meekly laying down their weapons: "We didn't fight," their leader told her. "What was the point?" There was no point, and yet some fought on. By mid-March, the First Army and Lee Carson were approaching the Mulde River. Beyond lay the last significant Nazi military resistance. The *Volkssturm* might be made up of old men and teenagers armed with anti-tank weapons they could hardly lift, but the holdouts also included hardened SS units ready to fight to the death. In his final broadcast, Hitler railed against "Jewish Asiatic Bolshevism," calling on "every able-bodied German" to resist the invaders with "the utmost fanaticism." And of all the places to make a futile and bloody last stand, none was more appropriate, or more defensible, than the vast castle on the hill built by ancient German princes as a symbol of overweening power.

As the Allies advanced, Colditz steadily filled up with Allied generals, British aristocrats, and other notables. Eggers remarked with dark irony that the Nazi leadership seemed to be making a "last minute shuffle through *Debrett's*," the bible of British genealogy, in search of more blue-blooded prisoners to take hostage. Someone in Berlin seemed to be laying down a grotesque insurance policy, collecting together individuals of value to be cashed in when the end came. Eggers wondered what the exchange rate might be. "Who was going to be offered for whom in the Final Bunker in Berlin? Who, or how many, would be suggested in exchange for the Führer? For Himmler . . . and so on?"

On January 19, 1945, four generals arrived in two army cars from the French officers' camp at Königstein. Eggers was told to expect a third car carrying a fifth French general, Gustave Mesny, commander of the North African Infantry, who had been captured in 1940. The car never appeared. The next day brought word that Mesny had been "shot on the autobahn" while attempting to escape. "He has been buried in Dresden with full military honors by a detachment of the Wehrmacht," Prawitt announced.

The reality was starkly different. Back in October, German general Fritz von Brodowski had been captured by French Resistance forces in eastern France, and subsequently killed in Besançon Castle, possibly in retaliation for the mass murder of 643 French civilians at Oradour-sur-Glane—an atrocity carried out by Waffen-SS troops ultimately under von Brodowski's command. Enraged, Hitler demanded the execution, in retaliation, of a captive French general. The SS discussed various ways of carrying out the Führer's order, including a plan to construct an airtight partition between the front and rear seats of a car, and place the intended victim in the back. "Odorless carbon-monoxide gas will be introduced during the drive into the inner compartment through a special apparatus to be controlled from the front seat. A few breaths will suffice to ensure death. The gas being odorless, there is no reason for the general to become suspicious at the decisive moment and break the windows in order to let in fresh air." The Reich was disintegrating, but SS executioners were still dreaming up imaginative and efficient ways to gas their enemies. Of the five French generals, Mesny was selected at random by SS Oberst Friedrich Meurer, chief of staff to Obergruppenführer Gottlob Berger of the SS High Command. In the end, the killing was quite simple. The car carrying Mesny, driven by SS officers disguised in Wehrmacht uniforms, stopped in a wood off the motorway between Königstein and Colditz.

Hauptmann Schweinitzer, an officer on Himmler's general staff, swiveled in the front passenger seat, shot the French general in the heart at point-blank range, and then dropped off the corpse at the Dresden military hospital. The assassination was not even a propaganda exercise or a warning to the Resistance, since it was immediately hushed up. Planned by Berger, the new *Über-Kommandant* of the prison camps, and carried out by his underlings, this squalid, secret, tit-for-tat murder served no purpose other than to slake Hitler's desperate bloodthirst as his Reich went down in flames.

The French generals were followed to Colditz a few weeks later by an equally distinguished military contingent of Poles, led by General Tadeusz Bór-Komorowski, commander in chief of the secret Polish Home Army that had resisted Nazi occupation for five long years. In August 1944, with Soviet forces advancing on Central Poland, Bór-Komorowski led the Warsaw Uprising against the Germans and took over most of the capital. The Red Army, however, stopped at the city's eastern edge beyond the Vistula River and ignored Polish pleas for help, enabling the Germans to regroup and launch a ferocious counterattack. The street fighting continued for sixty-three days. More than 16,000 Polish Resistance fighters were killed, along with thousands of civilians murdered by the Nazis in mass executions. Stalin may have deliberately allowed the uprising to fail, ensuring that his troops could march into Warsaw unopposed once the Polish Resistance had been destroyed. Without Soviet support, surrounded and outgunned, Bór-Komorowski finally surrendered in exchange for a German promise to treat his captured soldiers as prisoners of war under the Geneva Convention. He and 15,000 of his men were marched off to camps in Germany. Bór-Komorowski was a small, bald, wiry cavalryman who had received a medal on behalf of the Polish equestrian team from Hitler himself at the 1936 Berlin Olympic Games. He loathed the communists as much as he detested the Nazis. When Eggers dared to ask him whether he would prefer German or Russian occupation, he spat: "Even if you occupy my country for twenty years, both of you, my people will remain Polish." Julius Green thought the Polish general could have been mistaken for a "solicitor's clerk, until you took a close look and saw the steely eyes and air of ruthless determination." Bór-Komorowski and his entourage of five generals, nine other senior officers, and seven orderlies took up residence in the *Prominente* quarters. "It has been a pleasure to hear Polish voices again," wrote Padre Platt.

The days passed in a strange clatter of contrasts: buoyancy and gloom, industry and lassitude, fear and absurdity. Micky Burn rushed to finish his novel before the war ended: *Yes, Farewell* was an accurate fictionalized portrait of Colditz, but also a disguised socialist manifesto declaring the old class structure dead and buried. Its heroes were the orderlies, solid men of simple virtue. With his fellow communist Giles Romilly, Burn continued to lecture on the virtues of the Soviet Union. General Bór-Komorowski was persuaded to give a contrasting and equally passionate talk, simultaneously translated by his aide, on the perils of "Russian duplicity." The glider took shape in the attics. Florimond Duke lectured on Anglo-American relations, pointing out that "one of the main differences between the British and Americans was the language."

Duke's role as Senior American Officer had taken on new significance with the arrival of an American soldier facing imminent execution. In Szubin camp, Colonel William Schaefer had prevented a German NCO from pinning up the notice declaring that "escape from prison camps is no longer a sport," a serious breach of prison discipline. In Leipzig, he was court-martialed and sentenced to death, a verdict personally approved by Hitler. The condemned man was sent to Colditz to await execution, and now languished in solitary confinement, smoking endless cigarettes. "His nerves were not up to it," wrote Rudolf Denzler, the Swiss official. "He lost his hair and teeth."

The bread ration was reduced still further. Platt noticed that some officers were "squirrelling" supplies: "They are so afraid of the wolf that they dare not eat the food that is in their hands." Julius Green's imaginary dinners were taking on a hallucinatory quality, but the dentist continued to dream up impossible banquets as the food ran out. He now believed he had perfected the ideal imaginary menu: "Smoked salmon, minestrone, roast beef, pineapple and kirsch, followed by coffee and a good brandy."

The inhabitants of Colditz were hungry, but they were nowhere near as famished as the desperate lines of German refugees toiling through the town below, a wave of starving humanity hurled from their homes by the advancing Allied armies. "They looked a heart-rending sight trudging brokenly across the bridge. Some carried small bundles, but some could barely carry themselves." On February 10, a "very appreciative audience" packed into Colditz theater to see *They Came to a City,* J. B. Priestley's play about the hopes and fears of people moving to a model city.

Three days later, more than 1,200 British and American bombers converged on Dresden, the last major German city as yet unscathed by bombing. Over the next two days, some 25,000 people were killed and a cultural landmark was obliterated in one of the most ferocious acts of war ever carried out. "It is not possible to describe!" said one survivor. "Explosion after explosion. It was beyond belief, worse than the blackest nightmare." The prisoners could see the conflagration taking place thirty miles to the east; those who could not bear to watch felt the bombardment reverberating through the castle walls. "The old *Schloss* rocked, dropping dust and plaster," wrote Platt. Many of the German guards were from Dresden. Eggers gave his clerk permission to return to the city to search for his family. "When he got home, he found the house burned out and his family all dead." Appalled by the carnage taking place on the horizon, the padre requested permission to take a "parole walk" in the countryside. For the first time in months, Platt left the castle and walked beside the Mulde, a guard trailing behind him. "A chaffinch burst into song. Coal tits were singing their eager, nervous little ditty, and flitting through the apple trees." Here was innocent birdsong in a tranquil valley, while just a few miles away men burned one another to death in multitudes.

A rumor swirled around the castle that all the prisoners would soon be transferred to the "Bavarian Redoubt" where the Nazis were expected to make their last stand. Colonels Tod and Duke requested a meeting with the Kommandant and asked what steps

would be taken when Allied forces reached Colditz. Prawitt replied vaguely, but also truthfully, that he had "no instructions
on this point." Rudolf Denzler returned for what he hoped
would be a final inspection. The Swiss official found the castle
feverish with uncertainty, but his presence seemed to lend the
prisoners courage: "His twinkling pince-nez and avuncular so-
ciability turned the edge of doubt."

"How much longer?" he was asked, as another formation of
Allied bombers droned overhead.

"Not much longer," he replied, with an optimism he did not
feel. Denzler knew the prisoners had never been in greater peril.
The rule of law was dissolving in Germany, and with it his abil-
ity to protect them: "The castle was like a ship threatened by a
storm just before reaching harbor," he wrote.

Former inmates were also watching from a distance, with
mounting unease, as the hurricane rolled closer to Colditz. From
Switzerland, Pat Reid wrote to the Foreign Office, expressing
"serious alarm for the safety and lives of the POWs at Colditz"
and demanding that something be done to protect them or enable them to defend themselves. "The officers and *Prominente* of
Colditz will be held as hostages," Reid predicted. "The POWs
will at a specified moment be moved from Colditz to the center
of the Nazi ring wherever that may be." His plan for liberating
the castle was radical: "Blow the garrison courtyard and the
guard house to bits by very low accurate bombing, drop arms in
the inner courtyard and give the officers a chance for their lives.
They will do the rest."

Pierre Mairesse-Lebrun had a similar idea in mind, but one
even more flamboyant. With the same panache that had sent him
sailing over the perimeter wire in 1941, he intended to liberate
Colditz in person, with his own army. The dashing French cavalry officer had crossed the Rhine south of Strasbourg with the
Liberation Army, and he now approached General Jean de Lattre
de Tassigny, commander in chief of French forces in Germany,
with a suggestion. "I knew of the *Prominente,* and I was convinced that they, if not every POW in Colditz, all known as
deutschfeindlich, would become hostages to be held as such, or

massacred in the last resort." Mairesse-Lebrun asked de Lattre to give him "two squadrons of tanks with supplies and ammunition for a lightning thrust to Colditz," some 300 miles to the northeast. "Germany was beginning to crumble," he wrote. "Whatever I did had to be done quickly." De Lattre approved the plan, and Mairesse-Lebrun was preparing for a glorious dash to Colditz, when the scheme was scuppered by the Americans, who feared, rightly, that this independent relief force might collide with the advancing Russians and trigger an embarrassing conflict.

The fears of Pat Reid and Pierre Mairesse-Lebrun were fully shared in London, Paris, Washington, and General Eisenhower's Supreme Allied Headquarters. What fate did Hitler intend for the vast population of men he still held prisoner? If the camps were simply abandoned, many inmates would undoubtedly die of starvation and disease, or face reprisals from the local population. If they were marched deeper into Germany ahead of the Allied armies, men already enfeebled by malnutrition would surely perish on the way. Would Hitler corral some or even all of them into his final stronghold as hostages, a human shield against aerial bombardment? Or would the SS simply slaughter them all, in a final, horrific *Götterdämmerung*?

In February, at Sunningdale golf course southwest of London, the newly formed Special Allied Airborne Reconnaissance Force began training 120 three-man teams to rescue thousands of endangered POWs. Recruited from British and American special operations units, the SOE and the OSS, these heavily armed agents would parachute into the collapsing Reich with radio sets and infiltrate the prison camps. Once inside, they would "contact the Senior British Officer and open radio communications with advancing Allied troops [who] would then drop arms and supplies and give air cover while the garrison was overpowered." The plan to seize control of the POW camps from within was appropriately codenamed "Eclipse." Three teams were allotted to Colditz, including one led by Patrick Leigh Fermor, the scholar, writer, and soldier who had already successfully operated behind the lines in Crete. With Henry Coombe-Tennant, an escaped

POW who would go on to become a Benedictine monk, Leigh Fermor began forging plans to liberate Colditz before the SS got there.

But they were too late.

In early March, Irmgard Wernicke and her messenger, the young German guard Heinz Schmidt, passed on a grim rumor circulating around town: SS squads had arrived with "orders to kill the prisoners when the time came." The Colditz Intelligence Unit run by David Stirling and Checko Chaloupka was proving highly effective. Astonishingly, the older Schmidt had successfully bribed the telephone operator of the Colditz switchboard to note down all calls to the Kommandant from Berlin and Dresden: "More and more often the calls came from SS and Gestapo sources." At the same time, another of Schmidt's spies inside the *Kommandantur* reported seeing a letter on Prawitt's desk, "signed by Hitler saying that the *Prominente* were under no condition to be allowed to fall into Allied hands." Something unpleasant was brewing.

If the order came to move the VIP hostages or carry out a massacre, it would certainly be relayed through the Dresden offices of Martin Mutschmann, the Gauleiter of Saxony, who had visited the castle in triumph to inspect the discovered French tunnel in 1942. As befits the founder of the SAS, David Stirling launched a preemptive strike: a "strongly worded and threatening" letter in idiomatic German, handwritten in Gothic script, and personally addressed to Mutschmann. "Your day in power is over," it began. "Now you face death." The letter went on to warn that "if any harm came to prisoners in Colditz the Allies would see to it that he was hanged." It was unsigned, but phrased as if it had come from the growing anti-Nazi German Resistance. Mutschmann was the most powerful man in Saxony, but he was also a coward, and with Armageddon looming some senior Nazis were actively exploring how to save their own hides. "We hoped it might give the Gauleiter some worried moments, and perhaps make him think twice in a crisis," wrote Jack Pringle. The letter was passed on from Heinz Schmidt to Irma Wernicke, who took the train to what remained of Dresden, and posted it.

The prisoners had spent more than four years trying to get out of the castle; now, it seemed, they might have to fight the Germans in order to stay in it. Colonel Tod began making resistance plans. If an attempt was made to move them, the staircases would be blocked with furniture. A battering ram was constructed in the attic, to be used if necessary to break down the door to the armory. Julius Green prepared an emergency medical kit of drugs and dressings, for use "in case of attack or forcible eviction." The glider was ready to fly; what had once been an escape tool was now seen as a way to send two men to get help if the SS closed in. "The glider is to be held in reserve in strict secrecy," Tod ordered. If the Germans attempted to seize the *Prominente,* evacuate the prisoners, or kill them all, the move would come without warning. "Whatever was going to happen to us would happen soon," wrote one officer. Irma and her network were closely monitoring local troop movements and other menacing signs, but alerting the prisoners in the event of an emergency would take time. "We could not wait for meetings with Heinz, which could only take place every other night when he came on guard."

The Intelligence Unit, and its spies in the village, devised an early-warning system. Three hundred feet below the castle, on the street at the foot of the hill, stood a lamppost, clearly visible from the windows of the British quarters. In collaboration with Irma, Heinz, and his father, a simple visual code was agreed. Every day, at 9 a.m., 12 p.m., and 4 p.m., a trusted man would appear at this signal site. If he simply leaned on the lamppost for a few minutes and then walked away, this meant "Nothing to report"; if he crossed the road, it would indicate "You are to be moved"; if he lit a cigarette, it sent the message: "German troops are pulling out." The fourth signal was the most complicated, and the most feared. If the agent walked in the center of the road, passed the restaurant, halted at the first telegraph pole on the left for half a minute, and then returned to the lamppost, he was signaling: "Extreme danger. Come out at all costs." This would be the trigger for the prisoners to launch a mass breakout, armed with whatever weapons they could find. The signal would be made only "if the castle was to be blown up," or the SS was mustering for a full-scale assault. Every day, three times a day, a lookout trained a homemade telescope on the lamppost. But even with forewarning the prisoners could not hold out for long: in the end, their fates would depend on whether the Colditz garrison opted to defend the inmates from the SS or surrender them.

One morning after roll call, Tod addressed the prisoners. "Gentlemen, there comes a time when things get so bad, all one can do is laugh." He continued, unsmiling: "The Germans have informed me that there will be over 1,000 French officers coming here in the next few days." The French prison camp east of Leipzig had been evacuated ahead of the Soviet advance, and its inmates herded westward. By the time they reached Colditz they had been driven, like cattle, for almost a week and "were in the most terrible state, unshaven, unwashed and smelling to high heaven in their filthy clothes." Eggers watched them tramp in like a "barbarian horde." Some 1,200 were crammed into the castle, with a further 600 imprisoned in a makeshift camp outside the town. The British were moved into the *Kellerhaus* basement to make room, but there were not enough beds for all; the overspill slept on straw spread on the floor of the chapel and in the latrines. "With 2,000 near-starving men on our hands," wrote Eggers, the food shortage was desperate. The drains swiftly blocked up. The hot water stopped. Famished prisoners brewed a gritty and tasteless broth from potato and turnip peelings scraped off the kitchen floor. When even more ravenous prisoners arrived, Eggers distributed a single slice of bread and jam to each, with his revolver drawn to prevent them from stealing one another's meager rations. The air raid sirens sounded day and night. "All is jostle & racket & apology & smell," complained the padre. When the fuel finally ran out, a handful of prisoners were allowed outside the walls, on parole, to collect fallen wood in the *Tiergarten*. One of the foragers wrote: "As we walked back into the yard the prison smell hit us in the face." Colditz was descending into a freezing, stinking, starving vision of purgatory.

Into this hellhole, on April 6, strode an oddly angelic figure, "a fair-haired young man with steel-blue eyes and a sensitive character," the last prisoner into Colditz and the latest addition to the exclusive ranks of the *Prominente*. Lieutenant John Winant Jr. had been a twenty-one-year-old sophomore at Princeton when he quit university to enlist in the U.S. Air Force; he flew thirteen missions over Germany before his B-17 Flying Fortress bomber was shot down near Münster in 1943. He parachuted from the stricken plane and was swiftly captured. Winant was just another POW, except that his father was the U.S. ambassador to Britain. A former governor of New Hampshire, tipped by some as a possible future president, John G. Winant Sr. had been appointed America's ambassador to the Court of St. James by Roosevelt in 1941, and would remain in that post throughout the war. Ambassador Winant was a popular figure and a champion of the war effort, whose desire for close Anglo-American bilateral relations even extended to having an affair with Churchill's daughter Sarah. So when news reached Britain that Winant's eldest son and namesake had been taken prisoner, "the American Embassy in London was flooded with letters and telegrams from well-wishers in the United States, Great Britain and other countries." The young pilot had spent eighteen months in a POW camp near Munich when he was abruptly transferred to Colditz.

John Winant was rather baffled to have been thus singled out, but it soon became clear why he had been brought there: the son of the American ambassador could be a valuable pawn. "He was in face and figure and in all else the Englishman's idea of an American college boy," observed Michael Alexander, with a flicker of English *hauteur,* when Winant was ushered into their quarters. The clutch of Colditz VIPs now included Polish and French generals, British aristocrats, politicians' relatives, members of the royal family, and one famous young American. The chips were down, and someone in Berlin was putting together what might prove to be a winning hand. "We never discovered exactly who it was among Hitler's entourage who was looking for a likely swap in his own personal interests [by] horse trading in hostages," wrote Eggers. The probable answer was Himmler himself, who had retained personal control of the department overseeing prisoner affairs.

Four days after Winant's arrival, the fighting to the west became clearly audible. The Americans had now reached Halle, twenty-five miles from Leipzig, and were advancing swiftly in the direction of Colditz. A ragged stream of German tanks and armored cars rumbled through the town heading south toward Chemnitz, where the Wehrmacht Area Command had set up a new headquarters, an army facing oblivion with nowhere to go. "People are constantly staring out of the windows in a westerly direction," wrote Gris Davies-Scourfield. "Others are busy packing." But not every German soldier was retreating. A force of 200 men from the 101st Motorized Rifle Battalion, led by SS officers and supported by tanks, moved into the town and began preparing for a last-ditch defense: the prisoners watched as members of the Hitler Youth dug trenches and foxholes in the slope opposite the castle. The SS barricaded the main street and established defensive positions inside houses on the outer edges of the town. The *Volkssturm* battalion was mustered, armed with a handful of rifles and a couple of *Panzerfaust* handheld anti-tank warheads. They unrolled barbed wire across the bridge over the Mulde, and then stood around uncertainly. Several tanks and motorized artillery took up positions in the woods overlooking the valley.

The SS officer in command appeared at the castle gates and demanded to see the Kommandant. His orders were to make a stand at the river, he told Prawitt and Eggers, and "he would need all the men and munitions that we could muster." Prawitt explained that his garrison had been reduced to just 200 men, all aged over fifty, armed with ancient French rifles and a dozen rounds of ammunition each, ten machine guns, and a few hand grenades. Some 700 of the French officers had been shifted to another camp, but the castle was still rammed with hungry, nervous, and increasingly unmanageable prisoners; he would need every guard just to keep them from mounting an insurrection. The SS Hauptmann reluctantly agreed, but something in the Kommandant's manner had alerted him to a hint of disloyalty. He left with a warning: "If white flags were raised on the castle, he would shoot the place up."

Every day, at 9 a.m., midday, and 4 p.m., the signaler leaned on the lamppost below the castle: nothing to report. Yet the feverish defensive preparations confirmed Irma Wernicke's warnings: "Colditz was becoming a battle zone." Once again, Willie Tod and Florimond Duke asked to see Prawitt. American troops would reach Colditz within days, if not hours. What were his intentions? Again, Prawitt temporized, saying he was "awaiting orders." He did not reveal that those orders had already been drawn up by Himmler himself, along with an emergency system of coded messages to put them into action.

If the Area Command HQ telephoned through the code word *Heidenröslein* to the Kommandant, this was the signal to evacuate the *Prominente*. The choice of word was deliberate. *Heidenröslein* is the title of a celebrated poem by Goethe. When a young lover goes to pick the "Rose of the Heath," the rosebud does not give up without drawing blood:

> Said the boy, "I'll now pick thee,
> Heathrose fair and tender!"
> Said the rosebud, "I'll prick thee,
> So that thou'lt remember me,
> Never will I surrender!"

On receipt of the coded signal, Prawitt's orders were to assemble the VIP prisoners at the outer gate. The SS would send a squad of stormtroopers and two buses to collect them. The *Prominente* would then be transferred farther east to the fortress at Königstein, behind the dissolving German front line.

The second coded signal was even more dramatic. If headquarters sent the letters "ZR," this stood for *Zerstörung-Räumung* (Destruction-Evacuation): all documentary evidence in Colditz should be burned, remaining food stocks and weapons gathered up, the prison evacuated, and the inmates moved out at gunpoint using "whatever transport is available." This amounted, Eggers noted, to "one antique vehicle, barely working, and two horse-drawn carts." The prisoners should then be taken "to the east." The order did not specify where.

As a Methodist minister, Padre Platt felt it was incumbent on him to exhibit a devout and dignified aspect at all times, but his diary entry for April 12, written in bed after the prisoners had been locked into their quarters, was as close as he ever came to giddy overexcitement.

> Army trucks, armoured cars and tanks have streamed over the bridge all day, an army in retreat. The German army personnel, armour and convoys are perhaps making for Berchtesgaden [Hitler's hilltop retreat in Bavaria] where, rumour says, the last stand will be made. By 10:00 am we had a rumour of an American army having reached the Elbe; by midday they were reported to be 12 miles from Leipzig. Artillery has been plainly heard since 1:30. The camp was in a furore of excitement and every inch of window-space was crowded with leaning, crushing bodies. Tonight we have a red-hot rumour of a large tank concentration four miles west of Colditz. The announcement of the death of President Roosevelt came over the air. Defence preparations continued around the village more furiously. Slit trenches could be seen everywhere in the fields on the higher slopes and bordering the woods. Boys and girls of all ages could be seen at work with spades and pickaxes alongside their elders in uniform. The Germans look as if they are going to make a serious stand in the country around the castle . . . The SBO has gone to interview the Kommandant—on what subject we do not know.

The subject was the *Prominente*.

That afternoon a one-word message had arrived on Gerhard Prawitt's desk: *Heidenröslein*.

17

Besieged

For two years, Oberstleutnant Prawitt had ruled Colditz as his fiefdom. Now he was in serious personal danger, under threat from the advancing Americans, the SS in the town, and more than 1,000 increasingly assertive prisoners. The code word ordering him to ship out the *Prominente* had come through at 5 p.m. He summoned Eggers to a council of war. They could ignore the order, but the SS would then undoubtedly storm the castle, probably arrest them both, and seize the special prisoners by force. If the VIPs realized what was happening, some or all of them would surely try to hide, or disappear among the teeming prisoners. "In those circumstances we should never catch them at all, even inside the castle, without bloodshed," said Eggers. The prisoners might riot: "No telling what they might do if this news got around. There could be a revolt." But if Eggers and Prawitt obeyed orders and delivered the *Prominente* to the SS they would be held legally responsible for whatever subsequently happened to them. The war was almost over, and there would be an accounting when it was lost. Neither man was a murderer: they knew that the future for these men in SS hands was at best uncertain, and at worst extremely short. But the habits of obedience were ingrained, and Himmler's order was explicit: the Kommandant must hand over the *Prominente,* and "would be answerable with his life if any escaped." Prawitt and Eggers agreed they would delay making a move until the prisoners were securely in bed. "By 10 o'clock the yard was clear and all the prisoners were locked in their quarters or the chapel," wrote Eggers. Colonels Tod and Duke were summoned to the Kommandant's office.

"Tall and emaciated," Prawitt saluted stiffly and invited them to sit. Through an interpreter, he informed the senior officers that the special prisoners would be leaving the castle at midnight. "The SS force in the village is supplying the guard to protect the *Prominente*." He was not at liberty to say where they would be going.

Tod's response was immediate and emphatic. "We demand that you ignore the orders."

Prawitt shook his head. The SS troop was just a few hundred yards away. If he did not follow Himmler's orders, then they would do so, with maximum force. "If I refuse to obey this order the SS will carry out reprisals, not only against me but against the entire castle. There will be many deaths throughout the camp, and still the *Prominente* will depart."

Tod and Duke remonstrated. Allied aircraft were strafing the roads. "It would be madness to send out two truckloads of prisoners through an ever-narrowing corridor between American and Russian forces . . . sending them to certain danger and possible death."

Duke chimed in: "It is your duty as a responsible officer to act independently, exercising your own best judgment."

Prawitt was unbending. "The move will take place tonight. The move will be completed by daybreak."

Now they appealed to Prawitt's Prussian sense of legal order, and his instinct for self-preservation. The Geneva Convention required a detaining power to give twenty-four hours' notice before moving prisoners, and to state their destination. "You will be held personally responsible for the abduction of the *Prominente*," said Tod.

Prawitt shrugged. They would be guarded by the SS, so the responsibility was theirs.

"And who will protect them from the SS?" Duke demanded.

This question gave Prawitt pause. The American had a point. If the SS simply executed the prisoners after he handed them over, the Allies might charge him as an accessory to murder. The buck might stop with him and so, as bosses have tended to do throughout the ages, he passed it on.

Prawitt gestured toward Reinhold Eggers. His security officer,

Hauptmann Eggers, would accompany the VIPs to their destination, and then "return to Colditz with a letter signed by the *Prominente* announcing their safe arrival at wherever it might be."

Eggers was stunned. In one stroke, Prawitt had removed himself from the firing line, and placed his subordinate directly in it. "My head was a target from both sides in this affair, from my own and from the Allies," Eggers wrote. "If the *Prominente* escaped, Hitler would get me and my family too. If the *Prominente* were killed, the Allies would finish me off as responsible for their deaths."

Tod went straight to the *Prominente* quarters, where additional sentries had taken up positions, to convey the bad news: the men had an hour to pack. He tried to sound reassuring. "The situation is changing hourly, and in our favor," Tod said. "The Swiss Protecting Power has had specific warning and requests to follow the movement of any prisoners. You will not be deserted." Charlie Hopetoun and Dawyck Haig were both unwell, and had to be hauled out of the sickbay. Maintaining status to the last, the *Prominente* officers insisted that they were "entitled to at least two orderlies" to pack and carry their luggage. The "other ranks" had been crammed into an attic. The orderly officer asked for volunteers, and two New Zealand soldiers, both Maoris, stepped forward. Eggers was astonished that anyone would voluntarily "take this trip with their officers into the unknown."

Young John Winant managed to separate himself from the other *Prominente* and hid in the attics. Florimond Duke was immediately summoned back to Prawitt's office.

"If he has not been found by the time the *Prominente* are ready to leave," said the Kommandant, "the SS will take up the search."

"And if they don't find him?" asked Duke.

"There will be shooting."

"You and your men are sworn to protect prisoners."

"What can my handful of old men do against 800 SS troops?"

Moreover, the SS would seize the opportunity to occupy the prison if the American ambassador's son failed to reappear. "That would please the SS commander," said Prawitt. "He could move his men into the castle, to put down the revolt. Once in, they would stay . . ."

Duke knew he was right. "The castle would be a great spot for a fanatical last stand."

Prawitt got to his feet. "In an hour, an SS detachment will arrive to escort the *Prominente*. If Lieutenant Winant is not ready to move, with the rest, then God help us all."

Refusing to surrender one American would place the life of every other prisoner in jeopardy. "I've decided the risk is too great," Duke told Guy Nunn, who went to find Winant in the attic.

At 1:30 in the morning, Captain John Elphinstone, the King's nephew and the most senior British officer of the group, led twenty-one men across the courtyard and through the gate to the waiting buses. The posse of *Prominente* now consisted of seven British officers of varied nobility and notability, the Polish contingent under General Bór-Komorowski, two Maori orderlies, and a lone American. The other prisoners crowded the windows, shouting encouragement as they departed. Giles Romilly described the moment in a series of snapshot images: "General Bór marching out impeccable. Castle attempting its Van Gogh look. Walls light greenish-yellow. Potato Cobbles. Potato-faces. Prawitt switching boot. A great moon emerging from behind clouds." They passed through two lines of stormtroopers. "There was no friendliness to their faces, a black Alsatian hung around their heels." Eggers, wearing "a crisp uniform" and an expression of deep anxiety, was the first aboard. Flanked by two motorcycle outriders and followed by an armored car, the convoy set off "as if on some hellish holiday excursion, down the hill, over the bridge, and through the deserted streets of Colditz."

Friday, April 13, was unnervingly quiet. The very air seemed "dead still, like the middle of a typhoon." Distant artillery fire boomed from the direction of Leipzig, but the air raid sirens had fallen silent. The night had been spent wondering what would become of the *Prominente*. Few slept. Padre Platt claimed to have seen two officers of the SS escort studying a map under the light and speculated that "they seemed to be indicating a road veering south in the direction of Berchtesgaden." Rumors swirled and eddied around the castle. Some said Soviet paratroopers were already dropping on Berlin. The optimists claimed the Americans were just over the brow of the hill. Others were doubtful that liberty was truly at hand. "We reckon it is 50/50 on all of us being moved today," wrote Platt. "But where can they move us to?" The most widespread theory was that they would be herded south, destined to become pawns, like the *Prominente*, in some horrific last stand in the Bavarian Alps. Reinhold Eggers returned in the evening, bringing with him a handwritten note from Elphinstone confirming that the group had been delivered to Königstein Castle and were safe, for the time being. Eggers liked to exude a schoolmasterly air of omniscience at all times, but even he admitted he had no clue what might be in store for the hostages.

The prisoners responded to the uncertainty by gorging themselves. For weeks, they had been eking out the remaining food stocks. Now they ate the lot. Whether the next day brought liberation, a forced march to some Nazi redoubt, or death, they would be well-fed. "It seems absurd not to eat everything up, for who could know how and when we might eat again," wrote Gris Davies-Scourfield, who carefully listed his consumption that day: cheese soufflé, bread and butter with jam, soup, cold salmon, mashed potato, fried Spam, French beans and turnip, cake, chocolate prune pudding, and "a delicious cup of coffee." It was another disturbed night, partly due to excitement and anxiety over what tomorrow might bring, but also on account of acute indigestion.

At 9 a.m. the next day, the lookout trained his telescope on the signal site. But instead of leaning on the lamppost as usual, the signaler crossed the road with slow, deliberate steps, and then turned to look up at the castle: *You are to be moved*. Sure enough, an hour earlier, a two-letter message to Prawitt had arrived from German Area Command Headquarters: "ZR." Destruction-Evacuation.

The *Prominente* were already on the move again. Hopetoun and Haig were too ill to travel, and remained in the sickbay at Königstein with one of the Maori orderlies. But the others were loaded back on the buses for a hopscotch odyssey through a series of camps, each mile taking them farther from the advancing Allied armies: south through Czechoslovakia to Kattau, then Laufen, and finally Tittmoning, a medieval fortress in southeastern Bavaria near the Austrian border. To the south, beyond Salzburg, lay Berchtesgaden, Hitler's "National Redoubt" high in the Bavarian Alps. The Alpine Fortress (*Alpenfestung*) built around the Bergdorf, or Eagle's Nest, consisted of a system of mighty defensive works including a command complex of 200,000 square feet hollowed out of the mountain beneath Hitler's private chalet. If the Nazi diehards dug in here with their hostages, it would be impossible to dig them out without a bloodbath.

Tittmoning was a prison for Dutch officers. One of the first to greet the new arrivals was Captain Machiel van den Heuvel, the officer who had engineered so many of the Colditz escapes. "Vandy" had a good idea where the *Prominente* were headed and, as usual, he had an escape plan ready.

The following evening, Giles Romilly and a Dutch officer hid in the ditch running along the inside of the ramparts. Soon after midnight, "under a moon of brilliant power and size," they lowered themselves ninety feet into the moat. On the way down Romilly tore the skin off his knuckles as the bedsheet rope twisted and sent him swinging into the rock face. "Moon, castle, space, whirled in one bowl." At the bottom, they scrambled down a bank, and onto the road. Following "a compass as tiny and miraculous as a wren's eye," they headed in what they hoped was the direction of the railway station. There, if their luck held out, they might catch a train to Munich. "The peace of the night amazed us. It was beyond reasonable hope."

While Romilly marveled at the embracing silence of the Alps, his companions immured themselves in Tittmoning Castle. Van den Heuvel led them to a deep window recess, where the ancient wall was some eight feet thick. "The Dutchman got down on his hands and knees and, by the light of a small torch, began to ease a knife blade between the great stone blocks that formed the wall. A stone slid out and revealed a hole just large enough for us to wriggle through, one by one." A short tunnel led to a chamber, three feet square and twelve feet high. When the Germans discovered they were missing, Vandy predicted, they would assume all the British prisoners, with Winant, had escaped by the same route as Romilly. He could supply them with sufficient food and water to remain hidden for a week; by the end of that time, the war might be won. The five officers crammed inside. The Maori orderly was not invited. The Polish contingent elected not to take part, and could not have been accommodated anyway. There was so little space that two had to lie side by side in the tunnel, one stood, the fourth perched on an upper ledge, and the fifth on a lavatory bucket. To avoid cramp, they changed places every two hours. Michael Alexander slept not a wink that first night, "wondering how long we would have to spend in this intolerably ill-appointed hole."

The Swiss official Rudolf Denzler was back in Berne awaiting the end of the war when a message arrived from the British delegate of the foreign interest section in Geneva. Marked "Very Urgent," it listed the names of the *Prominente* and described how they had been removed from Colditz by the SS and taken to an unknown destination. It ended with an earnest request: "Ascertain immediately where these prisoners are being kept, undertake everything possible to assure their safety and wellbeing, and warn the German authorities most solemnly that any failure in this matter will have the most serious consequences for those responsible." Denzler had a hunch where they might be headed. "We had every reason to assume that the leaders of the Third Reich were contemplating making a last stand in the Alps." He climbed into his little Swiss car and headed back into Nazi Germany.

The Colditz prisoners were ordered to assemble, with whatever possessions they could carry, in the inner courtyard at 10 a.m. By 11 a.m. none had appeared. At 11:10 the senior officers were brought to the Kommandant's office.

"Why is the parade not ready?" Prawitt demanded.

"I have changed my mind," Tod said quietly. "We are not prepared to leave the castle."

The warning from their collaborators in the village had given him time to formulate a plan with Florimond Duke and the senior French officer.

"Then the prisoners will be moved by force," Prawitt snapped.

Tod bit back. "By force? Have you no idea of what is happening out there? The Americans are only twenty miles away. They will be here in a few hours."

"That is not our information," Prawitt said stiffly.

Tod ignored him and continued. "If you attempt to use force, then I must warn you that we shall resist and then there will be bloodshed. How will you explain this bloodshed when the Americans arrive?"

"We have been waiting for this day for a long time," Duke added. "Now, with freedom only hours away, not you nor anybody else will ever get these men out of Colditz."

Given how much of that time had been spent trying to get out of Colditz this was quite a funny remark, albeit unintentional. No one smiled.

Prawitt picked up the telephone and asked to be put through to the Area Command Headquarters at Glauchau. The men in the room could hear only one side of the conversation, but the gist was clear.

"Yes, General, I have already given the order. Yes, General, but they refuse to obey. Yes, General, I have indeed warned them, but it makes no difference. There will undoubtedly be bloodshed."

The debate raged back and forth, with the Kommandant desperately trying to pass liability to the general, and the general passing it back.

Finally, Prawitt lost patience: "General, will you accept responsibility for what will happen here?"

There was a brief pause.

"Then neither will I!" Prawitt snarled and slammed down the receiver.

A man hollowed of all authority, the Kommandant slowly turned to Tod. "What do you want me to do?"

At exactly 11:30 a.m. on April 14, 1945, control of Colditz passed from the guards to the prisoners.

Eggers was quietly relieved. "We would never have got the prisoners out, and even if we had no one relished the prospect of trying to keep them together on a trek in the path of the advancing Russians." He began destroying evidence. All day, five guards shoveled stacks of documents into the boiler. By midnight, the vast sea of paper that told the bureaucratic story of the prison had gone up in smoke. But Eggers was a historian: the artifacts of the Colditz Museum were carefully packed into boxes and stacked in the cellar. With punctilious propriety, every item of personal property confiscated from the prisoners on arrival was returned to them, 1,400 objects in all: fountain pens, knives, British banknotes. The American colonel Schaefer, under sentence of death in the solitary cells, was released. In the theater, the men who had once stitched costumes and fake uniforms began sewing flags—Polish, French, and British—to fly from the ramparts when the moment of liberation came. Now the Germans began to pack: one small suitcase each. The wheel was turning at bewildering speed. The sounds of gunfire were coming closer. American artillery shells began bursting within sight of the castle.

"We think the SS might move into the castle," Tod told Prawitt. "We request that you give us the keys to the arsenal. We will arm the prisoners to defend it from the SS."

Again, Duke chimed in. "You have much more to fear from the SS than the Americans."

With extreme reluctance, Prawitt handed over the keys to the ammunition depot and weapons stores, on the understanding that these would not be distributed to prisoners unless the SS tried to take over the castle. In the meantime, the German sentries would continue to patrol as usual: the SS could not be allowed to know that Prawitt had already surrendered. "If they saw white flags or Allied flags exposed [they] would almost certainly storm into the castle, precipitating a bloody battle." The charade carried a risk: if the advancing Americans were unaware that the castle had changed hands, they might attack it.

There was one piece of paperwork to be completed: Tod handed the Kommandant a sheet of paper. "In consequence of the correct behaviour of Lieutenant Colonel Prawitt and his officers in handing over the camp, no reprisal measures will be taken . . . every protection will be afforded them and their families, the NCOs and men will be released as soon as possible." The Germans would be absolved of responsibility for whatever had happened in the past, save in two specific cases: the death of Michael Sinclair, and the fate of the *Prominente*. Prawitt signed. His defeat was complete. The document had no legal status and made promises that could not be guaranteed. At most it was a gentleman's agreement, a last gesture of military decency in a prison that had always prided itself on being run by gentlemen, for gentlemen.

Colditz had seen many unlikely theatrical productions over the years, but nothing as bizarre as the drama now unfolding: the German garrison was pretending to guard a prison no longer under its control; the inmates were acting as if they were still prisoners, while actually protecting their jailers against both the SS and the advancing American troops; Prawitt was performing the part of a Kommandant, a role now effectively taken over by Colonel Tod; the guards had become prisoners, and the prisoners their guards.

The Third Battalion of the 273rd Infantry Regiment, the sharp tip of the First Army, was advancing fast from the southwest supported by tanks from the 9th Armored Division. These American soldiers had been in Europe less than a month, but already they had seen hard fighting in the Ardennes, and witnessed terrible things. At Stalag Tekla, a slave labor camp near Leipzig, they found dozens of charred bodies: The inmates had been locked into a mess hall that had then been set alight; those who managed to escape the burning building were shot. Some appeared to have been electrocuted on the outer wire. Colonel Leo Shaughnessy, the commander of the advance force, was tasked with "clearing the countryside of resistance and uncovering groups of refugees and Allied prisoners." It was grim and bloody work. "Resistance increased as we approached Leipzig," he wrote. Shaughnessy lost a dozen men at Altengroitzsch, picked off by snipers in the buildings. "We were fighting a lot of 15 and 16-year-old boys," wrote one soldier. Most of the Americans were not much older, but battle-edged, wary, and, as they drew nearer to Colditz, increasingly enraged.

Lee Carson rode immediately behind the vanguard. She had once been an object of curiosity and lust, but now the GIs barely noticed the khaki-clad woman in the back seat of a Jeep, usually just a few hundred yards from the fighting. Carson wrote in the first person, her vivid eyewitness reports spiced with slang. "Leipzig is a crazy nightmare," she wrote from the shattered city. "Shops, homes and offices are being looted by swarms of civilians. American troops are getting a weird welcome, complete with wine, flowers, cheers and kisses, plus machine pistol and bazooka fire from packs of Hitler's baby gangsters under SS officer direction. Fires spotlight streetcorners. Tanks rattle and clank up side streets. There is rape and robbery in this town, and no safety for anyone."

On Saturday, April 14, the task force made camp west of the Mulde River. Shaughnessy was informed that a large body of prisoners was being held in the vicinity. The orders came through late that evening: "Take Colditz."

The next morning broke, wrote Eggers, with "the breath of spring." Gazing down from the battlements, he could see townsfolk barricading their homes against the gathering storm. "Nature carried on, but men and women took cover, wondering who would die by nightfall."

Soon after 9 a.m., the first Sherman tanks appeared on the western horizon, emerging from a wheatfield. Checko Chaloupka spotted them through his lecherscope and "let out a great whoop of joy." Colonel Shaughnessy deployed his artillery in the forest above the village of Hohnbach and ordered the battery commanders to target "the most prominent aiming point across the river, the towers of a rather large and imposing castle." Six Thunderbolt fighters streaked over the town, strafed the railway station and the German artillery dug in among the trees above the park, and swung away. There was no answering anti-aircraft fire. In both the *Kommandantur* and the prisoners' quarters, spectators crammed at the windows to witness the battle for Colditz. Some climbed onto the battlements. Just after midday the first two-inch American shell slammed into the guardroom by the main gate. A second crashed through the third-floor window of the room occupied by Douglas Bader. The legless fighter pilot was down in the courtyard, mocking the guards, repeatedly chanting: "Where is the Luftwaffe?" As Duke observed, "By goon-baiting to the bitter end he had saved his life." A third skimmed over the northwest ramparts and landed in the trees. The German 88mm guns in the *Tiergarten* fired back over the castle, peppering the woods beyond. Colditz was now smack in the middle of an artillery duel. Then the six-inch American howitzer shells began falling. One thumped down near the bridge over the dry moat, killing a German sergeant. Two more struck the *Kommandantur*. The American gunners were zeroing in. Colonel Tod ordered everyone down to the basements, but not before the homemade flags were unfurled from the windows and the letters P-O-W spelled out, in bedsheets, on the cobbles of the inner courtyard to catch the attention of overflying reconnaissance aircraft. The American barrage slowed, and then stopped. "We observed three Allied red, white and blue flags appear at the upper windows," wrote Shaughnessy. "This thrilling sight was the only signal we needed to know that the castle was the prison where the prisoners-of-war were being held." Characteristically, David Stirling ignored the shelling and stayed on the roof, with a "bird's-eye" view of the fighting below.

The American tanks and heavy machine guns took up positions on the edge of Colditz, while two rifle platoons entered the town from the west. The SS were waiting. The American infantry were spread out on the slope above the town allotments when two concealed machine guns opened up. "There were so many bullets coming at us that the trees were crackling like they were on fire," wrote Sergeant Roy Verdugo, whose men began dropping left and right. With covering fire, twenty-two infantrymen worked their way around the machine guns, and into the side streets. As the Americans inched forward, crouching low, hiding behind parked cars, hurling grenades around corners, they were picked off by snipers firing from the upper floors. A *Panzerfaust* shell blazed into a building "sending up gorgeous splinters of red, yellow and orange." The American commanding officer, twenty-three-year-old Lieutenant Ryan, was hit by shrapnel.

With his left eye hanging from its socket, he screamed: "Assemble in the houses. We're not leaving." Contact with Shaughnessy's command post was severed when a bullet ripped through the two-way radio. A squad of Germans, SS and Hitler Youth, charged down the main street toward the Americans and were obliterated by a bazooka shell. Several houses were now burning, and a thick pall of smoke drifted across the town. Emil Miskovic, a Polish-American sergeant from Chicago, was edging up the street leading to the bridge when "a young boy, possibly fourteen or fifteen years old, dressed in a German soldier's uniform, stepped out of his doorway and shot the sergeant in the head." Miskovic died instantly. The boy was gunned down, his body left "in the roadway in front of his home."

The prisoners returned to the windows and watched transfixed. Many had not seen battle since 1940. Commandos like Micky Burn and Michael Alexander had taken part in bloody special operations, and Stirling led his SAS in attacks on the North African airfields. But none had ever witnessed fighting like this: house-to-house, hand-to-hand, face-to-face combat, savage and intimate, pitting an unstoppable trained army against Nazi fanatics and indoctrinated children at the ragged end of a ghastly war. It was the most ferocious close-quarters fighting Lee Carson had yet seen. "The Yank force composed of tanks and infantry from the 9th Armored Division met fierce resistance by well organized bands of Hitler Youth under command of SS officers."

Outnumbered, the Americans pulled back, dragging their dead and wounded. The *Volkssturm* attempted to destroy the bridge with dynamite but succeeded only in blowing a hole through the roadway. Half a dozen SS stormtroopers climbed down onto the riverbank and tried to blast the supports with bazookas at close range, but still the moss-covered Adolf Hitler Bridge stood firm. From the castle heights, the spectators joined in a last chorus of goon-baiting: "Their boos and jeers could be distinctly heard by the SS," wrote Duke. Shells from the American howitzers pummeled the town, where Irma Wernicke and her family crouched in a basement. From the *Tiergarten* came "the welcome sound of infantry small arms and machine gun fire."

Oberstleutnant Prawitt came to find Colonel Duke, a final reversal of their roles.

"Your Americans will be here soon," he said.

"By tomorrow morning at the latest," Duke replied.

"I shall need someone to meet them. Someone who can explain that our guards won't resist." The words hung somewhere between an order, a request, and a plea for mercy.

At dusk the American troops crossed the river via the railway bridge north of the town, and began cautiously moving downstream. "We cleared the western side of the Mulde by midnight," wrote Shaughnessy. The cacophony subsided, and the fires burned out. The task force had lost more than a dozen killed, including two platoon sergeants, and twice that number wounded. "Colonel Shaughnessy gave orders for an attack at daybreak." The Americans settled down for the night in the abandoned houses close to the bridge, where defenders had dragged wire and old iron machinery across the road. The GIs posted guards and tried to sleep, "but the wind blowing through the metal debris made a creaking, groaning sound in the eerie emptiness of the night." Gunfire echoed in the darkness. Not the irregular crash and crackle of street fighting now, but volleys at regular intervals, coming from the old china factory on the northeast edge of town.

No one, it seems, had known about the slave labor camp for Hungarian Jews on the outskirts of Colditz.

The Hugo Schneider Aktiengesellschaft Metallwarenfabrik, or HASAG, started out in 1889 as a small metal-products factory. The company had prospered under Nazi rule, and by 1944 it was one of the largest arms manufacturers in the Reich, with eight factories in Germany and three in Poland. Under the management of Paul Budin, a member of the Nazi Party and a Sturmbannführer (Major) in the SS, HASAG mass-produced ammunition, small arms, and rocket launchers for the German army, using forced labor. More than 20,000 prisoners of various nationalities were made to work in the HASAG labor camps, where Budin ruthlessly applied the policy of "*Vernichtung durch Arbeit*" (extermination through work): in all camps there were regular selections, and those no longer considered "fit for work" were murdered. The Third Reich was HASAG's only customer: the company paid the SS for each laborer, and the Nazi regime paid HASAG handsomely for its products. HASAG was singled out as an "Exemplary National Socialist Enterprise" by the Nazi rulers, and Budin received a personal note of thanks from the Führer. Beginning in the summer of 1944, the arms company established seven satellite units, or *Aussenkommandos*, employing Jewish slave laborers from the Buchenwald concentration camp. The smallest of these, Aussenkommando 24, was located inside the old Steingutfabrik building at Colditz (once the largest china factory in Germany), with a labor force of around 700 Hungarian Jews producing armaments for the German war effort.

Conditions inside the HASAG camps were appalling. The prisoners lacked sanitation and running water. The morning "ersatz coffee" was so disgusting that some preferred to use it to wash themselves, before performing twelve hours of punishing physical work, assembling guns and explosives. Beatings were frequent. Supper was a bowl of thin soup with a small piece of bread. They slept in unheated wooden barracks on straw mattresses or bare wood. The dead were frequently left in the open for days, where they had fallen. One survivor, Charles Kotkowsky, described a world of utter degradation: "There were no baths to take care of millions of lice, so we had to undress and stand naked waiting at a wall. After freezing for half an hour, they unleashed several fire hoses on us and not everyone was able to withstand that. Each thrust of water in the cold weather knocked us against the wall." Life expectancy in a HASAG *Aussenkommando* was three and a half months.

Irma Wernicke and her spies appear to have been unaware of the camp's existence. Even Reinhold Eggers claimed he had known nothing about the Jewish laborers in the old factory, slaves for the Nazi war machine: "They were in the charge of an SS unit, with whom we in the castle had practically no contact at all," Eggers wrote. "This was an SS matter." It hardly seems credible that a small army of slaves could have passed unnoticed in a town that size; but people are skilled at seeing, and remembering, what they want to. A great deal has been written about Colditz over the years, but little has been recorded about the other camp, just a few hundred yards away, where Jews were being worked and starved to death. The German occupation of Hungary, in which Mission Sparrow played such an unheroic part, had been followed by the mass deportation of the country's Jews. Some 434,000 people, more than half the total Jewish population of Hungary, were transported to camps. Most were taken to Auschwitz, where 80 percent were gassed on arrival. Some were selected for slave labor. No one knows the exact number of Hungarian Jews taken to HASAG Aussenkommando 24 at Colditz, when they arrived, and how many had already perished from exhaustion, disease, and malnutrition. But as the defeated German forces prepared to pull out, the SS guards set about systematically murdering the Jewish prisoners, in batches of five.

The shooting stopped just before daybreak.

18

Endgame

The dawn was cold and clear. "There was absolute silence." At the castle, the first prisoners awake climbed to the ramparts, and looked down on the town through the pallid morning light. White flags, pillowcases, and bedsheets fluttered from the windows of the houses. In the darkness, the SS forces had slipped away and retreated eastward.

Private Bob Hoffman was manning a machine gun overlooking the woods above the *Tiergarten* when a group of Hitler Youth emerged from the trees, still in uniform, but now unarmed, leaderless, and "very frightened." A few hours earlier Hoffman would have killed them all. Now they were children again. "They looked like a boy scout troop," he recalled. "We told them to go home."

At 5 a.m., five miles to the west, Private Alan Murphey of the task force Intelligence and Reconnaissance section was woken in his tent and told to report for duty with three other soldiers. Colonel Shaughnessy's orders were to proceed to Colditz and set up an observation post. "Once there, occupy a building overlooking the bridge and await the arrival of the battalion communication section, who would run a wire and provide a field phone." Shaughnessy was not going to allow his men to be ambushed a second time. "No mention was made that there was a prisoner-of-war camp in Colditz," Murphey later wrote.

The four had trained together at Camp Shelby, Mississippi, as part of the 69th Infantry Division, "The Fighting 69th," before sailing for France on January 22, 1945, aboard the *Morowai*. They had seen action at Kamberg and the Rhine, before being attached to Task Force Shaughnessy. All were in their twenties.

Armed with M-1 rifles, hand grenades, and ammunition bandoliers crossed over their chests, the four GIs set off for Colditz town in the milky dawn. "When we reached the bridge, we saw our first Americans, a half-dozen infantrymen crouched behind the parapet that bordered the bridge's west bank."

The bodies of two German soldiers lay in the road, behind the pathetic wire and metal barricade.

"There are still snipers over there," said the sergeant in command. "I'm not going to risk my men."

A tough midwestern farmboy, Murphey was up for adventure. He turned to his companions: "Wanna try it?" Their orders were to remain by the bridge, but it was tempting to push on over the river. "We decided to cross. It was one of those quick decisions that you often have to make in combat."

They fixed bayonets, and on the count of three, they sprinted. "We raced up onto the bridge [and] had to jump over a dead German youth sprawled on his back to the left of a gaping hole in the roadway." The market square was deserted. White sheets hung limply from the windows. The four GIs made their way forward in single file, ducking into doorways. At the end of the square, a cobbled street rose steeply. "We had gone too far to turn back," wrote Murphey. They ran up the narrow alleyway, and then stopped. "The castle came into view, towering above us." Murphey had been so alert for snipers he had not spotted it before.

A two-man Anglo-American reception committee was waiting inside the main gate: the Californian captain Guy Nunn, one of the original "Sparrows," and Captain David Walker, wearing the full uniform of the Scottish Black Watch regiment. Both would go on to become novelists, and left vivid descriptions of what followed.

Nunn spotted the figures moving slowly toward the castle, and let out a low whistle. Murphey raised his hand, suspecting a trap, and the three GIs behind him froze. "This is a Yank," Nunn shouted. "There's a prison up here. The Kommandant wants to surrender. It's all yours."

Still Murphey hesitated. Nunn now came up with what he later considered a "stroke of genius."

"This is kosher," he shouted. No German guard would ever have used a Yiddish word.

The GIs moved forward. "They looked menacing. Their faces were smeared with lampblack. They bristled with hand grenades and ammunition."

A figure wearing tartan trousers and a bonnet with a red feather cockade stepped out from the gateway arch with his hand extended. "Welcome to Colditz," said Walker. "We've been waiting a long time. Would you like a cup of coffee?"

The German garrison was lined up in the courtyard of the *Kommandantur,* as if on parade. Eggers stepped forward and proffered a neatly typed sheet of paper. "Officer Special Camp IV-C—1,500 Allied officers and men, all unhurt. Nominal roll herewith." Murphey had never seen a live German soldier at such close quarters before, let alone accepted a surrender, but with all the authority he could muster he told Eggers to disarm his men and stack the guns in a room at the base of the watchtower. Prawitt stood erect and expressionless.

Leaving two of the Americans to supervise, Murphey allowed Nunn and Walker to lead him to the gate of the inner courtyard, which stood ajar. He pushed open the huge oak doors.

Tod had ordered the men to remain in their quarters, but a few of the senior officers were already milling around the courtyard. They turned as the apparition entered the gloomy interior of the castle: "A fresh faced man hardly out of his teens, festooned with weapons." They stared. "He was filthy from battle, steel-helmeted and armed to the teeth." Murphey was also very nervous. The prisoners suddenly surged toward him. Alarmed, Murphey unslung his M-1 and pointed it at the ragged mob converging on him: "Stay back! Stay back!" For a few seconds they all stood still, a strange standoff between Allies. "We're friends, friends," they urged. Murphey lowered his gun. "The next instant all hell broke loose." The men flooded forward, and Murphey was swamped by an ecstatic throng, laughing and cheering. Dozens of hands clapped him on the back, with such force his knees buckled. A few of the prisoners held back, disbelieving, stunned. Some wept. Hundreds of others had by now gathered at the windows, whooping and bellowing. At this moment Private

Frank Giegnas Jr. entered the courtyard. "As we stepped into view a roar of cheers greeted us from the windows overlooking the yard. I could see faces at every window." A working-class youth from New Jersey, Giegnas was carrying a large portrait of Adolf Hitler. He had found it on the wall of the German mess, and intended to keep it as a souvenir. A lively barter system existed among the GIs: watches, weapons, belt buckles, knives, and other items were all collected by the advancing army as trade items or mementoes. A framed Führer was worth several hundred cigarettes. But Giegnas had a theatrical bent. On a whim, he "raised the picture of Hitler high above his head with both hands, and turned in a slow arc so that all could see. Then, he crashed the picture across his raised knee. There was pandemonium. The shouts and cheers echoed in the narrow confines of the courtyard."

The events of the next few hours took on an unreal quality. "It felt like we were making a movie," said Robert Miller, one of the original quartet of GIs. Jeeps had started to arrive at the castle gates, disgorging more troops. Each American soldier entering the courtyard was loudly embraced, backslapped, invited to breakfast in the mess. Some of the former prisoners felt a twinge of embarrassment at the physical contrast between these beefy, corn-fed GIs and their own pallid and scrawny bodies. Colonel William Schaefer, so recently under sentence of death, was brought out to meet his countrymen, shaking uncontrollably, tears streaming down his face.

Prawitt and his senior officers were herded together at gunpoint and marched down to the town over the bridge "where the body of a boy of about fourteen lay spreadeagled, a Hitler Youth band on one arm, a flattened *Panzerfaust* beside him. The face of the child was palish green." Eggers wondered: "What made them die like this?" On the far bank stood the dead boy's mother, "torn with grief." Desperate to retrieve her son's body, her way was barred by an American corporal with orders not to let any Germans through. The town undertaker had already arrived with a horse-drawn hearse, "like a stage prop from a Wild West movie."

The advancing Americans had by now established a tempo-

rary command headquarters in the town hotel. The formal surrender of Colditz Castle took place in the saloon. Prawitt stepped
forward, saluted, and presented his sheathed saber and pistol to
Colonel Leo Shaughnessy of the 273rd Infantry. The Kommandant and his sixteen officers were then marched away to the jail,
through jeering, shoving crowds of GIs. One of Prawitt's epaulettes was ripped off. Locked into the cells where so many prisoners had been consigned to solitary confinement, Eggers
reflected that his world had now truly turned upside down: "I
must learn the feel of the other end of the stick. I was the POW
now." The town square, deserted and hostile a few hours earlier,
became a scene of jubilation, as the inhabitants emerged, greet-
ing the Americans with food and flowers. Just five months before, the townsfolk had turned out to celebrate the anniversary
of the Nazis' rise to power. Overnight, collective amnesia set in.
The swastikas and copies of *Mein Kampf* quietly disappeared.
The inhabitants of Colditz forgot their recent history, and then
rewrote it. "In the town it seemed there were no Nazis," Green
observed. "Everybody had hated them for years and had worked
secretly against them." In an imposing private house on the other
side of town a drinks party was underway, symbolizing the dramatic transformation in the town's politics. Private Murphey escorted Čeněk Chaloupka to meet in person, for the first time,
Herr Schmidt, linchpin of the Colditz spy network and "the gentleman who was to become the burgomaster when the allies took
charge of the town." Checko struck Murphey as "a Clark Gable
type, the black hair, good-looking etc." Schmidt warmly welcomed them with champagne. The Czech pilot seemed quite at
home in Schmidt's elegant parlor, but Murphey was suddenly
self-conscious. "I really hated to enter his beautiful home as dirty
as I was or sit on his furniture and drink a glass of wine."

Lee Carson was in a very bad mood. "This tall woman in
khaki uniform came marching up," recalled one of the GIs. "She
was just furious." Every journalist lives for a scoop, and she had
been denied one. "She was supposed to be there for the capture
of Colditz and to have the exclusive story," but Carson had arrived half an hour too late. The sight of the dead German boy
lying on the bridge had further upset her. "Shooting children is

murder," she told the military minder whose impossible job it was to try to control her. Carson brushed past the guard and marched into the courtyard.

The "arrival of a very attractive blonde, carrying a helmet and camera" sent excitement levels among the newly liberated inmates soaring to new heights. Most had not seen a young woman in five years, let alone one who appeared to have materialized from a glamour magazine; the entrance of this "rather smashing American female war correspondent dressed in a boiler suit" threatened to start a riot. Carson was immediately surrounded by a scrum of men, "most of whom," Julius Green noted wryly, "appeared to be Douglas Bader." The celebrated double-amputee flying ace was "amazed to see a girl, a real live girl, in battledress, in the courtyard." He swooped instantly: Carson had been in Colditz less than a minute before Bader offered her an exclusive interview.

The report of Bader's liberation was so glowing he might have written it himself: "Debonair wing commander Douglas Bader wants most of all to 'get another squirt at the bloody Hun' now that he is free from German internment. 'Just give me one more shot at those goons,' begged the 35-year-old fighter pilot who became one of Britain's great aces with two artificial legs. The laughing dark-haired hero was one of a thousand or so liberated from the great, grey Colditz prison."

Carson was taken on a tour of the prison's best-kept secrets: the radio hideaway where the news had been gathered nightly for two years, and then up into the attics. That morning, the glider-builders had fully assembled the Colditz Cock for the first time. The GIs queued up to stare at it, a complete aircraft constructed in absolute secrecy from floorboards, bedposts, and mattress covers, an astonishing feat of aeronautical engineering. "My god, it was incredible," recalled one American soldier. "I was thinking: 'How could they do that?'" Lee Carson took the first, last, and only photograph of the glider: the machine is poised as if staring out of the top-floor windows of Colditz, contemplating a flight it would never take.

As Lee Carson was leaving, Douglas Bader climbed into the back of the Jeep alongside her, carrying a holdall packed by his orderly, Alex Ross. Tod had given orders that no officer was to leave the castle without permission, but rules did not apply to Bader. By the next day he was back in Paris, and a day after that he returned to Britain and a hero's welcome: the first prisoner to make a "home run" from Colditz after its liberation, several days before anyone else.

Lee Carson's report flew around the world. "The Yank force drove to the camp despite well-organized resistance. Every town had to be fought through, but in less than 24 hours the tanks, with doughboys riding topside, blasted their way through to the medieval castle. Five American officers were rescued along with 350 British, a thousand French and a handful of Poles," she wrote.

But the last chapter of the Colditz story was still being written. Carson's report was headlined "Allied Hostages Hidden in Nazi Redoubt" and reported: "Twenty-one prominent British and American prisoners have been taken to Adolf Hitler's headquarters in the so-called national redoubt as hostages, taken from their cells and loaded into a truck for their trip to Hitler's last-ditch refuge. The American task force arrived 48 hours too late."

In Tittmoning camp, the disappearance of Giles Romilly and the five other *Prominente* entombed inside the wall provoked panic among their jailers, and a massive manhunt. Three thousand German soldiers combed the surrounding countryside. The castle was searched from cellar to battlements. After three days of frantic hunting, the five men were found, possibly through a tip-off, in their cramped hiding place. "How silly of you to try to escape now," said the Kommandant, aware that his own life would have been forfeit had they succeeded. Romilly was still missing. The remaining special prisoners were transferred, along with the Poles, to Laufen Castle near Salzburg, and placed in a special enclosure surrounded by barbed wire and double guards. The SS was not going to lose its grip on these valuable captives a second time.

But the *Prominente* also had a last line of defense, in the shape of one exceptionally dogged Swiss official. Rudolf Denzler appeared at the camp next morning, as ill-shaven and competent as usual, and demanded to see the prisoners. He explained that he had taken lodgings in the town and was keeping a close watch; if they were moved from the castle he would immediately inform his boss, the Swiss minister Peter Feldscher, head of the foreign interests section at the Swiss embassy in Berlin. He studied the prisoners benignly through his pince-nez. "Everything seems to be in order," he said. There was something naïve but deeply reassuring in Denzler's unshakable belief that official regulations would confound anything the Nazis might attempt. That faith was about to be put to the test, because when Denzler returned to see the prisoners the following day he was instead ushered into the Kommandant's office. On the desk lay a written order, signed by SS Obergruppenführer Gottlob Berger himself, stating that Oberst Fritz Meurer would be coming to collect the *Prominente* within twenty-four hours. Meurer was the SS officer who had organized the murder of French general Gustave Mesny three months earlier.

Denzler swung into action. From the telephone in the lobby of the Österreichischer Hotel in Salzburg he "informed Minister Feldscher of the new situation." He then drove thirty miles east to Schloss Fuschl, the private residence of the German foreign minister Joachim von Ribbentrop, to warn "the highest level of what was left of German Foreign Politics" that a major violation of international diplomacy was about to take place. Next, he tracked down every high-ranking German army officer he could find in the area, including the general in command of the Salzburg sector. At each stop, the response was the same: "Acting against the SS was dangerous." Finally, he reached the headquarters of Field Marshal Kesselring, in a hotel just a few miles from Berchtesgaden. Kesselring's chief of staff, General Wilhelm Seidel, was "friendly and pleasant," but unhelpful. Denzler wrote: "He was shrugging his shoulders which gave away his attitude: if injustice is done, it is done by others, I am washing my hands of this. The Wehrmacht was obviously powerless in a Reich within days of total collapse."

Two buses were waiting at the gates of Laufen camp the next morning. As the *Prominente* were being herded into them, a black Mercedes drew up and out "stepped a tall figure in a long black leather coat almost to his ankles. His cap bore the death's head emblem of the SS." Meurer had brought along his mistress, "a hard-faced blonde wearing trousers and smoking a cigarette through a long holder."

"The whole scene had a gangster-like atmosphere," wrote Elphinstone, the group's senior officer. "We entered the transport with the colonel fingering his revolver, watching us."

The buses started up, and Michael Alexander felt a lurch of fear. "We were now in a malignant world of purely arbitrary hostility." The protective hand of the Wehrmacht had been removed; they were now at the mercy of the SS. "But suddenly, as we drove out, we saw, crouching behind a kiosk, a familiar figure wearing an enormous gray trilby hat pulled down over his eyes. It was the faithful Mr. Denzler. As we passed, he gave us a conspiratorial wave. Our departure had been noticed. A lifeline was still out." Rudolf Denzler joined the back of the convoy: a tall Swiss bureaucrat in a small car, with spots of blood on his shirt collar.

Obergruppenführer Gottlob Berger was summoned to the *Führerbunker* in Berlin. The Red Army was closing in; the last act would be played out in the ruins of Hitler's capital. But the Führer had unfinished revenge in mind. Berger found Hitler "ill and demented, purple with rage, blaming everyone else for losing the war, ranting and raving about this betrayal and that act of disloyalty." According to Berger, the enraged Führer ordered him to fly to Bavaria, where the *Prominente* had been taken as hostages. "His hand was shaking, his leg was shaking and his head was shaking; and all that he kept saying was 'Shoot them all! Shoot them all!'" Berger commandeered Himmler's private plane, and flew south.

Munich, the "Capital of the Movement" in Nazi geography, fell to American forces without a fight. Giles Romilly was standing on a street corner in the northwest suburbs when the first American tank rolled into the city. "It traveled past slowly, unseeing and curiously gentle, like a blind man crossing a road. It was covered in flowers."

Romilly's escape from captivity had been long, hard, and boring: by train and on foot he and his Dutch companion had slogged west from Tittmoning, sleeping in bombed-out buildings and hay barns, scrounging just enough food to survive. In the villages the people were too exhausted and terrified to take much notice of two more refugees toiling westward. After a week, utterly spent, they reached the outskirts of Munich and knocked on the door of a house near an estate. "No special reason to pick it. We just did." The door was opened by a woman with a "pleasant face, neither pretty nor plain," who agreed to take them in as lodgers. She fed them, laid out deck chairs in the garden under an apple tree, and prepared clean beds in her spare room. Her name was Magda. "She never asked us who we were or what we were doing." Her husband was in the Waffen-SS. She had not seen him for three years. Romilly wondered "if her kindness to us had any motive," and concluded that there was none, save a desire for company. Amid the destruction and cruelty, he had accidentally stumbled into a small and unexpected patch of human sympathy.

Romilly presented himself at Sixth Army headquarters and felt "for the first time the anxiety of my new-born freedom." The Americans put Churchill's nephew on the first plane to Paris, and that evening he found himself the guest of honor in "the middle of a roaring party" at the chic Hotel Scribe. "Dazed, I gyrated in a haze of smiles, hands, drinks, cigarettes, glittering lights." Joltingly, he was back in some "wonderful Parisian fairy-story." But it could not feel real. The "dull, stinging oppression of the past" was rooted in his soul. "The story did not end," he wrote. Giles Romilly never fully escaped from Colditz. "My five years of absence were like a deep shaft, I at the bottom, able to see the free people overhead, not able to make them see or hear me."

The *Prominente* convoy wound slowly around the hairpin bends of the Bavarian Alps. Rudolf Denzler, "keeping them in sight as far as possible," tucked in behind the black Mercedes carrying Oberst Meurer and the "rather sinister-looking blonde woman." The roads were crowded with military vehicles of every description. They were now deep inside Hitler's Alpine Fortress. At strategic points, boulders had been piled up on the mountainsides;

when the order came, explosives beneath them would be detonated to create artificial landslides to block the passes and roads, sealing off the redoubt. The buses passed a signpost for Berchtesgaden and continued west deep into the mountains. It was late afternoon when they reached Markt Pongau camp, Stalag XVIII C. The prisoners were locked into "a dismal hut."

The Swiss, meanwhile, were struggling to trace the only man with the authority to intervene. SS Obergruppenführer Gottlob Berger "was not easy to find," wrote Denzler. "He was practically on the run and any talk of his whereabouts could be interpreted as treason." But after a few discreet telephone calls (the Swiss had informants inside German high command) the general was located, holed up in a remote farmhouse with his SS retinue. The Swiss minister put through a call and made an appeal, not to Berger's better nature, because he did not have one, but to his self-interest, which he had in spades. The only way to save the *Prominente*, Denzler knew, was to "convince Berger that it would be to his personal advantage if he handed over his prominent prisoners."

The next afternoon another black Mercedes pulled up outside the prisoners' hut. In the back sat "a portly figure propped up on pillows": Berger himself. Almighty Gottlob entered the hut, wrote Michael Alexander, "smoking a large cigar and swaying as if slightly drunk." He bowed as if in the presence of royalty (which he was), gestured at the prisoners to be seated, handed out whiskey and cigarettes, and then launched into a prepared speech. Any crimes committed by the Nazi regime, concentration camps and so on, had been the work of the Gestapo and the SD, not the Waffen-SS, of which he was a general. Indeed, "he disapproved of these activities." Germany had gone to war to hold back Bolshevism, "the Red Virus," and had no quarrel with Britain and America, let alone with his distinguished audience. He described his visit to the *Führerbunker,* and Hitler's demented order to kill them all. His refusal to do so, he claimed, had now earned him his own death sentence as a "defeatist." So he was now being hunted, as were they, by stormtroopers under the command of SS General Ernst Kaltenbrunner, a fanatical Nazi loyalist.

It was a remarkably cynical performance. War criminal, murderer, enslaver of children, and abject coward, Berger was trying to save his own skin, and dressing this up as an act of principle, even self-sacrifice; he was no longer the jailer of the *Prominente*, he insisted, but their savior. Swiss officials would convey them to the American lines; he would provide an SS escort "with orders to defend" them, and a letter of safe conduct signed by himself.

"Gentlemen," General Berger declared solemnly, rising to his feet. "These are probably the last orders I shall give as a high official of the Third Reich."

This was also the first time the craven Berger had disobeyed a Nazi order. He was acting not out of clemency or courage, but wily calculation. Delivering the *Prominente* to the Allies might just save him from the hangman's noose when the war was over.

Berger was not the only one scrambling for survival as the Nazi state collapsed. The bus drivers had slipped away with the buses. Oberst Meurer and his blond mistress had vanished in their Mercedes. Instead, the prisoners woke the next morning to find a waiting Buick with diplomatic plates containing a young Swiss official named Werner Buchmüller, "elegantly dressed and as charmingly casual as if he was just dropping in for a drink," summoned by Denzler to accompany the group as extra diplomatic protection. Denzler somehow managed to conjure up two army lorries, and from the trunk of his car Buchmüller produced two enormous Swiss flags, which he draped over the hoods. It was dark before they all set off, the British officers and the American Winant in one lorry, the Poles in the other, accompanied by the Swiss in the Buick and a squad of stormtroopers armed with anti-tank weapons. Various Nazi chiefs, including Kaltenbrunner, were "lurking somewhere in these mountains, each with his private band of desperate retainers" and might try to snatch them. "Berger held the royal flush," as Michael Alexander put it, and he was not going to surrender a winning hand.

Half an hour later the convoy shuddered to a halt. "We saw in the dim rays of the headlights the figure of an SS soldier waving a gun and signalling us to turn to the right." After jolting up a steep dirt track, they turned into the courtyard of a substantial farmhouse. "A door was thrown open, a shaft of light shone out" and the prisoners and their Swiss protectors entered a surreal scene. Before them stood a long table illuminated with lamps and candles, groaning with food and drink, "a feast such as prison-conditioned eyes had not seen for a long time": cold meats, smoked fish, crystallized fruit, bottles of French wine, and American whiskey. A huge fire roared in the grate. Alexander described a spectacle of debauchery from another age: "On the floor, about twenty SS men, boys almost, lay sprawled like retainers on a Saxon hearth. They were half undressed and seemed too tired, or too drunk, to be interested in our presence."

Gottlob Berger was back for an encore.

The pudgy Obergruppenführer entered the room wearing a white mess jacket that gave him, Alexander observed, "the appearance of an American businessman on vacation in Palm Beach." The general was sozzled, and launched into another ingratiating political homily, identical to the one he had delivered the previous day: "England and Germany are blood brothers of the same Aryan stock," he slurred. Berger paid no attention to the Swiss officials, and ignored General Bór-Komorowski and his entourage; the Poles were not about to win the war, and were therefore irrelevant. His peroration over, Berger clapped his hands and a white-uniformed retainer appeared carrying a scarlet leather case: inside, on a red velvet cushion, lay a large automatic pistol inlaid with ivory, the barrel chased with gold oak leaves in bas-relief, the butt engraved with Berger's signature and the insignia of the SS. This had been, the general proudly declared, a personal gift from the Führer, and now he was presenting it to his British friends "as proof of his good wishes." Each officer was offered a fat cigar. Alas, history does not record whether these were made by H. Upmann Ltd.

At 5 a.m. Berger finally staggered off to bed and the *Prominente*, gorged on Nazi food and drink, clambered back onto the lorries, taking with them a sinister SS souvenir from one of the nastiest parties in history.

At dawn, the convoy passed through a final German command post, manned by "exhausted-looking, sweaty troops," and came to the Inn Valley. "They watched us with a curiously detached air as we sailed past, immune under our neutral flag, toward our salvation and their probable destruction." The convoy entered a strangely tranquil no-man's-land. "A little white church shone in the morning sun." Twenty minutes later a line of three stubby American tanks came rumbling into view.

The next morning, clean and rested, the *Prominente* were having breakfast at the headquarters of the U.S. 53rd Division in Innsbruck, when a call came through for John Elphinstone. The Queen was on the line.

"Would it be possible to come home directly and quickly?" Elphinstone asked his aunt.

"The Queen said she would speak to the King," and by the following evening the royal former prisoners of Colditz were sitting down to a "family dinner party" in Buckingham Palace.

By then, Colditz Castle was empty.

The Americans had told the prisoners they would be leaving in two days' time, and to take only one item of luggage each. Micky Burn carefully packed the manuscript of his finished novel. Gris Davies-Scourfield wandered down to the cemetery to visit the grave of Michael Sinclair. Willie Tod pointed out that SS squads might be roaming the countryside, and suggested the men stay inside the castle: it was advice, not an order, and widely ignored. Checko Chaloupka, David Stirling, and Jack Pringle moved into a large abandoned townhouse and began a riotous forty-eight-hour party.

At the old china factory, the GIs discovered a handful of Jewish prisoners who had survived the SS massacre. Julius Green was appalled when they were brought to the castle sickbay. "Living skeletons were lying on the beds, quite unconscious, arms and legs like matchsticks and bodies covered in sores and bruises. One of them was an eminent Budapest doctor." They were now being treated by American medics, but Green could tell most would not live long. "They were in a dreadful state of emaciation, some of them with gunshot wounds and all desperately ill. Those I saw had been left for dead or had hidden." The Jewish dentist was not a man of violence, but the sight of the dying Hungarians triggered something savage in him. German civilians had been instructed to surrender weapons at the police station.

"I picked myself a nice automatic and a few clips and then went around with an American Jeep trying to see if any of the SS were about and requiring our attention." As usual, Green's tone was jocular, but his intentions were murderous: had this gentle dentist been able to find any stormtroopers, he would have killed them.

On April 18, the men were loaded onto U.S. Army trucks driven by Black American servicemen, who gunned their engines and set off "at full throttle." Dick Howe, the former escape officer, commandeered a motorbike and led the convoy out of the castle gates. Each of the trucks was equipped with a machine gun mounted on the cab. Julius Green was selected to sit behind the weapon and scan the roadsides in case of ambush. "I had never fired a machine gun and wasn't quite sure how this one worked."

A journey of 100 miles brought the convoy to an airfield near Chemnitz. After a night in a barn sleeping on soft straw, they climbed onto Dakota transport planes. Most had never been in an aircraft before. Green was airsick all the way to England. "I would have welcomed any German fighter that tried to shoot us down." At Westcott airfield near Aylesbury, "a really delicious" volunteer from the Women's Voluntary Service with a clipboard passed among the prisoners asking: "Is Captain Green here?"

"I indicated that indeed he was," Green later wrote, "and she should reject all imposters." The smiling woman told him to report to the War Office in the morning, where he would be debriefed on his intelligence activities inside Colditz. He caught the next train to London.

Like many returning prisoners, Green was bewildered to be suddenly roaming the streets of the capital, unfettered and unguarded. His mind ranged back over his captivity, the boredom, fear, and frustration, but also the occasional unlikely satisfaction, in humor, friendship, and espionage. Like every Colditz prisoner he had been put to the test, and wondered if he had passed. No one can predict how they will behave in enforced, unexpected, and lengthy captivity: Colditz contained every sort of person, and they responded in every kind of way, with courage or cowardice, anger or wit, kindness or cruelty, resistance or rebellion. "If I had been cleverer and braver, I might have been more useful," wrote Green. This was typically modest, and quite wrong. As a skilled dentist, few had been more useful; and as a Jew in Nazi hands and a spy sending back coded messages, none had been more brave.

London felt alien, friendly but foreign after so long spent behind barbed wire and stone walls. Britain was still at war. German bombs had gouged great holes in the city. Many of the shops and restaurants remained boarded up. Just three weeks earlier, one of Hitler's V2 rockets had landed on a three-story housing block in the East End, killing 134 civilians. That was the last bomb to fall on London. The night streets were being lit once more after five years of blackout, but people still scurried along the pavements, occasionally glancing anxiously upward. No one paid any attention to the lone soldier who wandered slowly through Piccadilly as if lost and searching for something.

Green knew he had changed: He was two and a half stone thinner, graver than the carefree soldier-medic who had left England in January 1940, and older than by the sum of the lost years. His frayed uniform hung off him like a sack. Whenever a passerby came near, he instinctively flinched, backing into doorways. Everyone else seemed to have somewhere to go. Throughout his imprisonment, Green had never been more than a few feet away from another prisoner. Humans need space as much as company, and now he had to navigate liberty, the suddenly limitless expanse of a life so recently confined. In Colditz, he had known the name of every other inmate, their voices and stories, their fears, their teeth and the smell of their breath. These hurried Londoners in a city waking from war no longer knew him, and never could. He was alone, and he was free.

He was also very hungry. "My first thought was to treat myself to the meal I had been dreaming about for four years."

Julius Green, dentist, gourmand, spy, and unsung war hero, settled into a corner table in a restaurant off Regent Street, and savored the taste of freedom: smoked salmon, minestrone, roast beef, pineapple and kirsch, followed by coffee and a good brandy.

Aftermath

The Red Army reached Colditz in May 1945. The town was now in the Russian zone, which would become the GDR, or East Germany, in 1949. Colditz was used, variously, as a prison camp for local criminals and others deemed undesirable by the communist state, a psychiatric hospital, an old people's home, and a storehouse for excess stock from the ceramics factory. The radio hide, bricked up when the wartime prisoners departed, was rediscovered in 1965, with the radio intact. The Colditz glider vanished after the war. No one knows its precise fate. At a time of scarcity in eastern Germany, it may have been chopped up for firewood. In 2012, a full-size, remote-controlled replica was launched from the roof of Colditz, and landed safely in the meadow over the river.

The great collection of objects and photographs amassed by Reinhold Eggers was dispersed, many of them sold as souvenirs to visitors. Starting in 2006, the castle was refurbished and remodeled, leading to the discovery of many more wartime artifacts, escape aids, and hiding places in the walls and roofs and under floors. The chapel was recently restored, leaving part of the French Métro tunnel visible through a glass floor. Colditz now houses a small museum. Life-size cardboard cutouts of Airey Neave and Douglas Bader stand in the inner courtyard, where the prisoners once played stoolball. The German barracks, the *Kommandantur,* is now a youth hostel.

The wartime history of Colditz is little known in Germany, despite its mythical status among the countries whose prisoners were held there. The precise number of successful escapers is still debated, depending on whether the total includes escapes that took place when prisoners were in transit, or as a result of repatriation on false pretenses. The best estimate is that a total of thirty-two men made "home runs," with just fifteen starting from inside the castle: eleven British, twelve French, seven Dutch, one Pole, and a Belgian. The last surviving inmate, Alan Campbell, who wrote poetry in Colditz and acted as the prisoners' senior legal adviser, died in 2013. But while the living memories of Colditz are gone, the story continues to emerge and evolve in declassified files, unpublished memoirs, diaries, and letters.

After the war **Pat Reid** worked as an MI6 officer, under diplomatic cover, in the British embassy in Ankara, before returning to Britain and resuming a career in civil engineering. His first book, *The Colditz Story,* was published in 1952. An instant bestseller, it was followed by two more, adventure narratives written in a breathless, engaging style, replete with tales of gallant escapes, schoolboy humor, and cheerful derring-do: "If you feel in the mood to launch into the feverish underground activity of a camp full of diehards, read on." Reid's writings formed the foundations of the Colditz industry. His books offered an account of prison camp life that was relentlessly upbeat, full of boyish enthusiasm, comic interludes, and plucky high spirits. Uncomplicated and irrepressible, Reid came to embody the place as the archetypal Colditz prisoner, leaving the false impression that everyone in it had been just like him.

Reid had always treated escaping as a game, and the popular image he forged of Colditz was powerful and enduring. It was also highly subjective, and partly inaccurate. Reid's book was adapted into a film starring John Mills as Reid. Not all former prisoners were pleased with the result. Airey Neave was furious that his own escape, the first by a British officer, was eclipsed in favor of the author's. Reid was technical adviser on the BBC television series *Colditz,* which ran from 1972 to 1974, starring David McCallum and Robert Wagner. This was the most successful television drama the BBC had ever broadcast, with an average of seven million viewers, over one-third of the entire British viewing public, tuning in to watch every week. Again, the series was not universally popular with ex-prisoners, but Reid's version was now firmly established, and ripe for parody. In *The*

Times, Alan Coren began his review: "Hurrah! The Christmas hols over it was back to The Fifth Form at St. Colditz for a new term . . ."

Reid cooperated with an advertising campaign for Galaxy Ripple chocolate bars featuring a Colditz escape map, wrote a children's book entitled *My Favorite Escape Stories,* and conducted lecture tours using a model of the castle and various memorabilia as props. He even authorized a gramophone record, *Colditz, Breakpoint,* a soundscape of songs, music, speeches, and general military background noise. "It will be something new," promised Reid on the sleeve notes. "A very personal experience which you will live, in your imagination, as a prisoner with me in Colditz." In 1973, Gibsons Games released a board game, Escape from Colditz, which bore the legend "Devised by Major P. R. Reid, M.B.E. M.C." and his signature. For a time, it was more popular than Monopoly. Reid made a small fortune and a large reputation from his wartime imprisonment, married three times, and died in 1990 at the age of seventy-nine. Reid put Colditz on the map and permanently embedded it in popular culture.

At the Nuremberg trials **Airey Neave,** now a lawyer on the International Military Tribunal and a revered war hero, read out the indictments against the accused Nazi leaders. In 1953, he was elected Conservative MP for Abingdon, and went on to become one of Margaret Thatcher's most trusted advisers. Neave advocated defeating republicanism in Northern Ireland by military means, a hawkish stance that earned him the hatred of the IRA and other paramilitary groups seeking an end to British rule. It was widely expected that if Thatcher became prime minister, she would appoint him secretary of state for Northern Ireland. On March 30, 1979, a month before the general election that brought Thatcher to power, Neave was killed when a bomb exploded beneath his car as he was leaving Parliament. The paramilitary Irish National Liberation Army claimed responsibility for the assassination. Thatcher was devastated by Neave's death. "He was one of freedom's warriors," she said. "He was staunch, brave, true, strong; but he was very gentle and kind and loyal. It's a rare combination of qualities."

Two weeks after returning from Germany, **Alex Ross** was back at his family home in Scotland when he was summoned to the local post office in Tain to take a long-distance call from Douglas Bader. Throughout their shared captivity Ross had carried Bader up and down stairs, cooked his meals, and washed his stump socks. At Bader's insistence, the orderly had remained in Colditz an additional two years. At last, he thought, Bader was calling to express his gratitude.

"Have you got my legs?" demanded the wing commander.

Ross explained that the American liberators of Colditz had permitted each man to take away only a single suitcase, and the spare tin legs had been left behind.

"You're a c—," said Bader, and hung up.

Ross worked as an army dispatch rider, then in a brickfield, and finally ran an ironmonger's shop in High Brooms, Kent. He never spoke to Bader again.

Douglas Bader's fame continued to soar after the war. In June 1945, the disabled flying ace led a victory flypast over London of 400 planes. A biography by Paul Brickhill, *Reach for the Sky*, painted him in colors of unalloyed glory and became the biggest-selling hardback in post-war Britain. It was later made into a film starring Kenneth More that smoothed out Bader's jagged personality. Bader declined to stand as a Tory MP, stating that the only political job he was interested in would be that of prime minister. He continually expressed his opinions as truths, which made him outspoken or appalling, depending on your point of view. He praised apartheid in South Africa, supported the white minority regime in Rhodesia, favored the return of the death penalty, and opposed immigration. He became friends with former foes, but at an Anglo-German gathering of war veterans in Munich, he glared around a beer cellar filled with former Luftwaffe pilots and loudly remarked: "My God, I had no idea we left so many of the bastards alive." But he had moments of humility, and many more of generosity. His fame, he admitted, had come about "not because I was better than others but because I was the chap with the tin legs." He used his celebrity well. Douglas Bader's stubborn and courageous refusal to allow physical impairment to inhibit his freedom became an inspiration to disabled and limbless people everywhere. He raised millions for charity. "I am just grateful that my story is known because it has enabled me to do the really worthwhile thing in life which is to have helped some others who had the same problem I had in 1931." He died in 1982: a total hero and, at times, a complete bastard.

In the closing months of the war **Walter Purdy** worked for the SS as a translator and wrote propaganda leaflets for the Gestapo. His application for German citizenship was turned down. Gretel gave birth to a son in June 1945. By that point even this monumentally unperceptive man had worked out that he might be in trouble. With the end of hostilities, he was picked up by American forces and returned to Britain, where he settled in a bedsit in Putney, living off a disability pension and passing his time in seedy pubs. Drunk one night, Purdy boasted to Betty Blaney, a thirty-one-year-old telephonist, about his wartime broadcasting for the Nazis. Betty tried to blackmail him. He reported this to the police, and both were arrested: she for extortion, and he for treason. Purdy came quietly: "I know I have been a bit of a sod in Germany," he told the arresting officers.

On December 18, he appeared in the dock of the Old Bailey on three counts of high treason. Purdy's defense was part fantasy and part fabrication: he had been secretly working for the Allies all along and sending messages back to Britain from a concealed wireless; he had carried out a series of sabotage missions on German targets; he even claimed to have plotted to kill William Joyce, "Lord Haw-Haw," with a hand grenade. The attorney general, Sir Hartley Shawcross, dismissed his testimony as a mass of "inconsistencies, improbabilities and contradictions." Julius Green attended the trial and remarked: "His whining protestations of patriotism and ludicrous attempts to explain his treasonable activities fooled no one." The jury took seventeen minutes to find him guilty. The judge described the accused as "a weak and vain man, who decided to sell himself to the enemy." Walter Purdy was sentenced to death.

Joyce was hanged on January 3, 1946. Purdy's execution was set for February 8. The executioner Albert Pierrepoint was summoned to Wandsworth jail. But thirty-six hours before Purdy's appointment with the hangman, his sentence was commuted to life imprisonment. The proof of treason was overwhelming, but the home secretary ruled there was insufficient evidence to convict him on the specific charge of betraying the Colditz prisoners. For a second time, Green felt relieved that Purdy had escaped the noose. "It was obvious to me during the trial that he was not an intellectual giant." To Green's way of thinking, killing a man for being very stupid seemed unfair.

Purdy was released in November 1954 after nine years in prison. He changed his name to Robert Poynter, married twice, had another son, and settled in Essex, where he worked for a water softener firm and then as a vehicle inspector at Ford's Dagenham factory. He told his family he had served on submarines during the war. He died in 1982, and his secret remained hidden for a further twenty-six years. In 2008, MI5 declassified his case files, including an internal Home Office memo describing Walter Purdy as "the greatest rogue unhung."

Reinhold Eggers was interrogated by U.S. officials, and was released four months later after demonstrating that he had never been a member of the Nazi Party. He returned home and resumed his old job as a schoolmaster. Halle, like Colditz, lay within the Soviet occupation zone that would become East Germany. Oberstleutnant **Gerhard Prawitt,** the last Kommandant of Colditz, slipped into West Germany with his family before the Iron Curtain came down, and settled near Hamburg, where he died in 1969. Eggers considered a similar move, but decided he was in no danger. "I had been no Hitler man," he wrote. "The communists had nothing against me." In 1946, he was arrested and interrogated by the NKVD, Stalin's ruthless security service. The Russians were convinced that, as the security officer in Colditz, he must have worked with the Gestapo, running spies among the prisoners. When he insisted that only three inmates, notably Walter Purdy, had been willing to spy for Germany, they were scornful: "We'll send you to Siberia and then the names of your agents will come back to your memory." A Soviet military tribunal sentenced Eggers to ten years' hard labor for aiding the fascist regime. He was sent to Sachsenhausen, the former concentration camp where the commandos of Operation Musketoon had been murdered. Here the brutality far exceeded anything prisoners had endured in Colditz. At least 12,000 of those crammed into "NKVD Special Camp No. 1" perished of disease and malnutrition within five years. Chained up with common criminals and Nazis, starved, and beaten, the fastidious schoolmaster could not believe where fate and bad luck had landed him: "In this hell, morals and manners deteriorated into rough violence." By 1951, Eggers was one of just 1,500 survivors, "skeletons weighing no more than 50 kilograms." He was finally released in December 1955 and ordered to leave East Germany, having spent twice as long in prison as any Colditz inmate. Eggers settled by Lake Constance, where he died in 1974 at the age of eighty-four.

Throughout her husband's long imprisonment, Margaret Eggers preserved his diaries, photographs, and notes. "It would have been far safer for her to have burnt all my papers, but she saved them," he wrote. In the wake of Pat Reid's publishing success, Eggers wrote his own memoir, *Colditz: The German Viewpoint,* which he followed up with a collection of reminiscences gathered from Allied prisoners and German guards. He kept in touch with many of those he had once guarded: "I found new friends among my former enemies." In his writings, Eggers offered a counterpoint to the dominant British perspective, as sober and precise as Reid's was jovial and impressionistic. Eggers had stuck to the rules and made Colditz a tolerable place to be imprisoned; but he had also done more than anyone else to prevent escapers getting out. Colditz was the "bad boys' camp," and the schoolteacher Eggers saw his role as keeping them in line: this made him a dangerous adversary, and quite irritating. Among ex-prisoners he was a divisive figure, loathed by some for his cunning and efficiency, but admired by others for retaining his humanity in an inhuman war. "This man was our opponent, but nevertheless he earned our respect by his correct attitude, self-control and total lack of rancor despite all the harassment we gave him," wrote one former inmate. When Pat Reid appeared on the British TV program *This Is Your Life,* the surprise guest was Reinhold Eggers.

SS Obergruppenführer **Gottlob Berger** was arrested by French forces a week after throwing his grotesque party for the *Promi-*

nente in the Bavarian mountains. Brought to trial at Nuremberg, he claimed he had resisted pressure to inflict harsher treatment on POWs and disobeyed Hitler's direct order to "kill them all." His role in delivering the *Prominente* to safety formed a central plank of his defense, and he insisted he had risked his life by defying the Führer. In April 1949, the tribunal found him guilty of genocide as "an active party in the program of persecution, enslavement and murder" of European Jews. The court found that he also bore "command responsibility" for the assassination of French general Gustave Mesny. Berger was sentenced to twenty-five years in prison. But on appeal, two years later, the Advisory Board for Clemency ruled that insufficient weight had been given to Berger's actions in the final days of the Nazi regime. "The defendant Berger was the means of saving the lives of American, British, and Allied officers and men whose safety was gravely imperilled by orders of Hitler that they be liquidated or held as hostages. Berger disobeyed and intervened on their behalf and in so doing placed himself in a position of hazard." The sentence was reduced to ten years, and he was released in 1951, having served just six. Berger worked in a curtain factory, wrote occasional articles for a right-wing magazine, and died at the age of seventy-eight. SS Oberst **Fritz Meurer,** Berger's chief of staff, went on the run. In 1953, a French court found him guilty in absentia of General Mesny's murder and issued an international warrant for his arrest. He was briefly imprisoned in Germany, but the investigation dragged on for years and in 1975 Meurer was declared unfit to stand trial.

One of **Lee Carson**'s last articles from Germany related the fate of **Paul Budin,** the general manager of HASAG, the arms manufacturer that had worked hundreds of Jewish laborers to death in the Colditz slave camp. "Something strange, almost unbelievable happened here Wednesday night," she wrote from Leipzig, five days after the liberation of Colditz. Carson described how the arms manufacturer and SS officer had hosted a party in his large Leipzig mansion. "Frightened by the approach of the Americans, as most good Nazis are frightened, and realizing that his factories and his life as Hitler's favorite were over, he invited his friends to an elaborate banquet. It was complete with champagne, caviar, and all the trimmings. A gay time was had by all." The guests numbered around a hundred people, among them Budin's wife and children. "Then, after the gentlemen had smoked their cigars, and lingered over fine French cognac, Budin touched a button which blasted himself and his friends to Valhalla. The banquet room had been mined and set for push-button detonation." The explosion also destroyed the HASAG company files, including the record of how many enslaved laborers had perished at Aussenkommando 24 in Colditz.

When American forces finally linked up with the Soviets at the Elbe River, Carson was there to report it. She never forgot the sight of the dead boy sprawled on the bridge at Colditz. "In the mad melee Americans fought gray-bearded men and children, while thousands of trained Nazi soldiers surrendered," she wrote. On her return to the United States in 1946 she was awarded the International News Service Medal of Honor. Lee Carson retired from journalism in 1957, married a CIA officer, and died of cancer, at the age of fifty-one, in 1973. Her funeral in Philadelphia was attended by her fellow war reporters, still drooling over her combination of looks and talent. "Miss Carson was built like a movie star," wrote one. "It can be argued whether Lee was the greatest woman war correspondent of World War II. But there is no question that she was the best-liked news chick who ever beat a male reporter to a story—or the best seat in the Jeep."

In October 1945, **Micky Burn** received a letter from his one-time lover, Ella van Heemstra. Her family had suffered grievously under Nazi occupation and Ella's daughter Audrey, who had dreams of becoming a dancer, was suffering from jaundice, anemia, and an infection caused by malnutrition. Ella asked Burn if he could help her obtain penicillin, a wonder drug that might save Audrey's life. Burn sent thousands of cigarettes, which Van Heemstra sold on the black market and bought the medicine. The girl recovered and went on to become an actress: she is better known as Audrey Hepburn. Burn remained a man of erratic short-lived passions, political and sexual. He returned from Colditz convinced he was exclusively attracted to men, but then immediately fell in love with a woman, to whom he remained married, despite his several homosexual liaisons, for the next three decades. He embraced Catholicism, but then renounced the faith over the church's stance on homosexuality. He campaigned for the Communist Party but then disavowed Marxism, too, after witnessing the reality of communist rule firsthand as a correspondent for *The Times* in Budapest and Belgrade. His communist convictions were badly shaken by the defection of the KGB spy Guy Burgess, his former lover. His Colditz novel, *Yes, Farewell,* was published in 1946, the first of many books, plays, and poems. He moved to Wales, where he established a mussel-farming cooperative run on socialist principles in Porthmadog Harbour. It was a financial disaster. Reviewing his 2003 autobiography, *Turned Towards the Sun, The Times* observed that the book's moral "is that there are no easy answers to the paradoxes with which existence is constantly confronting the human tenants of this planet." Nazi-sympathizer turned communist, journalist turned novelist, mussel breeder, commando, poet, dilettante, and "scribe" of the secret Colditz radio, Micky Burn was never bored and continued to try everything, at least once, until his death at the age of ninety-seven.

Čeněk Chaloupka, seducer, spy runner, and black marketeer, did not marry Irma Wernicke after the war—an outcome that surprised nobody who knew him except, perhaps, Irma herself. Checko somehow obtained a Spitfire and flew back to Czechoslovakia in it. He rejoined the Czech air force and served in the 1st Air Division near Prague. In February 1946, ten months after leaving Colditz, he took a C-2 aircraft on a training flight and crashed. He was killed instantly. Years later it emerged that Chaloupka had never been an officer at all. **Irma Wernicke** got out of Colditz just before the Soviets moved in. The truth about her espionage activities on behalf of the prisoners was emerging, the town was suffused with bad blood, and once it became clear that she would not be living under Allied protection, the dental assistant knew she, too, had to escape. On the night the Red Army arrived "she fled, under cover of darkness." She was living in West Germany and working as a dental nurse when she met Tony Koudelka, another dashing Czech adventurer, an army deserter, and former soldier in the French Foreign Legion. They married in 1953, emigrated to the United States, and settled in Castaic, north of Los Angeles, where Koudelka joined the LAPD and moonlighted as a security guard for future president Ronald Reagan. She worked as a dentist for a trade union. In 1993, a year before Irma's death, a collection of former prisoners presented her with a signed book of Colditz photographs, "to remember her unique courage in helping us during the uncertain days of long ago and to thank her with all sincerity on behalf of every Allied Officer who was confined in Colditz castle and for whom she risked her life."

Julius Green returned to Scotland, where he married Anne Miller. They had two sons and spent the rest of their lives in Glasgow. He briefly entered business, but resumed his dental practice in 1950. In 1971, he published *From Colditz in Code,* a memoir of wry self-mockery and quiet fortitude. Green died in 1990 at age seventy-seven. His history remains all but unknown, eclipsed by the tales of louder and more obvious actors. But then history is like dentistry: you never know quite what you will find until you drill down.

With a large private income and a larger determination to enjoy himself, **Michael Alexander** became a pillar of the group of bohemian writers and artists known as the "Chelsea Set." An inveterate ladies' man, he happily reminisced about the sexual experiences with men he had enjoyed in Colditz. In a hovercraft, he explored the Yucatán peninsula of Mexico and the upper reaches of the Ganges; he circumnavigated the coast of Scotland in a small inflatable boat. Alexander worked for various publishers, rescued an old friend from the French Foreign Legion in North Africa, founded the British Inflatable Boat Owners' Association, located the remote area of Firozkoh in Central Afghanistan, and was elected a fellow of the Zoological Society of London; but he never did anything that might have been mistaken for a job. His literary output was vast and eclectic, including an anthology on India, a book about Hogarth's engravings, and a biography of Duleep Singh, Queen Victoria's Indian protégé. He opened a restaurant (briefly), married (briefly), and lived in a derelict Scottish castle (briefest of all). Having endured drab imprisonment for so long, he spent life after Colditz exploring as many of its colors and flavors as he could find.

Back in London, **Florimond Duke** "checked in with OSS and had one fine dinner in Claridge's before he flew home." He was writing up his report on Mission Sparrow in Washington when some unexpected news arrived from Hungary, now under Soviet control. A Hungarian military officer had approached an American diplomat in the street. "I have six thousand dollars in gold belonging to one of your officers," he said, in a North American accent. "I want to return it before the Russians get their hands on it." Major Kiraly dropped off the money at the American military mission the next day, "declined a receipt," and then disappeared. Duke moved to New Hampshire, where he served on the legislature, and then retired to Scottsdale, Arizona. Every year on April 15, he joined Colonel **Leo Shaughnessy** to celebrate the anniversary of the liberation of Colditz. "My task force did not capture Colditz," Shaughnessy insisted, "the prisoners had already done so." Duke had never been one for philosophical introspection, but as he grew older he began to wonder: "How did I survive?" In a book published shortly after his death in 1969, he wrote: "Part of it was just plain luck. But part of the answer lies with the true protective power of men of goodwill and high moral purpose—men like Denzler."

Rudolf E. Denzler never received any recognition for his wartime achievements, and never sought any. In a conflict involving, as he put it, "all the power, cruelty and inhumanity inherent in modern warfare," he was proud that inside Colditz he had managed to uphold the rules he venerated: "In this limited area, the spirit of chivalry of the 1929 Geneva Convention lived on." Having saved so many lives, with so little fanfare, he quietly slipped back into the anonymity of Swiss bureaucracy.

Michael Sinclair was posthumously awarded the DSO for his "relentless devotion to escaping whilst a POW," becoming the only lieutenant to receive a medal for courage during captivity. In 1947, his remains were moved to the Berlin war cemetery. **Charles Hopetoun** and **Dawyck Haig,** too ill to be moved from Königstein with the other *Prominente,* both recovered and were subsequently liberated by American forces. Hopetoun became director of an insurance company and 3rd Marquess of Linlithgow. Haig had a breakdown after the war, a fine modern painter who never quite escaped the shadow of his famous father. **Gris Davies-Scourfield** remained in the army, serving in Germany, Malaya, Ghana, and Cyprus, and ended his career as a brigadier. **Jack Best** resumed farming, first in Kenya and then Hertfordshire. The orderly **Solly Goldman** emigrated to the United States, and swapped his cockney accent for an entirely American one. **Tony Rolt** returned to the motor racing circuit and competed in three Formula 1 World Championship races. **Peter Allan,** the diminutive, kilt-wearing Scotsman who had staged the first escape inside a mattress, became a traveling representative for Bell's Scotch whisky. **Machiel van den Heuvel** was promoted to major in the Dutch army and killed in action in 1946 during the Indonesian War of Independence. **Tony Luteyn** settled in Australia. **Hans Larive** took a job with Royal Dutch Shell. General **Tadeusz Bór-Komorowski** never returned to now communist-controlled Poland. In London, he was prime minister of the Polish government-in-exile from 1947 to 1949, and an upholsterer. The French cavalry officer **Pierre Mairesse-Lebrun** served in de Gaulle's intelligence service and spent much of the rest of his life on horseback. As local commander of the Forces Françaises de l'Intérieur, **Alain Le Ray** liberated the city of Grenoble, and pried the last German forces out of the Alpine forts. The first Colditz escaper served in Indochina and Algeria, and retired in 1970 with the rank of general. **David Stirling** founded a number of failed businesses, took part in covert military actions in the Middle East, and was knighted in 1990, the year he died. His SAS became the model for special forces worldwide. The inventor **Christopher Clayton Hutton** attempted to publish a memoir describing the escape tools he had created for MI9 but became, in his words, "enmeshed in a labyrinth of minor officials" and threatened with prosecution under the Official Secrets Act. His autobiography, *Official Secret,* was finally published in 1960. Clutty retired to the eastern edge of Dartmoor, passed days on end inventing things in his shed, and died in 1965. His escape aids have become sought-after collectors' items.

Frank Flinn never fully recovered from the experience of Colditz, and was one of the few to admit it honestly. A gentle, shy man, he had escaped by being declared insane, and his mental health remained fragile. "The long-term effects were definitely there," he said. "Horizons shrink when you are in prison, and all the things around you make sense, but you get into a wider world, and the traffic is too noisy. Your mind is attuned to four walls, and it expands too rapidly." He was pronounced unfit to fly and left the RAF at the end of 1945, suffering from acute survivor's guilt. "You're alive, but so many have died," he said. "I don't think I really came to terms with it." "Errol" Flinn established a business making syrup for the ice cream industry in St. Helens before opening a kitchenware shop in Southport. He died in 2013, at the age of ninety-seven. **Giles Romilly,** the first of the *Prominente* to be incarcerated and the only one to escape under his own steam, was also irreparably damaged by imprisonment. He developed claustrophobia and "a heightened fear of crowds." Doctors prescribed barbituric acid, and he became addicted. With Michael Alexander, he co-wrote a book about the Colditz experience, entitled *The Privileged Nightmare,* but his journalistic and literary career failed to take off. His marriage disintegrated in acrimony and in 1963 he kidnapped his two children and fled to America. A year later, he sent them back. His ex-wife sequestered his property and assets. Churchill's communist nephew survived by selling Bibles and the *Encyclopaedia Britannica* door to door. The addiction worsened. "His whole life revolved around drinamyl, sodium amytal and Nembutal," said his son. In 1967, he died at the age of fifty from an overdose of tranquilizers in a lonely hotel room in Berkeley, California.

While some were changed forever by Colditz, Padre **Jock Platt,** armored by his Christian beliefs, emerged virtually unaffected. Imprisonment had been a trial sent by God, and he had met it. After the war, he served as a Methodist minister in St. Leonard's, Bromley, and Somerset, before retiring to Dorchester, where he died in 1973, "a man of deep faith who could never be turned away from his convictions."

The redoubtable **Jane Walker** was still hiding in a Polish village on the banks of the Vistula when the Red Army marched through on its way to Berlin. Mrs. M had no intention of living under Soviet rule in communist-controlled Poland, and the seventy-one-year-old spy decided it was time to go home. She made her way to Lublin and hitched a ride on a boxcar with a POW transport headed for Ukraine. On the way she obtained a fresh disguise and, as *The Times* reported, presented herself at the British Military Mission in Odessa "dressed, curiously enough, as an NCO in the RAF." There she boarded a British ship for Port Said, and on April 22, 1945, she docked in Gourock, the first time she had seen her native land in four decades. Walker was appointed MBE for "helping hundreds of Allied prisoners escape from German-occupied territory," received a personal invitation to the coronation of Queen Elizabeth II, appeared on the BBC show *This Is Your Life*, and retired to Bexhill-on-Sea on the Sussex coast, where she died at the age of eighty-five. "She was a great patriot," wrote Gris Davies-Scourfield, one of many who owed his survival to Mrs. M. "She lives on in the memories of all who knew and loved her in dark and dangerous days."

Birendranath Mazumdar was held for four months under house arrest in a Swiss hotel, awaiting trial on charges of embezzlement. Finally, the Swiss colonel overseeing the care of British soldiers in Switzerland came to see him. "They want me to be removed from the medical register and ruin my whole life," Mazumdar told him. The Swiss officer arranged for the Indian doctor to be moved to a nursing home. "They can't court-martial you now," he said. In November 1944, he was transferred to Marseille, and put on a troop ship back to England. Colonel Foote, meanwhile, had written to Z section of MI5 suggesting that "the behavior of Captain Mazumdar gave rise to suspicion." Mazumdar had been back in Woolwich barracks for just two weeks when the suspect now identified as "Z/240" in a file labeled "Indian Subversion" was summoned to the War Office.

"Z/240 was very hard to deal with," wrote the MI5 officer who conducted the cross-examination. "He disliked being interviewed and expressed the opinion that he was being subjected to treatment that no British POW had to put up with." Reluctantly, Mazumdar described again the failed attempts to recruit him in Berlin. The interviewer concluded that Mazumdar posed no security threat and deserved "credit for remaining loyal," yet the odor of suspicion still clung to him. "It seems impossible that Z/240 has forgotten as much as he pretends."

"You are ruining your chances of getting a medal," the MI5 officer warned.

Mazumdar exploded. "Do you think I escaped and went through all these things just to get a bloody medal?" he shouted, and walked out.

Biren Mazumdar was discharged in 1946. By then, **Subhas Chandra Bose** was dead: his Indian National Army had fought the British in Burma, and then surrendered with the Japanese. In circumstances that have never been fully explained, a plane carrying the Indian nationalist leader crashed in August 1945 in what is now Taiwan. Bose died from third-degree burns.

In 1947, India won its independence. Mazumdar might have then returned to the country of his birth, no longer under British rule, but instead he chose to remain in England. In the bank one day, he was served by an attractive young cashier named Joan, who recalled their first meeting: "He stood there at the counter. He was always beautifully groomed—three-piece suit, gloves; never smoked without his gloves on." They married and moved to Wales, where Mazumdar worked as a GP, and later to Essex. They had two sons. After Biren's retirement, the Mazumdars settled in the little village of Galmpton in Devon. He seldom talked about Colditz, but before his death in 1996 Mazumdar made a series of tape recordings describing his wartime experiences. In one of these, he recalled a highly symbolic incident.

Shortly before Indian independence and still in British uniform, Mazumdar visited his hometown of Gaya. His brother's family was also staying in the family house, and on the day they were leaving Mazumdar bought first-class tickets at the station, installed them in a compartment on the train to Calcutta, and went to buy food for their journey. He arrived back at the platform to see his relatives being hustled out of their first-class seats by a British sergeant major, to make way for an Englishman and his mistress.

"What happened?" Mazumdar asked.

"They told me to get out," his brother replied.

Mazumdar rounded on the British soldier and gave vent to all the frustrations built up over so many years of captivity and prejudice. "Stand to attention! Salute a senior officer!" His tirade continued for several minutes, as the soldier cowered. "You are dismissed."

Mazumdar turned. The packed platform had fallen silent. The porters had dropped their bundles and the Indian crowd was staring in awe. Then the applause started, building to a deafening roar, as they stamped their feet and cheered.

"*Shabash!*" they shouted. "*Shabash!*"

APPENDIX

The 5-6-O Code

A coded letter was indicated by a numerical date, e.g., 15/5/41, and an underlined signature.

The number of words in the secret message, and the decoding grid, were indicated by multiplying the number of letters in the first two words in the first full line of the letter. "How are you?" would indicate a nine-word message in a 3 x 3 grid. "So pleased to hear . . ." would indicate a fourteen-word message in a 2 x 7 grid. The message was contained in the fifth and sixth words of the letter, starting with the second sentence.

The first decoded word, the fifth in the second sentence, was placed in the top left corner of the grid; the sixth word after that alongside it; the fifth word after that next . . . and repeated fifth, then sixth, and so on. Once the grid was filled out, the message was read diagonally in a zigzag from the bottom right corner.

Example:

This letter was sent by Julius Green to his mother in Fife and passed on to MI9. It contained information on German U-boat defenses gathered from captured naval officers.

15/5/41

Dear Mum,

How are you all keeping?

I will not be home as soon as I thought.

Escorted by guards I got out of the train near here and was glad after almost two-days train travelling to arrive and meet some English fellows again. Submarine, destroyers, merchant ships, even merchant raiders are represented. Seeing sailors disguised as soldiers is very amusing but a bit grim when you think of how they lost their own togs. They are a charming crew. I am in a hut with the RN & RM officers . . .

Best love to all, <u>Julie</u>

Solution

	H	O	W
A	HOME ←	ESCORTED	OUT
R	AND	TWO-DAYS	MEET
E	SUBMARINE	RAIDERS ←	DISGUISED

DISGUISED RAIDERS MEET SUBMARINE TWO-DAYS OUT AND ESCORTED HOME

The 5-6-O code, however, had a complex refinement. The O in the name was a letter, not a number. If the decoder found the word "the" (the definite article) in the sequence of deciphered words, this was the indication that the code had changed from a word code to a spelling code, and the rest of that sentence should be ignored.

The decoder needed to draw up a grid, 3 x 9, starting with the letter O in the top left corner, thus:

O 111	P 211	Q 311
R 112	S 212	T 312
U 113	V 213	W 313
X 121	Y 221	Z 321
. 122	A 222	B 322
C 123	D 223	E 323
F 131	G 231	H 331
I 132	J 232	K 332
L 133	M 233	N 333

Each letter of the alphabet and, crucially, the period, corresponded to a three-digit number, with every combination of 1, 2, and 3 represented.

The initial letters of the first three words in the next sentence corresponded to columns 1, 2, or 3 of the grid, to produce a three-digit number that, in turn, denoted a specific letter. For example, "Mother rang up" produces M = 2, R = 1, U = 1. The number 211 = P.

A full stop (122) was the indication to ignore the rest of the sentence, and revert to the word code, writing down every fifth and sixth word as before.

The decoded word "but" indicated "message ends." A dash was counted as a word.

Example:

This letter was sent to Julius Green from his "father" in the summer of 1943, referring to a map he had sent earlier of a synthetic oil production plant at Blechhammer North, and an unpaid bill to a Mrs. Hobbs.

8/7/43

Dear Julius,

So pleased to get your letter

Informing us you'd received the scripts for the plays, also the iodine, which Mrs. Simpson sent you. Mother rang up saying you're grateful for the gift, and also how really pleased you'd be, she told Mother that she had sent you some music. Next week I will be sending you more cigarettes. You will have plenty, if they remit them to you promptly, as the last lot I sent you a fortnight ago should reach you soon. Hope the other oddments followed on, because you should have got your parcel containing your cheese-cap and slacks which I sent in January addressed to "Marlag und Milag Nord." You remember poor old Mrs. Smith—her painful illness is following its usual course. Like others who suffer she's heroic. I hope the "Legal and General" received the cheque I sent them the other day, it was to pay the interest and capital due to them and it will reduce it further, I've also asked them to let me know when the premium is due on your policy. They're quite businesslike usually so you need not worry. Judith's birthday was on the 27th June, she was 4 and is getting quite a big girl. We all simply love her, however we haven't really spoiled her. We fixed up a little party, and mother baked her a beautiful birthday cake which had four candles on it. Judith was very excited, of course, and so were all the little guests. You'll be home again soon, Julie, at least I only pray you will . . .

Mother Kathleen and Judith send you their love.
<u>Dad</u>.

Solution:

The first two words "So pleased" indicate a fourteen-word message in a grid 2 x 7.

The fifth word of the following sentence is "the," so the rest of that sentence should be ignored, and the spelling code started from the next sentence.

The initial letters of the first three words ("Mother rang up") correspond to columns, 2, 1, and 1, producing 211, = P; the next three words ("saying you're grateful"), produce 222, = A; "for the gift" = I; "and also how" = D. The first word is therefore PAID, and should be placed in the top left-hand space on the grid. However, the next three words ("really pleased you'd") produce 122, the full stop, the sign that the decoder should revert to the 5-6 word code, starting with the next sentence. The fifth, sixth, and fifth words are "be," "will," and "remit." These are then inserted into the grid. The sixth word after that is "the," so revert to the spelling code as before . . . and so on.

The completed grid is as follows:

	S	O
P	PAID	be
L	will	remit
E	HOBBS	Mrs.
A	following	others
S	hope	received
E	N	blhmr
D	of	MAP

MAP OF BLHMR N RECEIVED HOPE OTHERS FOLLOW-
ING MRS HOBBS REMIT WILL BE PAID

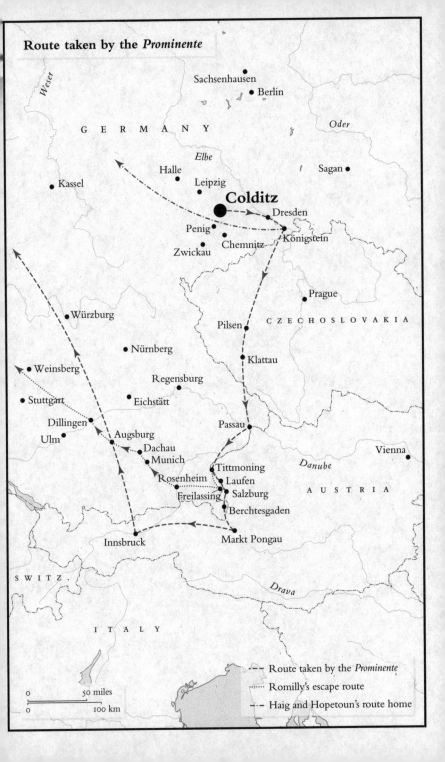

Route taken by the *Prominente*

Sachsenhausen

Berlin

G E R M A N Y

Oder

Weser

Elbe

Sagan •

Halle

Kassel •

Leipzig

Colditz

Dresden

Penig

Königstein

Chemnitz

Zwickau

Prague •

Würzburg •

Pilsen

C Z E C H O S L O V A K I A

Nürnberg •

Klattau

Regensburg •

Eichstätt •

Weinsberg •

Stuttgart •

Dillingen •

Augsburg

Passau

Ulm •

Dachau

Vienna •

Munich

Danube

Rosenheim

Tittmoning

A U S T R I A

Freilassing

Laufen

Salzburg

Berchtesgaden

Innsbruck

Markt Pongau

S W I T Z.

Drava

I T A L Y

0 — 50 miles
0 — 100 km

– · – Route taken by the *Prominente*
· · · · · Romilly's escape route
– · · – Haig and Hopetoun's route home

Acknowledgments

Once again, I owe a huge debt to many people, in Britain, America, Germany, and France, for their help with this book. Lucian Clinch performed miracles of research despite the constraints of lockdown; Regina Thiede, curator and archivist of Colditz, was most welcoming on my extended visits to the castle, and exceptionally helpful; Robert Hands read the original typescript, as he has done for eight of my earlier books, and saved me from countless toe-curling errors; I am particularly grateful to Joan Mazumdar for sharing her memories of Birendranath Mazumdar and permitting me to quote from his recorded recollections; once again, Cecilia Mackay has performed wonders in collecting and arranging the photographic inserts; John Green kindly translated swathes of dense German; the publishing teams at Viking in the U.K., Crown in the U.S., and Signal in Canada have done another superlative job; Daniel Crewe, Kevin Doughten, and Doug Pepper are the best editing combination in the business; Jonny Geller has been a rock of sage support at every stage. I would also like to thank the following for providing encouragement, sustenance, and inspiration during the researching and writing of this book: Alexandra Anisimova, Jo Barrett, Paul Barrett, Venetia Butterfield, Henry Chancellor, Derry Clinch, John Duke, Natasha Fairweather, Antonia Fraser, Ian Katz, Kate Macintyre, Magnus Macintyre, Natascha McElhone, Roland Philipps, Joanna Prior, Anne Robinson, Juliet Rosenfeld, and Michael Shipster. My beloved children, Barney, Finn, and Molly, have once again carried me through this story with endless joy and good humor, despite having to spend much of lockdown being forced to play the Colditz board game (tip: it's best to be the Kommandant). Never once did they ask: Is there no escape from Colditz?

A Note on Sources

The source material for Colditz is vast and eclectic, but of variable quality. In addition to the many books written by former prisoners, guards, and later historians, most classified materials, including the records of MI9, have now been released into the National Archives. By far the best general account of the camp is still *Colditz: The Definitive History* (2001) by Henry Chancellor, a book that emerged from the Channel 4 series *Escape from Colditz*. There are no Colditz prisoners still alive, but seventy-six people were interviewed for that series and the interview tapes amassed over twelve years are now held in the Imperial War Museum: a remarkable repository of human memory that I have used extensively in the preceding pages. John Duke kindly lent me a scrapbook compiled by Reinhold Eggers and presented to his grandfather Florimond Duke shortly before the latter's death: this contains several hundred original photographs, diagrams, and maps, complete with handwritten notations by Eggers himself. The Duke scrapbook has proved an invaluable resource in the writing of this book. For clarity I have occasionally combined or compressed quotations and standardized spellings.

PRIMARY SOURCES

National Archives, Kew

WO208/3288: MI9 report on Oflag IVC, Colditz.
WO208/3297: The Escapers' Story: A Compilation of Various Escape Reports.
WO208/3298–WO208/3327: MI9 Prisoner of War Escape/Evasion Reports.
WO208/332–WO208/3340: MI9 Prisoner of War Liberation Reports.
WO208/3341: MI9 Miscellaneous Intelligence Reports.
WO208/3342: MI9 Prisoner of War Interrogation Reports.
WO208/3343–WO208/3345: Miscellaneous Intelligence Reports.
WO208/3346: South African prisoner of war reports.
WO208/3347: Forces repatriated from Eire.
WO208/3348–WO208/3352: Escape Reports.
WO361/1838: Reports on Colditz by the International Red Cross.
DEFE2/364: File on Operation Musketoon.
WO311/382: Killing of British POWs in Germany after capture in Norway during Operation Musketoon, destruction of Glom Fjord power plant.
WO208/4440: File on Gottlob Berger.
PREM3/364/12: File on British prisoners held as political hostages.

National Archives, College Park, MD

Case Number 41-64, Vol I (OF), 40961789: Documents on Oberst Prawitt.

Halle University Archives

UAHW, Rep. 21, Nr. 682: File on Reinhold Eggers.
UAHW, Rep. 46, Nr. 37 (1929–1931): File on Reinhold Eggers.

Imperial War Museum Archives, Lambeth

Documents.1805: Papers of Reinhold Eggers.
Documents.1927: Papers of Lt. Commander Stephens.
Documents.2715: Colditz Certificates.
Documents.4275: Papers of Lieutenant Colonel M. Reid MBE MC DL.
Documents.6295: Papers of Major Bruce.
Documents.8814: Court-Martial Records.
Documents.11592: Papers of Flight Lt. Fowler.
Documents.19686: Papers of Brigadier General L. de Laveaux.
Documents.20390: Papers of Baron de Crevoisier de Vomecourt.
Documents.22101: Papers of Reverend JE Platt MBE.
Documents.23729: Papers of Mrs. Allan.
4432: Interview with Howard Gee.
4816: Interview with James Moran.
5378: Interview with Edgar Hargreaves.
9893: Interview with Montagu Champion Jones.
12658: Interview with Reinhold Eggers.
15336: Interview with John Wilson.
16800: Interview with Birendra Nath [*sic*] Mazumdar.
16910: Interview with John Hoggard.
16974: Interview with Jerzy Stein.
17312: Interview with Joseph Tucki.
17585: Interview with John Pringle.
17597: Interview with Francis Michael Edwards.
21742: Interview with Alex Ross.
21743: Interview with Francis Flinn.
21744: Interview with Michael Burn.
21747: Interview with Corran Purdon.
21748: Interview with John Chrisp.
21749: Interview with John "Pat" Fergusson.
21752: Interview with Kenneth Lockwood.
21768: Interview with Anthony Luteyn.
21775: Interview with Grismond Davies-Scourfield.
21777: Interview with Kenneth Lockwood.
21780: Interview with Ota Cerny.
22332: Interview with Dominic Bruce.
28416: Interview with Leslie Goldfinch.
29186, 21740, 16828: Interview with Franciscus Steinmetz.
29193: Interview with Peter Tunstall.
29195: Interview with George Drew.

29204: Interview with Jean-Claude Tine.
29209: Interview with Charles Michael Alexander.

Polish Underground Studies Movement (1939–1945) Study Trust

PRM/163.

USAF Base Maxwell, AL

Reel No. 44642.

SELECT BIBLIOGRAPHY

Baybutt, Ron, *Camera in Colditz,* London, 1982.

Beaumont, Joan, "Rank, Privilege and Prisoners of War in War and Society," *War & Society,* 1:1 (1983), pp. 67–94.

——, "Review Article: Prisoners of War in the Second World War," *Journal of Contemporary History,* 42:3 (2007), pp. 535–44.

Bishop, Patrick, *The Man Who Was Saturday,* London, 2019.

Booker, Michael, *Collecting Colditz and Its Secrets,* London, 2005.

Brickhill, Paul, *Reach for the Sky: Douglas Bader, His Life Story,* London, 1955.

Burn, Michael, *Yes, Farewell,* London, 1946.

——, *Turned Towards the Sun,* Norwich, 2007.

Campbell, Alan, *Colditz Cameo: Being a Collection of Verse Written by a Prisoner of War in Germany, 1940–45,* Sussex, 2004.

Catlow, T. N., *A Sailor's Survival: Memoirs of a Naval Officer,* Leicester, 1996.

Champ, Jack, and Colin Burgess, *The Diggers of Colditz,* London, 1985.

Chancellor, Henry, *Colditz: The Definitive History,* London, 2001.

Chrisp, J., *Escape,* London, 1960.

Davies-Scourfield, Gris, *In Presence of My Foes: From Calais to Colditz via the Polish Underground,* Barnsley, 2005.

Duke, Florimond, and Charles M. Swaart, *Name, Rank, and Serial Number,* New York, 1969.

Eggers, Reinhold, *Colditz Recaptured,* London, 1973.

——, *Colditz: The German Viewpoint,* Los Angeles, 1975.

Ferguson, Ion, *Doctor at War,* London, 1955.

Foot, M. R. D., and J. M. Langley, *MI9: Escape and Evasion 1939–1945,* London, 1979.

Froom, Phil, *Evasion & Escape Devices Produced by MI9, MIS-X & SOE in World War II,* Atglen, 2015.

Green, J. M., *From Colditz in Code,* London, 1971.

Haig, Dawyck, *My Father's Son: The Memory of the Earl Haig,* Barnsley, 1999.

Harewood, George Henry Hubert Lascelles, *The Tongs and the Bones: The Memoirs of Lord Harewood,* London, 1981.

Hutchinson, John F., *Champions of Charity: War and the Rise of the Red Cross,* Abingdon, 1997.

Kübler, Robert, *Chef KGW: Das Kriegsgefangenenwesen unter Gottlob Berger, Nachlass,* Lindhorst, 1984.

Larive, E. H., *The Man Who Came in from Colditz,* London, 1975.

Le Brigant, Général, *Les indomptables,* Paris, 1948.

Le Ray, Alain, *Première à Colditz,* Grenoble, 2004.

Mackenzie, S. P., *The Colditz Myth: British and Commonwealth Prisoners of War in Nazi Germany,* Oxford, 2004.

Makepeace, Clare, *Captives of War: British Prisoners of War in Europe in the Second World War,* Cambridge, 2017.

Morison, Walter, *Flak and Ferrets,* London, 1955.

Neave, Airey, *They Have Their Exits,* London, 1955.

Nichol, John, and Tony Rennell, *The Last Escape: The Untold Story of Allied Prisoners of War in Germany 1944–1945,* London, 2003.

Pattinson, Juliette, Lucy Noakes, and Wendy Ugolini, "Incarcerated Masculinities: Male POWs and the Second World War," *Journal of War and Culture Studies,* 7:3 (2014), pp. 179–90.

Perrin, André, *Évadé de Guerre via Colditz,* Paris, 1975.

Platt, J. Ellison, and Margaret Duggan, *Padre in Colditz,* London, 1978.

Pringle, Jack, *Colditz Last Stop: Four Countries, Eleven Prisons, Six Escapes,* London, 1988.

Reid, Miles, *Last on the List,* London, 1974.

Reid, P. R., *Colditz: The Full Story,* London, 1985.

——, *The Colditz Story,* London, 2014.

——, *The Latter Days at Colditz,* London, 2014.

Rogers, Jim, *Tunnelling into Colditz: A Mining Engineer in Captivity,* London, 1986.

Rolf, David, *Prisoners of the Reich: Germany's Captives, 1939–1945,* Barnsley, 1988.

——, "The Education of British Prisoners of War in German Captivity, 1939–1945," *History of Education,* 18:3 (1989), pp. 257–65.

Romilly, Giles, and Michael Alexander, *The Privileged Nightmare,* London, 1956.

Ruft, Reiner, *The Singen Route,* Munich, 2019.

Schädlich, Thomas, *Tales from Colditz Castle,* 2016.

Shavit, David, " 'The Greatest Morale Factor Next to the Red Army': Books and Libraries in American and British Prisoners of War Camps in Germany During World War II," *Libraries and Culture,* 34:2 (1999), pp. 113–34.

Stanley, Peter, *Commando to Colditz,* Sydney, 2009.

Sternberg, Antony, *Vie de château et Oflags de discipline: Souvenirs de captivité,* Paris, 1948.

Turner, John Frayn, *Douglas Bader,* Barnsley, 2009.

Walker, David, *Lean, Wind, Lean,* London, 1984.

Walters, Guy, *The Colditz Legacy,* London, 2006.

Williamson, David G., *The Polish Underground, 1939–1947,* Barnsley, 2012.

Wilson, Patrick, *The War Behind the Wire: Voices of the Veterans,* Barnsley, 2020.

Wood, J. E. R., *Detour: The Story of Oflag IVC,* London, 1946.

OTHER MEDIA

Colditz: The Complete Collection, 2010.

Colditz, 2005.

Turned Towards the Sun, 2015.

Index

PRISONERS
OF THE CASTLE

BEN MACINTYRE

A BOOK CLUB GUIDE

Questions and Topics for Discussion

1. Had you known about Colditz before reading *Prisoners of the Castle*? What surprised you most about this book? Did the story defy your expectations? Was there anything about World War II that you learned, especially about the lives of POWs? Please explain.

2. Which prisoners resonated with you most, and why? Who was the most courageous, the most obnoxious, the funniest, and the most tragic?

3. Do prisoners of war have a moral duty to escape? Why or why not? Are there particular circumstances that might affect your answer?

4. Tunneling out. Rappelling down ramparts. Walking through front gate disguised as a German soldier. Which method of escape most impressed you, and why? Which method would you choose, and why?

5. Name three qualities that you believe best help someone survive being a POW. Explain why you chose them.

6. The Colditz fortress prison was considered escape-proof, much like *Titanic* was considered unsinkable. Now it's your turn to fill in these blanks:

The Colditz fortress prison was considered escape-proof, much like _____ was considered _____.

7. *Prisoners of the Castle* seamlessly moves between intense drama, daring adventure, a bit of romance, and unexpected moments of comedy. How do you think this enriches the reading experience? Which parts did you like most?

8. Were you surprised that class structures and ranks remained intact among the prisoners at Colditz? Why do you think this was the case? In your opinion, did these categories and hierarchies help or harm POWs?

9. There were many heroes outside Colditz, including a "perfectly ordinary" (in the eyes of the Nazis) Polish housewife who was actually an agent of British intelligence; a sawmill worker who became "the most prodigious inventor of escape equipment in history"; the dental assistant (and lover to a Czech fighter pilot) who, surprisingly, was also a spy; and the Swiss official assigned to make sure the Germans complied with the Geneva Convention. Which most inspired you, and why?

10. Were you surprised to learn that the German authorities adhered to the Geneva Convention in Colditz? In your view, can "rules of war" have a significant mitigating effect on wartime atrocities, or do you think any effect is purely arbitrary?

11. A man of conviction with an impeccable sense of duty, Birendranath Mazumdar faced a different set of challenges at Colditz and beyond. Despite being a committed Indian nationalist, Mazumdar came to Britain's defense and joined the British Army when war was declared, proving heroic under fire. How do you explain the way he was treated *by his own side* both during captivity and after he escaped? Was it solely because he was a person of color, or were there factors in addition to racism? How do you think he persevered in the face of such adversity?

12. At Colditz, "reading matter was supplied via the Red Cross, and Penguin Books set up a system whereby . . . individual prisoners received a monthly parcel containing a selection of ten books." What would your ten books be?

13. Did you think that the British prisoners should have gone through with the execution by hanging of traitor Walter Purdy? Why or why not?

14. How did you feel about the fate of Germany's Leutnant Reinhold Eggers (supreme security chief of Colditz) at the hands of the Russians?

Read on for an excerpt from
BEN MACINTYRE'S *ROGUE HEROES*

"Reads like a mashup of *The Dirty Dozen* and *The Great Escape*, with a sprinkling of *Ocean's 11* thrown in for good measure." —MICHIKO KAKUTANI, *NEW YORK TIMES*

BEN MACINTYRE

THE HISTORY OF THE SAS,
BRITAIN'S SECRET SPECIAL FORCES UNIT THAT SABOTAGED
THE NAZIS AND CHANGED THE NATURE OF WAR

ROGUE
HEROES

NEW YORK TIMES BESTSELLER

"A ripping good read."
—*The Washington Post*

CROWN
NEW YORK

Into the Dark

On a November evening in 1941, five elderly Bristol Bombay transport aircraft lumbered along the runway of Bagush airfield on the Egyptian coast, and then wheeled into the darkening Mediterranean haze. Each aircraft carried a "stick" of eleven British parachutists, some fifty-five soldiers in all, almost the entire strength of a new, experimental, and intensely secret combat unit: "L Detachment" of the Special Air Service. The SAS.

As the planes rumbled northwest the wind began to pick up, bringing the electric inklings of a brewing storm. The temperature inside dropped quickly as the sun slipped below the desert horizon. It was suddenly intensely cold.

The fledgling SAS was on its first mission. Code-named Operation Squatter, it ran as follows: to parachute at night into the Libyan desert behind enemy lines, infiltrate five airfields on foot, plant explosives on as many German and Italian aircraft as they could find, and then, as the bombs exploded, head south to a rendezvous point deep in the desert where they would be picked up and brought back to safety.

Some of the men strapped in and shivering in the rushing darkness at eighteen thousand feet were regular soldiers, but others were not: their number included a hotel porter, an ice-cream maker, a Scottish aristocrat, and an Irish international rugby player. Some were natural warriors, nerveless and calm, and a few were touched by a sort of martial madness; most were silently petrified, and determined not to show it. None could claim to have been fully prepared for what they were about to do, for the simple reason that no one had ever before attempted a nighttime parachute assault in the North African desert. But a peculiar camaraderie had already taken root, a strange esprit compounded in equal parts of ruthlessness, guile, competitiveness, and collective determination. Before takeoff, the men had been informed that anyone seriously injured on landing would have to be left behind. There is no evidence that any of them found this odd.

The wind had reached gale force by the time the bucking Bombays neared the Libyan coast, two and a half hours after takeoff. Storm-driven sand and pelting rain completely obscured the flares on the ground, laid down by the Royal Air Force to guide the planes to the drop zone, twelve miles inland. The pilots could not even make out the shape of the shoreline. German searchlights on the coast picked up the incoming planes, and flak began exploding around them in blinding flashes. A shell ripped through the floor of one plane and missed the auxiliary fuel tank by inches. One of the sergeants made a joke, which no one could hear, though everyone grinned.

The pilots indicated that the parachutists should prepare to jump—although, in truth, they were now flying blind, navigating by guesswork. The parachute canisters—containing explosives, tommy guns, ammunition, food, water, maps, blankets, and medical supplies—were tossed out first.

Then, one by one, the men hurled themselves into the seething darkness.

Chapter 1

Cowboy Soldier

Five months before Operation Squatter, a tall, thin soldier lay, grumpy and immobile, in a Cairo hospital bed. The twenty-five-year-old officer had been brought into the Scottish Military Hospital on June 15, 1941, paralyzed from the waist down. A letter to his mother from the War Office stated that he had suffered "a contusion of the back as a result of enemy action."

This was not, strictly speaking, true. The injured soldier had not set eyes on the enemy: he had jumped out of a plane, without a helmet or proper training, ripped his parachute on the tail, and plummeted to earth at roughly twice the recommended speed. The impact had knocked him out and badly injured his spine, leaving him temporarily blinded and without feeling in his legs. The doctors feared he would never walk again.

Even before his parachuting accident, the officer's contribution to the war effort had been minimal: he lacked the most basic military discipline, could not march straight, and was so lazy his comrades had nicknamed him "the Giant Sloth." Since being posted to Egypt with the British commando force, he had spent much of his time in Cairo's bars and clubs, or gambling at the racecourse. The nurses at the hospital knew him well, for he frequently popped in during the morning, whey-faced and liverish, to request a blast from the oxygen bottle to cure his hangover. Before his parachute jump landed him in the hospital, he had been under investigation to establish whether he was malingering and ought to be court-martialed. His fellow officers found him charming and entertaining; his senior commanders, for the most part, regarded him as impertinent, incompetent, and profoundly irritating. On completing officer training, he had received a blunt appraisal: "irresponsible and unremarkable."

Lieutenant David Stirling of the Scots Guards was not a conventional soldier.

The writer Evelyn Waugh, a fellow officer in the commando force, came to visit Stirling about three weeks after his admission to the hospital. Waugh had been misinformed by the matron that one of Stirling's legs had already been amputated, and he would likely lose the other. "I can't feel a thing," Stirling told his friend. Embarrassed, as Englishmen tend to be when faced with disability, Waugh kept up a steady stream of meaningless small talk, perched on the edge of the bed, and studiously avoided the subject of his friend's paralysis. Every so often, however, he would sneak a surreptitious glance to where Stirling's remaining leg ought to be, and whenever he did so Stirling, with extreme effort, would wiggle the big toe of his right foot. Finally, Waugh realized he was being teased, and hit Stirling with a pillow.

"You bastard, Stirling, when did it happen?"

"Minutes before you came. It takes a bit of effort, but it's a start."

Stirling was regaining the use of his legs. Others might have cried for joy; for Stirling, however, the first sign of his recovery was an excellent opportunity to play a practical joke on one of Britain's greatest novelists.

It would take two more weeks before Stirling could stand upright, and several more before he was able to hobble about. But during those two months of enforced inaction he did a great deal of thinking—something that, in spite of his reputation as a feckless gadabout, he was rather good at.

The commandos were intended to be Britain's storm troops, volunteers selected and trained to carry out destructive raids against Axis targets. Prime Minister Winston Churchill had decided that the ideal theater in which to deploy the commandos would be North Africa, where they could conduct seaborne raids against enemy bases along the Mediterranean coast.

In Stirling's unsolicited opinion, the concept was not working. Most of the time the commandos were inactive, awaiting the order for a great assault that never came; on the rare occasions when they were deployed, the results had been disappointing. The German and Italian troops fully expected to be attacked from the sea, and were primed and waiting. The commando forces were simply too large and cumbersome to launch an assault without being spotted; the element of surprise was immediately lost.

But what if, wondered Stirling, the combat troops attacked from the opposite direction? To the south, stretching between Egypt and Libya, lay the Great Sand Sea, a vast, waterless expanse of unbroken dunes covering forty-five thousand square miles. One of the most inhospitable environments on earth, the desert was considered by the Germans to be virtually impassable, a natural barrier, and they therefore left it largely unprotected, and entirely unpatrolled. "This was one sea the Hun was not watching," Stirling reflected. If mobile teams of highly trained men, under cover of darkness, could be infiltrated onto the enemy's desert flank, they might be able to sabotage airfields, supply depots, communications links, railways, and roads, and then slip back into the embracing emptiness of the sand sea. A commando force several hundred strong could attack only one target at a time; but a number of smaller units, moving quickly, raiding suddenly and then retreating swiftly, could destroy multiple targets simultaneously. The opportunity to attack the enemy in the rear, when he least expects it, is the pipe dream of every general. The peculiar geography of North Africa offered just such a possibility, reflected Stirling, as he lay half paralyzed in his hospital bed, trying to wiggle his toes.

Stirling's idea was the result of wishful thinking more than expertise; it had emerged not from long hours of reflection and study, but from the acute boredom of convalescence. It was based on intuition, imagination, and self-confidence, of which Stirling had plenty, rather than experience of desert warfare, of which he had none.

But it was an inspired idea, and the sort of idea that could only have occurred to someone as strange and remarkable as Archibald David Stirling.

PHOTO: © JUSTINE STODDART

BEN MACINTYRE is a writer-at-large for *The Times* (U.K.) and the bestselling author of *Agent Sonya, The Spy and the Traitor, A Spy Among Friends, Double Cross, Operation Mincemeat, Agent Zigzag,* and *Rogue Heroes,* among other books. Macintyre has also written and presented BBC documentaries of his work.